Beside Quiet Waters

Daily

Devotions

for a

Year

Richard E. Lauersdorf

NORTHWESTERN PUBLISHING HOUSE
MILWAUKEE, WISCONSIN

Second printing, 2007

Cover photo: ShutterStock, Inc.
Art Director: Karen Knutson
Designer: Pamela Wood

Library of Congress Control Number: 2005927689
Northwestern Publishing House
1250 N. 113th St., Milwaukee, WI 53226-3284
www.nph.net
© 2005 by Northwestern Publishing House
Published 2005
Printed in the United States of America
ISBN 978-0-8100-1758-0

For all who seek refreshment daily

beside the quiet waters

in the green pastures of God's Word

Many of us as children learned to sing
"I Am Jesus' Little Lamb."
One of the verses of this simple,
yet sweet, song states:

When I hunger, Jesus feeds me,
Into pleasant pastures leads me;
When I thirst, he bids me go
Where the quiet waters flow.

(*Christian Worship* [CW] 432:2)

Over the years we have learned what
rich nourishment abounds in the green
pastures and quiet waters of God's
Word. In it the Shepherd richly refreshes
us throughout the days of our lives.

May our loving Shepherd use this book
of daily devotions to satisfy our
hungry, thirsting souls.

> LIFT UP MY EYES TO THE HILLS. . . .
> MY HELP COMES FROM THE LORD,
> THE MAKER OF HEAVEN AND EARTH. *Psalm 121:1,2*

Look Up, Not Down

It's not easy to look up when entering a new year. We'd much rather follow the lead of the world and look down—to ourselves. From little on, we do this. "I do it myself," pouts the little one whose shoe we are trying to tie. "Leave me alone," responds the teenager to whom we are trying to give advice. "That's not the way we do it," objects the senior citizen when changes are proposed. Human beings tend to look to themselves. And all too often Christians tend to follow that same lead.

Now listen to the psalmist. He didn't write, "My help comes from *me.*" It's, "My help comes from the LORD." Forget this and we're in trouble. Who are we that we can help ourselves? How mighty is our right arm and how foolproof our plans? How often this past year didn't we fret and even fail because we looked in the wrong direction? How cautious and concerned aren't we already about the new year because we look down to insufficient mortals instead of up to an almighty God?

Want to enter the new year with confidence? Then look up—to God. He made heaven and earth. He surely can and will take care of us. Even more, look at the nail wounds in his outstretched hands. They speak of a love that is solid and supreme. Nothing the new year can bring can rip us loose from those loving hands.

Almighty Shepherd, lead us with your
love and power safely into this new year. Amen.

THE LORD WILL KEEP YOU FROM ALL HARM—
HE WILL WATCH OVER YOUR LIFE. *Psalm 121:7*

Look Back, Then Ahead

When years change, we naturally look back. Were there no joys in the year that sped by so swiftly? No moments of meaningful love shared with a spouse? No proper pride in the achievements of family members? No successes in our jobs or professions? No lighter moments on the lake or at the ball game? Let's not forget from whom such blessings flowed this past year and how easily he can grant them also in the new year, if they should be for our good and his glory.

Does the backward look involve something painful? Were there times when I blew it in my dealings with my fellowman, perhaps even with those closest to me? Times when I tried so hard and yet fell right back into sin's old ruts and felt so bad afterward? Times when the load of trouble seemed two hundred pounds heavier than I could carry? Tell me, where are some of those troubles now? Many are gone, lifted by the loving hand of an almighty God. Some may be still with me, yet I made it through the past year in spite of them. A gracious God helped me to bear them and even to grow because of them. Will such a Lord forsake me in the year ahead?

I don't know what might happen to me or whether I'll still be here when the next year rolls around. Nor do I need to. It's enough for me to know not what the new year holds but who holds the new year. It's the Lord who went all out to save me and whom I can trust now to go all out to fill the new year with what he knows is good for me. His love and forgiveness do not change with the calendar.

Thank you, loving Shepherd, for blessing the
year past and now also the one coming. Amen.

"FRIEND, YOUR SINS ARE FORGIVEN." *Luke 5:20*

Starting With A Clean Slate

In my grade-school days the teacher assigned each student a weekly task. One was cleaning the blackboard at the end of each day. I still remember how hard it was to get all the chalk off the board. Today it's wiping the markers off the white board, but you still may have to scrub hard. Another task was removing the garbage in the wastebaskets.

How can I enter a new year with confidence if I don't know that God has wiped the slate of my life clean? Or what can I do with the shattered glass of my unclean thoughts, the dirty plastic of my unkind words, the soiled paper of my unloving deeds that filled the trash bin of the year past? How can I clean those up, and how many bags would it take? Even if I tried, I could never pick up all the garbage of my sin. How horrible if I had to carry that smelly load with me into this new year!

But how sweet it is to hear my Jesus say, "Friend, your sins are forgiven." I'm still his friend, he reminds me. I can still look up at his loving face and expect his loving help. All because of what he did for me on Calvary's cross. There he collected my sins, not to stuff them into some plastic bags designated for some landfill but to get rid of them forever. With his perfect payment he has erased my sins completely. They're gone in God's sight as though they never happened.

Jesus had to scrub hard to clean my slate. He did it because he loves me. Regardless how I try, I'll never be able to understand such undeserving love for me, a sinner. But I can enter the new year with confidence and thank him each day for taking my sins away.

Good Shepherd, assure me each day of
your forgiveness so that I have your peace. Amen.

COMMIT YOUR WAY TO THE LORD;

TRUST IN HIM AND HE WILL DO THIS. *Psalm 37:5*

Flying With The Lord

We were sitting at a chilly outdoor café, high in the Alps of Switzerland. As we enjoyed our hot drinks, we were enthralled by the hang glider flyers using a nearby peak. Strapped to a bare frame covered with nylon, they jumped calmly off and glided smoothly to the Alpine meadows below.

Watching them made me think of the psalmist's words. Flying a glider is like trusting the Lord. Those flyers weren't afraid to entrust themselves to that flimsy vehicle of plastic, leather, and nylon. From experience they had learned that the upthrust of the mountain air would carry them in smooth circles to the land below.

How much more so for us as God's children! We can commit our way to the Lord, rolling the challenges of each new day onto his almighty shoulders. We can do this because we've learned by experience to trust him. Did he fail me in any of the days gone by? When I rolled the wheelbarrow overflowing with my sins to him each day, was he not there assuring me through his gracious Word that his Son's blood had covered all my sin? When I raised my face stained with the tears of trouble to his throne, was he not there reminding me through his Word that he would work all things out for my good? When I knew not where to turn or what to do, was he not there with his promise, "Never will I leave you; never will I forsake you" (Hebrews 13:5)?

I don't know if I could ever learn how to fly with a hang glider. But I do need to learn how to fly with the Lord. I do want to grow in trusting him better each day.

Gracious Shepherd, lead me each day to trust you more
for the needs of both my body and my soul. Amen.

> TEACH US TO NUMBER OUR DAYS ARIGHT,
>
> THAT WE MAY GAIN A HEART OF WISDOM. *Psalm 90:12*

God's Unique Blessing Of Time

Somewhere I saw a greeting card with the following verse: "God give you one year of happiness, 12 months of prosperity, 52 weeks of success, 365 days of good health, 8,760 hours of joy and gladness, and 525,600 minutes filled with his peace, love, joy, and blessings."

Made me think of what a unique blessing from God time really is. Each year he puts before me 52 weeks filled with opportunities to learn his Word so that I might be filled with his love. Each week he hands me seven new days to walk in my Savior's footsteps and shine with his light. Each day he grants me 24 new hours to grow in his grace and knowledge of the Savior sent to die for me. Each day he gives me 86,400 wonderful seconds to do unto others as he has done unto me.

Time is God's unique gift to me. I have no say in how many months or days, hours or seconds he grants me. This new year is his time, to measure as he sees fit for me. I do, however, have something to say about my use of his gift. Can I use his gift of time any better than to live in his Word? There I gain a heart filled with true wisdom. Only his Word teaches me that life is the precious time of grace he grants me in which to be readied for heaven. Only his Word makes me wise unto salvation through faith in Christ Jesus. So I will use my moments and my days to learn more fully of, love more deeply, and live more closely to my Savior Jesus.

Eternal Shepherd, help me use the time
you grant me to draw closer to you. Amen.

> THE STAR THEY HAD SEEN IN THE EAST WENT
> AHEAD OF THEM UNTIL IT STOPPED OVER THE
> PLACE WHERE THE CHILD WAS. *Matthew 2:9*

Guided By A Star

Have you ever visited a computer Web site designed to give you a detailed map to the place you want to go? I often use it when heading off to preach in some distant city. Not only does the site show you what highways and streets to take, but it also puts a star right over the desired address.

The Magi from the East that first Epiphany had a star, not on some Web site but in the heavens. The same Lord, who in love had laid his Son as a baby in the manger, now led these first Gentiles to his side. And he used a miraculous star to do so. We don't know exactly what that star was. But we do know where it guided the Magi—to their only Savior from sin.

Do I want to join the Magi in kneeling down and adoring my only Savior? Do I want to watch as God's Son walks the dusty roads of Palestine, wears a crown of thorns, is wrapped in a burial shroud because of my sins? Do I want to marvel as Jesus emerges victorious from the grave, exhibiting his full payment for sin, his power over Satan, his pushing open of heaven's door? There is a way. "Your word is a lamp to my feet and a light for my path," wrote the psalmist (119:105). Wherever I open that Word, I find the Savior. When God gave his Word, it was to make me "wise for salvation through faith in Christ Jesus" (2 Timothy 3:15).

Better than any Web site, brighter than any star in the sky is the Word God has given me.

Guiding Shepherd, guide me daily this
new year by your Word to your side. Amen.

> YOU GUIDE ME WITH YOUR COUNSEL,
> AND AFTERWARD YOU WILL TAKE
> ME INTO GLORY. *Psalm 73:24*

Just Think Where I'm Going

Life is fragile. As soon as I'm born, I begin to die. Each day I live brings me one day closer to death. Like some endless current, the stream of life carries me toward the ocean of eternity.

Such a thought seems to offer scant comfort as I stride deeper into a new year. How hopeless life would be if its only destination were the grave. But wait! There's more. The psalmist dares to speak of glory. He refers to heaven where I will not only see but share in the glory of the Lord. In heaven awaits an existence for me at God's right hand where there is only fullness of joy and eternal pleasures (Psalm 16:11).

But only when God guides me with his counsel. At the head of the list of what a gracious God wants for me is my salvation. He sent his Son, not only for the world but for me. He gives me life, not just to exist but to equip me for eternal life through faith in the Savior. He promises to keep me in faith so that I can share in his glory in heaven.

One night a missionary was called to the deathbed of an elderly Christian. Picking his way through a dark alley, he finally reached her one-room hut. There on a blanket lay the dying believer. Seeing the dirt and poverty, the missionary said, "I'm sorry." But the woman responded, "Sorry for what? Just think of where I'm going." When God will call me home and from where doesn't really matter. What does matter is that I'm ready through Jesus.

*Gentle Shepherd, guide me with
your counsel all the way to heaven. Amen.*

> NOW LISTEN, YOU WHO SAY, "TODAY OR TOMORROW WE WILL
> GO TO THIS OR THAT CITY, SPEND A YEAR THERE, CARRY ON
> BUSINESS AND MAKE MONEY." WHY, YOU DO NOT EVEN
> KNOW WHAT WILL HAPPEN TOMORROW. *James 4:13,14*

See God's Hand In Everything

Can't you almost see them? Those business executives gathered around the conference table. The colored charts and statistics neatly bound in print before them. The future all planned down to the smallest detail. There's nothing wrong with planning. We do it too. We pencil our dreams on the calendar of time. But those men left something vital out. It was all, "We will go; we will spend; we will carry; we will make money." Where was the Lord slotted into their plans?

Such planning without the Lord is arrogant. It denies man's dependence on God and prevents asking him for guidance. Plans that paint self in bold colors but God only in the small corners of the landscape of the future are hollow and headed for failure.

I don't know what this year will bring. For that matter, I don't even know what tomorrow will offer. Should I use such ignorance as an excuse to do no planning, no hoping, no nothing? Or should I instead look to my gracious God? He knows what all the future holds for me. Indeed, he's planned that future. And he's done it in such a way that it will serve my good. I need only to look at his Son stretched out on Calvary's cross in payment for my sins to be assured of this comforting truth.

Guiding Shepherd, help me plan my days
asking for and assured of your gracious help. Amen.

> INSTEAD, YOU OUGHT TO SAY, "IF IT IS THE LORD'S
> WILL, WE WILL LIVE AND DO THIS OR THAT." *James 4:15*

Leave Everything
In God's Hand

"If it is the Lord's will, we will live and do this or that" is the key phrase in a Christian's planning. My life, every feature of it and any future in it, depends on God's will. In all my plans and pursuits, he is to be the rightful partner. Just as I pray in earthly affairs "your will be done," so I must plan for the future saying, "If it is the Lord's will." Only such planning pleases God and leaves everything in his hand.

"If it is the Lord's will." My forefathers used that phrase frequently. In life's daily choices, as well as in its deep crises, they said simply, "If it is the Lord's will." James, in the verse above, suggests that I might do well to follow their example. No, he doesn't mean merely to add another cliché to my vocabulary, one that means little when I speak it and others hear it. He's not offering a phrase to wave like some magical wand in the face of the year ahead to chase all failure away. What he has in mind is living with the conviction that God must do the guiding and with the confidence that his will is always right.

One day a man was complaining to his friend that the problems of today and the plans for tomorrow were keeping him awake at night. His friend replied that he himself had no trouble at all sleeping. "What do you do?" the first man asked. "Count the sheep?"

"No," came the reply, "I talk to the Shepherd." The guidance of a Shepherd who died for me will always be right.

Loving Shepherd, take my hand and lead me day by day. Amen.

THE EYES OF THE LORD ARE ON
THE RIGHTEOUS AND HIS EARS ARE
ATTENTIVE TO THEIR CRY. *Psalm 34:15*

What God Does Not Forget

How forgetful are you? Somehow names escape me more frequently as my birthdays speed by. I don't always remember what my wife told me yesterday. And I check my desk calendar more frequently to make sure I don't forget an appointment.

What if God would forget things the way I do? What if just for one hour he forgot and took his hands off this complex world he once created? What if just for one day he forgot to put the sun to bed at night and get it up in the morning? What if just for one season he forgot to cause the seed to sprout and the rain to water it?

Or what if he forgot about me? What if he lost track of me, one little cipher in this world of billions? What if he let my house number slip from his memory or lost sight of me in the madding crowds of life? What if he forgot or didn't care about my blisters and blunders, my dreams and desires? What a shambles this world would be and what a hopeless shuffle across it my life would become.

But God doesn't forget. He remembers the world he created and sustains it by his powerful Word. His believers, even the lowest of them, he calls by name. His wisdom, colored by his love, sends their daily care. And that includes me. His love washed me clean through Jesus' blood. Now his eyes are always watching over me and his ears are ever open to my prayers.

Lord, don't let me forget you, who
always watches over me, body and soul. Amen.

> "I WILL FORGIVE THEIR WICKEDNESS AND WILL REMEMBER THEIR SINS NO MORE." *Jeremiah 31:34*

What God Does Forget

Have you ever thought about the all-knowing, all-wise God forgetting something? It can happen. He himself says so. Of my many sins he declares, "I will remember them no more."

Do those words excite me? Or is my reaction, "It's good to hear that God forgives and forgets my sin, but . . ." Is sin only something next door in someone else instead of something very real in my daily life? Is it only like some slight smudge on the back of my hand instead of dirt imbedded deeply under every fingernail? Satan loves to blunt my conscience so that sin is less and less recognized and God's forgiveness more and more rejected.

Or is my reaction, "Can God forgive me? Isn't my sin too big?" Like some nightmare, those "special sins" of the past can come back again and again to haunt me. When the devil can't keep the message of God's forgiveness from me, he tries to tell me that it doesn't count for me.

But to the penitent, to whom each sin is eternally serious and its burden unbearably grievous, God's words about not remembering sins are wondrously sweet. Let me mark this well! When God forgets my sins, it's because he remembers what happened on Calvary's cross. Because he well remembers Jesus' total payment for my sin, he can say of me too, "I will forgive their wickedness and will remember their sins no more."

*Lord, thank you for sending Jesus to pay for
my sins so that you remember them no more. Amen.*

> "I HAVE LOVED YOU WITH AN
> EVERLASTING LOVE." *Jeremiah 31:3*

His Endless Ways Of Love

We were standing on the shores of Lake Superior, watching the waves. One after another they washed the shore. As long as we stood there marveling, those waves just kept coming.

How much like God's incredible love! It just keeps coming, not because of what we are but because of what God is. His very nature is love, and that love is so supreme. It embraces sinners who hate him. It reaches for the undeserving. It pays for the unworthy. It covers even me!

How might I go about describing this awesome love? To begin I might look back into eternity at a love that planned the salvation of a lost world not even yet made or born. Next I might look down to Calvary, to a love that shouldered my sins, shuddered in hell's pains because of them, shouted of their payment, "It is finished." Then I might look ahead to another eternity filled with the songs of saints to the One who loved them and washed them clean by his own blood.

All my life his love just keeps coming. It came to me at the baptismal font and put the sign of the Savior's cross on my heart. It speaks to me through the pages of his Word. It assures me at the Communion Table, by giving me his body and blood, that my sins are truly gone.

We could have stood longer on that Lake Superior shore watching the waves, but I had to move on. From those endless waves of God's love, we want never to turn aside.

Lord of endless love, hold us close, fill us
with wonder, bathe us with your saving love. Amen.

> JESUS ANSWERED, "I AM THE WAY. . . .
> NO ONE COMES TO THE FATHER
> EXCEPT THROUGH ME." *John 14:6*

Heaven's Direct Flight

I've become rather picky when it comes to flying. Too many times I've had to race across the concourses in the airport at Minneapolis or Detroit to catch or even to miss a connecting flight. No more, if I can help it. It's too risky. Only direct flights for me.

Yet why do I still at times think I need a connecting flight to heaven? The Savior has told me clearly that he's the one way to the Father. Scripture declares plainly that only his blood and righteousness can lift me up to heaven. Jesus is my direct flight, my only flight, with no other connections needed.

See how smart Satan is? He knows that if he can't keep the message of Christ's salvation away from me, he can at least try to confuse me about its sufficiency. "You have to do something too to save yourself," he whispers in my ear. "Christ will fly you part of the way, but you have to take a connecting flight," he suggests cleverly. And such nonsense appeals to me. My sinful nature wants me to think that I can, indeed, that I must, do something on my own to reach heaven's airport. Such insidious propaganda can keep me running in anxiety across the concourses of life.

*Lord, help me to say, "No more." Lord, help me to say,
"Only a direct flight to heaven aboard my Savior Jesus." Then
senseless anxiety will be replaced by sweet comfort. Please, Lord. Amen.*

GOD PLACED ALL THINGS UNDER HIS FEET
AND APPOINTED HIM TO BE HEAD OVER
EVERYTHING FOR THE CHURCH. *Ephesians 1:22*

More Than Menominee County

We were driving through upper Michigan on our way to Sault Ste. Marie, Canada. where we once served. Shortly after we crossed a county line, a hand-lettered sign caught our attention. "Jesus is Lord of Menominee County," it read.

It's true. Jesus is Lord of Menominee County. Yet isn't that statement too limited? Jesus is Lord of every county in Michigan, every state in the USA, every country in the world. The ascended Lord Jesus rules over everything. God has placed all things under his feet, an old expression meaning that he rules with his almighty power over all. And best of all, Jesus uses his power to rule everything for the best interests of his church.

By God's grace I'm part of his church. With his marvelous love God has added me to his family of believers in Christ. Now he assures me that the almighty ascended Jesus runs the world and everything in it for the benefit of all believers, including me.

So why do I fret and worry when I read the morning headlines or watch the evening news? Why do I sweat and strain when I look at the problems of today and speculate about what tomorrow might bring? I have an ascended Lord, who rules not just over Menominee County but the whole world. He especially has the well-being of believers in mind. Thank God, Jesus is Lord of my life.

Lord, keep reminding me of how almighty you are
and of how you rule over everything for your church. Amen.

> JOHN SAW JESUS COMING TOWARD HIM AND
> SAID, "LOOK, THE LAMB OF GOD, WHO TAKES
> AWAY THE SIN OF THE WORLD!" *John 1:29*

What Would You Like To Hear?

Contrary to some opinions, preaching a sermon is not easy. A faithful pastor spends many hours preparing his weekly message for his parishioners. One seminary professor drummed into our ears that we were to spend one hour in preparation for each minute of sermon. A pastor expends such effort because he wants to present God's Word correctly to his people.

There is no better way to sum up the message of God's Word than to say, "Look, the Lamb of God, who takes away the sin of the world!" "Christ died for our sins" is the central truth around which all the other truths of Scripture revolve. The apostle Paul preached this message. He said, "I passed on to you as of first importance: that Christ died for our sins" (1 Corinthians 15:3). Peter had the same message. He said of the Lamb, "He himself bore our sins in his body on the tree" (1 Peter 2:24). So did John the apostle. He reminded his people, "Jesus Christ laid down his life for us" (1 John 3:16).

Always a pastor will point listeners to the spotless Lamb, who sacrificed himself on the cross for the world's sins. No sermon is complete without lifting the eyes of sinners to Calvary's cross. Where else would I want my pastor to point me when sins oppress me? What else would my needy soul want to hear than those blessed words: "Look, the Lamb of God, who takes away the sin of the world!"?

Lord, give us faithful pastors who, like
John the Baptist, know where to point us. Amen.

> JESUS SAW THEM FOLLOWING AND ASKED, "WHAT DO YOU WANT?"
> THEY SAID, "RABBI" (WHICH MEANS TEACHER), "WHERE ARE
> YOU STAYING?" "COME," HE REPLIED, "AND YOU WILL SEE." *John 1:38,39*

What Do You Want?

When Jesus saw those two disciples of John the Baptist following him, he asked, "What do you want?" Hoping against hope for an invitation, they responded, "Where are you staying?" "Come and see," the Savior encouraged. And they did. What they received from him that day was marked deeply in their hearts. They could even remember the exact hour when they had been introduced to the Lamb of God and came to know him as the One who took away their sins.

What would I answer if Jesus asked that same question of me? Would it be "Pardon for my many sins"? "Come and see," he says, "whether I will not cleanse you from all unrighteousness." Or would it be "Peace"? "Come and see," he replies, "whether I will not give you peace with God, which transcends all understanding." Would it be "Help in temptation"? "Come and see," he invites, "whether I meant it when I said that I will with the temptation also provide a way out so that you might stand up under it." Is it "Comfort at the grave of a loved one"? "Come and see," he assures me, "whether I will not comfort you as one whom his mother comforts."

I may not be able to pinpoint the hour as those disciples did when I first sat believingly at Jesus' feet. Nor is that important. Better by far is what that Lamb of God gave and keeps on giving me. Important beyond imagination are the truths of salvation he has for my soul.

*Lord, keep leading me to
your Lamb, my Savior. Amen.*

> ANDREW, SIMON PETER'S BROTHER, WAS ONE OF THE TWO WHO
> HEARD WHAT JOHN HAD SAID AND WHO HAD FOLLOWED JESUS.
> THE FIRST THING ANDREW DID WAS TO FIND HIS BROTHER
> SIMON AND TELL HIM, "WE HAVE FOUND THE MESSIAH" (THAT
> IS, THE CHRIST). AND HE BROUGHT HIM TO JESUS. *John 1:40-42*

Whom Will You Tell?

We don't hear much about Andrew. He never preached a sermon like his brother Simon Peter on Pentecost. He never worked great miracles like Peter. He never wrote epistles as Peter did. But Andrew had the distinction of being the one who brought his brother to Jesus.

Perhaps I can't remember the "Andrew" who cared enough for my soul to tell me about Jesus. Was it Christian parents who brought me to the baptismal font? Was it my mother who held me on her lap and crooned the Savior's name in my ear? Was it a pastor or teacher who took the time to tell me about the Savior? Was it a spouse who loved me so much that she wanted me to know the One who loved me even more? The name of my Andrew doesn't really matter all that much. What does matter is the question, To whom will I be an Andrew?

It's not hard to be an Andrew and tell someone about the Lamb who takes away sin. All I need to do is repeat Andrew's words: "We have found the Messiah." I don't have to argue like some learned theologian. After all, the Bible is fact, and you don't argue facts. You simply state them. I don't need to convert someone to faith. All I need do is point to that Lamb and let the Holy Spirit do the rest. But like Andrew, once the Lamb is in my heart, point I must and will.

Lord, make me an Andrew. Help me to tell
all I can about the Lamb who takes away sin. Amen.

[YOU] THROUGH FAITH ARE SHIELDED BY GOD'S
POWER UNTIL THE COMING OF THE SALVATION THAT IS
READY TO BE REVEALED IN THE LAST TIME. *1 Peter 1:5*

Don't Cut Those Whiskers

Ever wonder why cats can move so gracefully in the dark? It's because of their whiskers. Those sensitive hairs, attached to nerves in the skin, alert the cat to nearby objects. Also those whiskers, nearly as wide as a cat's body, help it gauge whether it can fit through tight openings. So don't cut your cat's whiskers.

As a believer I have something much better than a cat's whiskers. I can find my way through the narrow gate that leads to heaven, while others stumble around in the darkness. I'm not only alerted to but closely attached to the most necessary object in anyone's life. That's Jesus, my Savior. I can walk safely through life because I know the eternal salvation that's coming when my days or the days of this world end.

I can do these things, I said. But that's not true. Rather, it's the power of my loving God that does them for me. His Holy Spirit through the power of the gospel has created faith in me. His Holy Spirit through the same powerful means promises to continue such faith in me. My salvation through Jesus' work is his gracious gift. So is also my continuing faith in the Savior.

There is one thing I can do—not cut my connection with the gospel in Word and sacrament. Without whiskers a cat might be lost in the darkness. Without an ongoing connection with God's powerful gospel, I'd be more than lost in this world's darkness. I'd be lost in hell.

*Lord, shield me by the power of
your Word unto eternal salvation. Amen.*

> JESUS HAS BECOME THE GUARANTEE
> OF A BETTER COVENANT. *Hebrews 7:22*

Great Deposit–
Great Return

When I was in Sweden teaching in the seminary of our sister church, I had to get used to returning plastic and glass bottles to the grocery store. In the store entrance stood a machine that spit out the coins as you slipped in the bottles. How different from the "no deposit—no return" practice that I was used to.

Thank God he doesn't operate with a "no deposit—no return" policy when it comes to mankind. He would have good reason to do so. Why should he want us in heaven with him after our first parents in the garden turned their backs on him? Why should he want creatures like me, sullied with sin and soiled by unbelief, to be his on earth and finally in eternity? How could I complain if he just tossed me into the garbage can of hell?

But that's not my loving God. On Calvary's holy mountain he put down a deposit on me. Even more, there he made his own Son the guarantee—the reliable security—for my salvation. With the precious blood of his Son, he signed the blessed covenant, his will and testament, in which he promised me salvation. He made me. He paid for me. He promises that he will take me as his very own to his heavenly home. And Jesus is his guarantee.

Talk about deposits! What can be more precious than Jesus' atoning blood? Talk about returns! What can be more precious than eternity at his side?

Lord, thank you for Jesus. Lord, help me
trust your promises made sure by his blood. Amen.

> "SALVATION IS FOUND IN NO ONE ELSE, FOR
> THERE IS NO OTHER NAME UNDER HEAVEN GIVEN
> TO MEN BY WHICH WE MUST BE SAVED." *Acts 4:12*

No Substitute For Jesus

While a seminary student, I earned my tuition by working summers as a section hand for the old Milwaukee Road railroad. One of our backbreaking tasks was to replace the worn-out wooden ties under the rails. Today the railroads are experimenting with ties made out of milk jugs, plastic coffee cups, and grocery bags. Their thinking is that such recycled material will last longer than wood.

Mankind likes to experiment. Often good comes out of their efforts. In one area no experimentation is needed. Nor can any good whatsoever come if man tries. That's in the serious matter of our salvation. Not satisfied with God's payment for sin through the sacrifice of his Son, people search far and wide for something better. They try science, assuming that they can better themselves if they put their minds to it. They try charity, hoping that good will can turn aside ever-present animosity among nations. They try education, reasoning that the more knowledge they acquire the better off they'll be. Only to end up in dismay when all their self-trusting efforts fail.

Peter's words still stand because they are God's words. When the apostle told the Jewish leaders there was no substitute for the Savior, he uttered a lasting truth. Railroad ties may change, even for the better. For me, the sinner, there can be no substitute for Jesus. Only his holy life offers the perfection I need to stand clothed in righteousness before my heavenly Father. Only his precious blood offers the payment I need to stand sinless in his sight.

Lord, keep me covered with Jesus'
all-sufficient blood and righteousness. Amen.

> THANKS BE TO GOD, WHO . . . THROUGH US
> SPREADS EVERYWHERE THE FRAGRANCE OF
> THE KNOWLEDGE OF HIM. *2 Corinthians 2:14*

Love That Smell

Onions smell. When I dice them for my wife because of her arthritic hands, I just can't seem to get the smell off my fingers. Did you know that pungent is better when it comes to onions? That the more robustly flavored ones contain the highest levels of disease fighting antioxidants?

Paul was not speaking about onions when he wrote our verse. He was speaking about ministers of the gospel and so, in turn, also about each one of us. As believers we are to smell. Let's use Paul's word; it sounds better. As believers we are to spread a fragrance as we go through life. That fragrance is the sweet knowledge of our loving Lord. From our words and our works, people are to learn something about their only Savior. What sensation can be more pleasant for anyone than knowing and trusting Jesus?

When God converts my fist of unbelief into a hand of faith, he pours sweet-smelling treasures into it. Pardon for my sin, peace for my soul, and the promise of heaven have a fragrance that nothing can top. That fragrance, however, is not intended just for me. God has given me two hands, one to hold these treasures and one to hand them on to others. He doesn't want me to smell sweet just for myself. He wants me to share the perfume of salvation with everyone I can.

I may not like the smell of onions, but I sure do love the fragrance of salvation.

Lord, thank you for making me smell sweet
to you. Help me share that smell with others. Amen.

> THIS IS WHAT THE LORD SAYS—HE WHO CREATED
> YOU, O JACOB, HE WHO FORMED YOU, O ISRAEL:
> "FEAR NOT, FOR I HAVE REDEEMED YOU." *Isaiah 43:1*

Made And Remade By The Lord

"God made me, and he don't make no junk," said the poster in a religious bookstore. How true! Each of God's children is important in his sight. There's no pecking order, no list of dignitaries, no higher or lower class, just people on whom he has lavished his love.

Just look at the "me" he made. Supposedly my skeleton has 206 bones. My heart beats about 100,800 times a day, handling 5,000 gallons of blood. My body has more than six hundred muscles and about an equal number of nerves. In my blood vessels course approximately 24 trillion red cells carrying oxygen to nourish tissues. That doesn't sound like junk but something God's wisdom put magnificently together and God's power keeps marvelously functioning.

There's more, much more! When my first parents infected me with their sin, God didn't cast me aside like some useless piece of rusted junk. When sin put me into Satan's clutches and closed heaven's door, God didn't put an eternal padlock on the latch. Instead, he sent his Son, Jesus, to redeem me. To Bethlehem's crib he came. On to Calvary's cross he went. Into the cold, clammy grave he was deposited. How much God, who made me, must love me! His awesome love has remade me into his beloved child and heir of his heaven.

Junk? Hardly. Sounds like something his love has made precious in his sight.

Lord, thank you for making me and
then remaking me because of your love. Amen.

> "I HAVE SUMMONED YOU BY NAME;
> YOU ARE MINE." *Isaiah 43:1*

He Knows My Name

In this world of five billion plus, I am no longer a name. I'm a number. From the beginning to the ending of life, I'm given a number. In the hospital it was a number on a wristband so that I wouldn't be mixed up with another baby. I live in a house that has a number. That number better be on the mail or it won't find my door. When I gained my driver's license, again a number was recorded in the state capital. And what about my social security number? More than anything else those nine digits are used to identify me.

How refreshing and how comforting to hear God say, "I have summoned you by name"! I'm not just a number to him, but a name. Just think of what that means. God knows every one of my needs. He knows the heartaches and heartbreaks of my life, the toils and troubles I have to wrestle with. He knows how much my shoulders can carry. He knows how to strengthen me under life's burdens and when to lift them to keep them from crushing me.

There's still more. When Jesus carried the world's sins to the cross, God included in them my sins. When my parents brought me to the baptismal font, God wrote my name in the book of heaven. When God sends his angels on my last day, they'll carry me home to heaven where a room with my name written on it awaits me.

I suppose I can live being just a number in this crowded world. But I cannot live without my God calling me by name.

Lord, let it ever be so because
of your grace and love. Amen.

> THEN HE SAID, "MAY THE LORD NOT BE ANGRY,
> BUT LET ME SPEAK JUST ONCE MORE. WHAT IF ONLY
> TEN CAN BE FOUND THERE?" HE ANSWERED, "FOR
> THE SAKE OF TEN, I WILL NOT DESTROY IT." *Genesis 18:32*

Pray Humbly

Do I know how to pray? "Of course," I might answer. "I've been doing it from my mother's knee." Prayer is a blessed privilege God gives only to his believers. Only his children can crawl up on his lap in prayer and lay everything in his hands. Yet I can use reminders of how to pray correctly. That's what Abraham offers us in our verse.

Did you notice how Abraham prayed? There was no brash demanding—no "you have to or else." Instead, it's the plea, "May the Lord not be angry." Humbly aware of his unworthiness, Abraham prayed to the Lord and yet with faith's strength squeezed God's arm.

Like Abraham, I need to realize that I'm a beggar. Only when Jesus goes with me dare I knock on the Father's door in heaven. When he opens, Jesus will tell him, "Father, answer, not because of him, the sinner, but me, the Savior." Because of my Savior, I can go boldly to the Father.

Mindful of this important truth, my prayers will not be crowbars to pry something loose from God but containers to carry my loads to him. First and foremost, when I come to him, will be my thanksgiving for giving me Jesus to cover all my sins and make me capable of even talking to my gracious Father. Then will follow my humble, yet confident, prayers.

Lord, teach me to pray humbly relying
on your love for me in Jesus. Amen.

> THEN HE SAID, "MAY THE LORD NOT BE ANGRY,
> BUT LET ME SPEAK JUST ONCE MORE. WHAT IF ONLY
> TEN CAN BE FOUND THERE?" HE ANSWERED, "FOR
> THE SAKE OF TEN, I WILL NOT DESTROY IT." *Genesis 18:32*

Pray Unselfishly

The Lord had come to Abraham's camp that day for several reasons. One was to announce that Sarah was finally to bear a son. Another was to share with his earthly friend news about the coming judgment on Sodom and Gomorrah. Still another was to give Abraham an opportunity to pray unselfishly for others.

Abraham seized that opportunity. How fervently he prayed for his nephew Lot! "Serves him right," Abraham might have gloated about that selfish nephew who had taken advantage of him and who was now living in those wicked cities. There were also the inhabitants of those cities whom he had once risked his life to rescue. "Not worth it," Abraham might have said of them. Yet he prayed for them. "Prayer is unselfish," we learn listening to Abraham's prayer.

Or is it? Recalling my prayers of this past week, do I find more "they" and "theirs" or "I" and "mine"? So quickly do my needs bend my knees and take up all the space that I forget about others. Even when I pray about others, isn't it often "us" and "ours," like those in my home or church family. From Abraham comes the reminder that those who are close to God will have a lost world close to their hearts and in their prayers. Let me take that reminder to heart as I tug on God's sleeve, asking him to spread the message of the Savior to the lost and to speed the work of the Holy Spirit in their hearts.

Lord, remind me so to pray. Amen.

> THEN HE SAID, "MAY THE LORD NOT BE ANGRY,
> BUT LET ME SPEAK JUST ONCE MORE. WHAT IF ONLY
> TEN CAN BE FOUND THERE?" HE ANSWERED, "FOR
> THE SAKE OF TEN, I WILL NOT DESTROY IT." *Genesis 18:32*

Pray Persistently

I wanted a football so badly. My parents weren't rich. Christmas gifts usually were essential items of clothing like socks and shirts. But I wanted a football and reminded especially my mother of my desire almost every day. Imagine my joy when a football showed up under the tree.

Six times Abraham prayed and each time his faith and courage grew. He started with 50 and went all the way down to 10 righteous for whom he prayed. It wasn't that he was haggling with God but that God was leading his believer on in persistent prayer. The Lord was teaching his friend to exercise a faith that sees the invisible, believes the incredible, and receives the impossible.

Too often I pray like some mischievous child ringing a doorbell and running away before anyone can answer. Abraham reminds me to put faith's finger on the doorbell of prayer and keep it there. When I carry earthly requests to God, I must add to my persistence the words, "Your will be done." But when it's for my spiritual needs, those words aren't necessary. I know how much he wants me to have his forgiveness. How much he wants to strengthen me in the face of temptation. How much he wants to comfort me in my sorrows. But from me he looks for persistence in prayer that shows I trust his will.

I don't know if my parents would have given me that football without my persistence. Thank God I do know how he answers my persistent prayers.

Lord, remind me to pray persistently. Amen.

> IN HIM WAS LIFE, AND THAT LIFE
> WAS THE LIGHT OF MEN. THE LIGHT
> SHINES IN THE DARKNESS. *John 1:4,5*

Light for the Dark Road

We were coming home from our granddaughter's basketball game. It was raining so hard that I had trouble seeing the faded white lines marking the lanes on the busy Milwaukee street. "Why don't they repaint those lines?" I complained to my wife as we struggled in the wet darkness to get home safely.

Do I want to reach my heavenly home safely? Are there any clear lines on the street to eternity? God has given me more than lane markers in Jesus. In Jesus he has given me life and light. Those two belong together. When John speaks of life in Jesus, he means more than what I need for my physical existence. He means life as God meant it for mankind before sin ruined his perfect creation. That life is also my light. Like a houseplant soon shrivels without the sun's light, so I cannot exist without my Savior. No Jesus—no life and light. With Jesus—eternal life and light.

Where can I find the life and light of Jesus? Only in God's Word. Scripture's chief purpose is to show me the way to heaven through Jesus' payment for my sins. Like some bright, shining lines drawn on the highway, God's Word points me to the Savior. Nor do the lines ever have to be repainted. Scripture's message of my only Savior shines clearly in the darkness of this world. Unbelief's darkness may still shroud the world, but not my life. I can travel safely to my heavenly home with Jesus.

Lord, thank you for bringing me from sin's darkness into Jesus' wondrous life and light. Amen.

> THE DISCIPLES WENT AND WOKE HIM,
> SAYING, "LORD, SAVE US! WE'RE
> GOING TO DROWN!" *Matthew 8:25*

A Sure Cure For Seasickness

Any landlubber can tell you that the only sure cure for seasickness is to stay on dry land. I had to learn the hard way. Out salmon fishing on Lake Michigan, I watched the waves rising. Finally they rocked our boat so roughly that I had to lean my head quickly over the side.

The disciples were obviously more seasoned sailors than I was. Nothing is said about them becoming seasick. But they did become afraid. The storm on the Sea of Galilee that day was rougher than any they had ever gone through. In fact, they didn't think they would get through this one. "We're going to drown," they frantically told Jesus as they awoke him from his nap. Yes, they should have known that with Jesus in the boat all would end well. But they forgot.

Sound familiar? Have I ever looked at the waves instead of the One who rules over them? Have I ever thought I was sailing alone in the boat of life instead of with my Savior? Have I ever despaired, thinking I had done all I could and forgetting to turn to him who can do anything? Especially when my soul is churning, how I need Jesus! When I've fallen into that same pet sin again, I need to turn to the One who has paid for my repeated mistakes. When some sudden temptation has made me seasick, I need to know the Savior's blood covers it also.

The good feeling when seasickness passes is far surpassed by the calm my soul finds in Jesus.

Lord Jesus, sail with me on life's sea
and keep me safe till heaven's shore. Amen.

> "THE PHARISEE STOOD UP AND PRAYED ABOUT HIMSELF: 'GOD: I
> THANK YOU THAT I AM NOT LIKE OTHER MEN—ROBBERS, EVILDOERS,
> ADULTERERS—OR EVEN LIKE THIS TAX COLLECTOR. I FAST TWICE
> A WEEK AND GIVE A TENTH OF ALL I GET.'" *Luke 18:11,12*

Worshiping God– What Not To Do

Each September we received a new vicar at St. John's. My job was to help train this seminary student in the field for one year. As part of his orientation, I'd tell him, "You're going to learn from my actions what to do and from my mistakes what not to do." The same thing is true as we watch those two men worshiping in the temple. Let's start with the Pharisee.

"He prayed," it says. Nothing wrong with that. But notice, "He prayed about himself." "God, I thank you," he went on. That sounds good too. But notice again for what he gave thanks. He wasn't thanking God at all but expecting God to thank him. Simply condensed, his prayer was, "See, God, how good I am and how well I have done." Then with his prayers finished, he went home empty handed; sinful, but not willing to admit it, much less ask for pardon.

How sneakily my worship can slip into something like that of the Pharisee. Time to ask some important questions. Do I worship in order to seek absolution for my sins or to announce my goodness? To do a favor for God or to learn of the great favor he has done for me by sending the Savior? As soon as I think there's something in me that God must commend and that will commend me for heaven, then I've become like that Pharisee. Then I also will go home empty handed without God's blessings.

*Merciful Lord, help me bring my sins to
you and carry home your abundant pardon. Amen.*

> "BUT THE TAX COLLECTOR STOOD AT A DISTANCE. HE WOULD
> NOT EVEN LOOK UP TO HEAVEN, BUT BEAT HIS BREAST AND
> SAID, 'GOD, HAVE MERCY ON ME, A SINNER.'" *Luke 18:13*

Worshiping God— What To Do

There in the back of the temple stood that tax collector. In the shadows, utterly ashamed, he wouldn't even raise his eyes to heaven. The best he could do was beat his breast in sorrow. Then came his prayer— one shuddering sigh, "God, have mercy on me, a sinner." Only seven short words, but they clearly showed the man's heart. In the Greek original he was even more emphatic. It was not "me, *a* sinner," but "me, *the* sinner." He felt himself as chief of sinners. His only plea was "God be merciful to me. Forgive my many sins out of your great mercy."

Do I want to go home from worship as that publican did? Do I want to hear the Lord say of me, "I tell you, this man . . . went home justified before God"? Then I need to look honestly at myself and recognize how my many sins have grieved my holy God. Then I need to look trustingly at Jesus and rejoice in how his blood has paid for my sins as numerous as they may be. Then, and only then, I can go home as the publican did, an accepted, cleansed, renewed child of God. And God will go with me.

I can worship God in many ways at my church, in my home, and in my daily life. But always at worship's center is confession of my utter unworthiness and reception of God's marvelous mercy. Then I'll know the fullness of those words, "The Lord look on you with favor and give you peace."

Lord, teach me to worship you as did that tax
collector so that I can go home with your peace. Amen.

"THE SEED IS THE WORD OF GOD. THOSE ALONG THE
PATH ARE THE ONES WHO HEAR, AND THEN THE DEVIL
COMES AND TAKES AWAY THE WORD FROM THEIR HEARTS,
SO THAT THEY MAY NOT BELIEVE AND BE SAVED." *Luke 8:11,12*

Routine Hearing

Can't you almost see the sower in Jesus' parable, taking his measured steps across the field, rhythmically scattering his handfuls of seed? Some falls on the hard path at the field's edge. No soft bed there, only hard surface on which to lie waiting for birds to swoop down and snatch it.

Remember Jesus is telling his parable for people like me who hear his Word. I'm not to be like some hard path on which the seed only bounces and becomes food for the blackbird called the devil to snatch away. The devil tries to do just that. If he can't keep me from hearing God's Word, he tries to close my ears so that I don't really listen. The pastor speaks about sin, but he must mean somebody else's misdeeds. The pastor preaches once again, "Christ died for your sins," but my mind drifts because I've heard that blessed message so often. The pastor tells me to forgive, but he can't be referring to that relative who has hurt me. Might it be embarrassing if some Sunday during the sermon my mind would say out loud what I'm really thinking about?

What's the antidote for such routine hearing? There is one. It begins by praying, "Lord, open my heart to hear." It continues by working at listening to his Word, something that requires effort just as hard as preaching the sermon. It carries home the message, thinking about and trying to follow it all week. Above all, it savors the chief part of that message, that of a Savior who died for me.

Please, Lord, open my heart to hear
and through your Word to me draw near. Amen.

"THOSE ON THE ROCK ARE THE ONES WHO RECEIVE THE WORD WITH JOY WHEN THEY HEAR IT, BUT THEY HAVE NO ROOT. THEY BELIEVE FOR A WHILE, BUT IN THE TIME OF TESTING THEY FALL AWAY." *Luke 8:13*

Shallow Hearing

In the land where Jesus walked there was plenty of soil like this. Only a thin layer of dirt covered the ground—just enough for the seed to sprout but not enough to sustain it. The first dry wind or hot spell that came along would cause the tender shoot to shrivel up and die.

The devil doesn't throw in the towel when God's Word sprouts in people's hearts. He turns up the heat. He blows on their fledgling faith with the heat of temptation, trouble, or ridicule. Sometimes he tries to wilt budding faith by overemphasizing faith's responsibilities. "Take up your cross; keep my commandments; love not the world—that's more than you bargained for," he argues. And some shallow hearers end up like the youngster who dreamed about being a fireman only later to turn aside when learning about the dedication to duty that required.

Again Jesus is telling his parable for people who like me hear his Word. Some days—like the days of my confirmation, wedding, or hospital stay—that Word makes a deep impression on my heart. The shoot of faith stands up boldly, eager to say, "Savior, lead I follow thee." But then sickness strikes, trouble thunders, loved ones leave, and the heat gets to me.

What's the antidote for such shallow hearing? There is one. It's more hearing of that powerful Word. Through it the Holy Spirit works, not only to create but to continue faith. Through it he works to tie me closer to the One who has saved me from the greatest trouble—my sin.

Please, Lord, open my heart to hear
and through your Word to me draw near. Amen.

"THE SEED THAT FELL AMONG THORNS STANDS FOR THOSE WHO HEAR, BUT AS THEY GO ON THEIR WAY, THEY ARE CHOKED BY LIFE'S WORRIES, RICHES AND PLEASURES, AND THEY DO NOT MATURE." *Luke 8:14*

Crowded Hearing

Some seed sprouted and started growing in the soil. So also did the weeds. And soon they outdistanced the sprouts of grain. Greedily the weeds soaked in the sunshine from above and selfishly sucked up the moisture from below. The result was predictable—death by strangulation for the grain.

Remember Jesus is telling this parable for people like me who hear his Word. If Satan can't kill off the seed of God's Word from below or wither it from above, he tries to choke it off with the weeds of cares and riches and pleasures. He tries to convince me that I can live the new life without giving up the old. He tries to entice me into listening with one ear to God's Word and the other to the world. He tries to assure me that I can enjoy the only Savior from sin and the sweet pleasures of this world at the same time. What he doesn't tell me is that the end result can only be death for my faith by means of suffocation. It's no secret that such crowded hearing has sucked the moisture out of many hearts and is one of the great problems in the church today.

The antidote for such crowded hearing? There is one. It's remembering that faith requires more than just annual pruning. It's recognizing that the only plant food for faith is found in the sprinkling can and fertilizer bag of God's Word and sacraments. And it's doing such pruning and feeding on a regular basis. I can live without the things of this world but not without the Savior.

Please, Lord, open my heart to hear
and through your Word to me draw near. Amen.

> "BUT THE SEED ON GOOD SOIL STANDS FOR THOSE WITH A
> NOBLE AND GOOD HEART, WHO HEAR THE WORD, RETAIN IT,
> AND BY PERSEVERING PRODUCE A CROP." *Luke 8:15*

Fruitful Hearing

In many parts of the Midwest, there are fields like Jesus mentions next in his parable. It's good loam, well prepared. In it the seed sprouts and grows. Soon tender stalks wave in the wind. On them the kernels start forming, filling out into golden grain, holding promise of a fruitful harvest.

Do I need any explanation for this picture? It happens all around me. Pray God, it's happening also in me. The Word of God sprouts in hearts and shows in lives. Faith grows and flourishes. Its fruits of Christian love and service flower daily. This part of the picture I can understand, but the rest I cannot. How there can be any fruitful hearing at all is beyond me.

Behind that fruitful hearing lies the power of God the Holy Spirit. He and he alone breaks up the stony soil of unbelief in my heart. He and he alone causes the Word to sprout and grow there. He and he alone lovingly cultivates and cares for me as his precious seedling through Word and sacrament. He and he alone brings fruit out of that Word in my life. It may be more or less fruit than in others. But a harvest there will be. Behind such fruitful hearing is always his miracle.

No antidote is needed for such fruitful hearing. Just thanksgiving to God for clearing my heart of unbelief, creating in it faith in the Savior, cultivating it with his powerful Word so that I can bear abundant fruit for him.

Please, Lord, keep opening my heart to hear
and through your Word to me draw near. Amen.

"GOD WILL WIPE AWAY EVERY TEAR
FROM THEIR EYES." *Revelation 7:17*

God's Absorbent Handkerchief

My mother had one, and it surely came in handy. When I was little and had skinned my knee or had my feelings scorched, I would run crying to her. Bending down to hold me close, she would pull out her handkerchief to wipe the hot tears from my eyes. Looking back now, I recognize it wasn't so much that absorbent cloth but her loving care that soothed my "owies."

What a pleasing, though imperfect, picture of Christ, the wiper away of all my tears! Folded closely to his breast, my "owies" not only feel better but are taken away. When my soul sheds hot tears of remorse over my sins, he wipes them away with his forgiveness. How can I continue crying when I see the cross embroidered on his handkerchief? Yes, repeated sins, even new sins, arise each day in my life, but his love is always there when I come crying in repentance to him.

When I bring my other tears to him, again he is there. Tears I have— every day. Tears of rejection caused by people closer or farther away. Tears of misfortune caused by sickness or sorrow. Tears of frustration caused by pain or problems. His soothing touch wipes them all away. He may not always remove the causes for my tears, but it helps to know he cares and shares.

How I look forward to the eternal day when God's handkerchief will wipe my tears totally away! I can't even imagine what life totally without tears will be like as I make my way through this vale of tears. But I know it's coming. Jesus, the wiper away of all my tears, has said so.

*Lord, hold me close and dry my
tears with your loving hand. Amen.*

"WHOEVER DRINKS THE WATER I GIVE HIM WILL NEVER THIRST. INDEED, THE WATER I GIVE HIM WILL BECOME IN HIM A SPRING OF WATER WELLING UP TO ETERNAL LIFE." *John 4:14*

A Well That Never Stops

Poor Edwin Drake. He was crazy enough to think he could find oil by drilling down to bedrock. Though his backers pulled the plug, he persisted. On August 30, 1859, he attached 20 feet of pipe to a hand pump and brought up eight barrels of oil from the first well in the United States. Others made fortunes from his work, but Drake died penniless.

In our verse Jesus compares himself to a well of life-giving water. He's even so bold as to claim that those who drink of him will never thirst again. He's speaking of spiritual thirst, the kind suffered by every human being. Sin does more than parch human souls. It dooms them to the fires of hell where their thirst never ends. Who of us would want to end up there?

Others may call me crazy, but I've learned by God's grace how Jesus quenches thirst. He's like an artesian well that just keeps flowing. His forgiveness for my sins has no end. His promise of heaven has no restrictions in small print. Nor do I have to drive any piping to receive his life-giving water. His Word channels it to my thirsty soul.

Edwin Drake died penniless. Not me! I'm rich already here on earth. All the treasures God offers in Christ bubble like springwater within me. In heaven they will flow endlessly, as I praise my Savior for quenching my thirst.

Lord, lead me to drink of you
and be filled with eternal life. Amen.

"THE BLOOD OF JESUS, HIS SON,
PURIFIES US FROM ALL SIN." *1 John 1:7*

The Miracle Stain Remover

Did you know that a remarkable stain remover used in hospitals for years is now available over the counter? It's called Stain Rx and comes 16 ounces for $12. To test it, strawberries, blood, and coffee were mashed into a white T-shirt. A splash of this stain remover took out the berry blotches, and a cold water wash left the shirt nearly spotless.

Sounds good, but nowhere near as good as the stain remover mentioned in our verse. Sin's stain is much stronger and penetrates more deeply than blood or berry juice. The original sin inherited from my parents and my actual sins of thought, word, and deed, not only stain my soul. They saturate it and doom it to the throw-out basket of hell. I need more than a splash of chemicals mixed with perfume to make me dazzling white again.

Thank God, I know what this miracle sin remover is. Though I know, I can never hear often enough that it's Jesus' precious blood. His blood is precious because it's the blood of the God-man. God himself became man to take on my sins, take them into hell's torment, and take them away from me forever. Only such precious blood can remove sin's stain.

Thank God, I know where to find this miracle remover for my sin. Not on some supermarket shelf or discount store counter but in his Word. On the pages of God's Word, Jesus' cross stands high. Wherever I turn in that precious Word, I find my Savior's precious blood.

Wash me, O Savior, and make
me whiter than snow. Amen.

THROUGH HIM [JESUS] TO RECONCILE TO HIMSELF
ALL THINGS . . . BY MAKING PEACE THROUGH
HIS BLOOD, SHED ON THE CROSS. *Colossians 1:20*

God's Mathematical Equation

Math certainly has changed. Not much pencil and paper or figuring in your head anymore. Now you punch a calculator or a computerized cash register, and the correct figure comes up. A person can't help wondering what would happen if the world ever ran out of batteries. Or if the electricity went out—how they'd ever make change at the fast-food place.

God still figures his math the same way he always has. As someone once put it, "1 cross + 3 nails = 4 giveness."

Those three nails and that one cross don't really make for my salvation. It's the One whom the nails pinned to that cross and what he did there that count. Also let's not forget the divine love involved. How do I adequately describe a love that caused a holy God to send his best to a cross? How can I ever fully plumb the depths of a love that made his precious Son, Jesus, suffer sin's punishment that I deserved? How do I fully savor a love that made perfect peace between God and me possible? When I pin a cross to my clothing or position one on the wall, it's to remind me of Jesus, whom God sent to make things right between him and me. When I hear about those nails, it's to remind me of what Jesus suffered to make this peace possible.

I don't need paper or pencil, computer or calculator to follow God's wonderful equation. I do need words like our verse to remind me that his math is correct and constant. Because of God's love and Jesus' blood, 1 cross + 3 nails = 4 giveness.

Lord, fasten my heart on your love and
your Son's cross, and your peace will be mine. Amen.

THEN MOSES SAID, "NOW, SHOW ME YOUR GLORY."
"BUT," [GOD] SAID, "YOU CANNOT SEE MY FACE,
FOR NO ONE MAY SEE ME AND LIVE." *Exodus 33:18,20*

An Impossible Sight

Does God have a face? The Scripture readers among us will quickly respond, "God is a spirit without flesh and bones." Didn't people in the Bible at times see God? Again careful readers of the Bible will reply, "They saw a form or manifestation of God, but not the intangible, invisible Lord." Just as invisible electricity shows itself in visible sparks, so God manifested himself at times to people. Limited human eyes aren't capable of seeing the eternal Lord. Sinful human eyes would not be able to stand the sight of the holy Lord.

Haven't you ever felt like Moses? Haven't you ever wished you could see your Lord face-to-face? Here I sit, reading a devotion about him, listening to him speak to me. But I can't see him. Often I talk to him, pouring out my heart to him. But I can't hear him speak back to me. Some day I hope to meet him in heaven. But how do I know he is there?

One day an atheistic professor wrote on the board in his university classroom, "God is nowhere." After a break another sentence, written by one of the students, was found under his words. Using the same letters, but in different form, it read, "God is now here." God granted Moses as much of a vision of his glory as the prophet could absorb. He's given me an even fuller view. On the pages of his Word, I can learn not what God *looks* like but what he *is* like. He's my loving, gracious God, who sent Jesus to pay for my sins and prepare me to see his glory in heaven.

Lord, show me your love through your
Word so that I will see your glory in heaven. Amen.

THE LORD SAID, "I WILL CAUSE ALL MY GOODNESS TO PASS IN FRONT OF YOU, AND I WILL PROCLAIM MY NAME, THE LORD, IN YOUR PRESENCE. I WILL HAVE MERCY ON WHOM I WILL HAVE MERCY, AND I WILL HAVE COMPASSION ON WHOM I WILL HAVE COMPASSION." *Exodus 33:19*

An Incredible Sight

Years ago I read a book entitled *If You Could See What I Hear*. It told how a blind man learned to overcome his handicap. When he fell in love, he traced his beloved's face with sensitive fingers to feel what she looked like. From her actions he was also able to determine her character and feelings toward him. Though his eyes couldn't see her, his heart did.

When Moses requested to see God's face, God in answer pointed the prophet to his mercy and compassion. Mercy is the attribute of God that looks down on sinful man's helpless condition and in tender love offers relief. Compassion is the characteristic of God that offers free pardon to totally undeserving man. Both mercy and compassion describe the Lord and constitute his highest glory. Both God's mercy and compassion are centered in the Savior from sin. No wonder Jesus once said, "Anyone who has seen me has seen the Father" (John 14:9).

In Jesus I'm granted a fuller vision of God than what Moses had. God's mercy and compassion shine forth in bold detail in the Savior. If I want to know how God feels toward me, I look at Jesus. If I want to know what God's love has done for me, I look at Jesus. Though I'm not able to see Jesus in person, yet eyes of faith can trace his features on the pages of his Word. And seeing Jesus, I behold the incredible sight of my loving God.

God of mercy, God of grace, show me
the brightness of your face in Jesus. Amen.

> "WE CANNOT HELP SPEAKING ABOUT
> WHAT WE HAVE SEEN AND HEARD." *Acts 4:20*

An Invigorating Sight

In the 1800s an artist named Ralph E. W. Earl became known for his one-subject paintings. For 20 years he painted pictures of Andrew Jackson. There was Jackson as the hero of the battle of New Orleans. Jackson as president talking with his guests. Jackson strolling the streets of Washington. And many more. As a result Earl was labeled the "king's painter."

Isn't this precisely my role as one who is grateful for seeing my Savior's face? How can I look at the incredibly lovely face of Jesus and go back to business as usual in life? Now life has become the canvass on which I paint my Savior again and again. Behind all and before all, I want to share him with others. Like Peter and John, my response will be "I just can't stop talking about him and all that he has done for me."

Think what meaning this puts into my life. I'm not just here to occupy space and breathe for so and so many years. My role in life is not just to marry and have a family. My days are not just to be filled with occupation, recreation, and relaxation. Above all, I'm here to tell others what I have seen and heard in Jesus about my loving Lord.

Nor do I really need a push to do this. The incredible love that God has shown me fills me with invigorating power. My request is not only "Lord, what do you want me to do?" but also "Lord, help me do it."

Lord, fire me up with the heat of your love
so that I show others your saving face. Amen.

> WE KNOW THAT WHEN HE APPEARS,
> WE SHALL BE LIKE HIM, FOR WE
> SHALL SEE HIM AS HE IS. *1 John 3:2*

An Indescribable Sight

I can still see it. The plane had landed and was unloading servicemen who had been held captive in Vietcong prison camps. I don't know why the news cameras were allowed at such a touching, intimate time as this. But one captain, gaunt and haggard, beamed with joy as he saw his wife's face for the first time in three years and embraced her tightly.

The Bible tells me, "No eye has seen, no ear has heard, no mind has conceived what God has prepared for those who love him" (1 Corinthians 2:9). One obvious implication of that statement is that one day my eyes will see, my ears will hear, and my heart will know fully all those things. Here on earth I have to walk by faith. In heaven it will be wonderful sight. With glorified eyes I will see what God has so graciously given me faith's eyes to believe while here on earth.

The best sight will be that of my Savior's face. When I step off the plane in heaven's airport, Jesus will be there in living color, warm and complete in his mercy to embrace me. How do I go about describing such a scene? What words can I use to detail in depth the love that I'll see displayed in every feature of his face? How can I begin to capture what my existence will be like in heaven, permanently at his side? The word *indescribable* doesn't cut it. Seeing my Savior face-to-face is much greater than that.

Till that blessed day comes, I have to be content with the eyes of faith.

God, help me never to forget that faith comes only one way—
"from hearing the message, and the message is heard through
the word of Christ" (Romans 10:17). Amen.

> "ARE NOT TWO SPARROWS SOLD FOR A PENNY? YET NOT
> ONE OF THEM WILL FALL TO THE GROUND APART FROM
> THE WILL OF YOUR FATHER. . . . YOU ARE WORTH
> MORE THAN MANY SPARROWS." *Matthew 10:29,31*

Perched In Faith

Why don't birds fall off their perches when they go to sleep? Somewhere I read that birds have a muscle in each leg that automatically tightens when they settle on a tree branch. This muscle curls their toes securely around their perches and keeps them safe.

Because I'm no ornithologist, I can't verify the truth of that theory. I can, however, tell you why a child of God is always safe. It's because he's worth far more to God than any or all of the sparrows. At the time of Jesus, sparrows were about as worthless as today. Poor people purchased sparrows for food because they were cheap. But hardly anyone cared when a sparrow fell lifeless to the ground. The Creator did. He makes, watches over, and measures the length of life for each of those insignificant creatures.

Worth more than a sparrow? By myself, no. I'm only false and full of sin. I deserve not my Maker's care but his condemnation. Yet, in his love, God has paid a tremendous price for me. He reached deep into the pocket of his love and paid out not pennies but the precious blood of his own Son. When I by faith know this saving truth, then another one follows. He who has made me so precious in his sight will keep me safe through life.

Now that's a truth to curl the toes of faith around.

*"I am trusting you, Lord Jesus; Never let me fall.
I am trusting you forever And for all." Amen.* (CW 446:6)

I KNOW WHOM I HAVE BELIEVED, AND AM
CONVINCED THAT HE IS ABLE TO GUARD WHAT I
HAVE ENTRUSTED TO HIM FOR THAT DAY. *2 Timothy 1:12*

Right Plane, Right Place, Right Time

When I exercise in the morning, I usually watch a news channel. The travel report often details how many planes are in the air, where they are heading, and how late many of them will be. Watching the report, you wonder if all those planes know where they're going and if any of them ever arrive on time.

Paul knew that he was on the right "plane," heading in the right direction, and would arrive there at the right time. He put it a bit differently. His words "what I have entrusted to him" refer to his salvation. The apostle, with the confidence of faith, had placed the important matter totally into the hands of Jesus. By God's grace and the Spirit's working, Paul knew which plane flies to heaven—only the one labeled "Jesus." Paul also knew this plane would arrive safely at heaven's airport. "He is able to guard what I have entrusted to him for that day," Paul said confidently of Jesus. No, he didn't know what time his flight would arrive. But that too, he put into his Savior's hand, trusting that at the right time the Savior would return to claim him.

When I know that Jesus has paid for my sins, overpowered my death, opened wide the door to heaven, I can lean back in peace on the flight to heaven. I can even leave the time of my arrival in his hand instead of scanning each day with anxiety. Above all, I can know that I'll arrive at the right place. My Jesus will deliver what he has paid for and promised me.

*Lord Jesus, my Savior, help me entrust my
entire salvation into your competent hands. Amen.*

THIS IS LOVE: NOT THAT WE LOVED GOD, BUT THAT HE LOVED US AND SENT HIS SON AS AN ATONING SACRIFICE FOR OUR SINS. DEAR FRIENDS, SINCE GOD SO LOVED US, WE ALSO OUGHT TO LOVE ONE ANOTHER. *1 John 4:10,11*

Have A Heart

Everyone has one. It's a muscle about the size of a fist, located near the center of the chest. This muscle beats about 70 times a minute, 100,000 times a day, pumping blood along 100,000 miles of blood vessels in the body. We can't live without a heart.

Because of its importance, we often associate love with the heart. That's why so many valentines today are shaped like a heart. When God wanted to show his love for me, he did more than send me a heart-shaped card. His valentine was not brightly colored, pressed paper but the precious form of his own Son. His card didn't just say he loved me; it showed me how much. His heart doesn't just speak of love for me on one special day but every day. God's valentine to me is Jesus, God's loving heart made visible. It is God's loving heart doing for me what I couldn't do—God's loving heart saving me from my sins and for his heaven. What a valentine for me—today and every day!

Now God wants me to send valentines to others. My heart is to model his heart of love. It's to love others unselfishly the way God has loved me. Though my sinful nature often gets in the way, I keep on trying. The more I appreciate God's valentine to me, the more my heart will respond in grateful love to those around me. "Have a heart," he tells me. "I did."

Lord, on this day of love, show me your great
love in Jesus that I might love others more. Amen.

> GOD DEMONSTRATES HIS OWN LOVE FOR
> US IN THIS: WHILE WE WERE STILL SINNERS,
> CHRIST DIED FOR US. *Romans 5:8*

What Do You Mean By *Love?*

How loosely we use the word *love!* We say that we just love the new furniture we purchased. The special cheeseburgers we enjoy at our favorite spots. The movies we saw last week. We also speak of loving a spouse, though hopefully in a different way than those burgers and fries.

So often we do more talking about love than living it. Someone once said, "Love talked about is easily ignored, but love demonstrated is irresistible." What if God had only talked about his love for me? What if he had only promised to heal the great gulf sin had dug between him and me? What if he were all words and no actions? Then there'd be no Jesus in the Bethlehem cradle and on the Calvary cross in payment for my sins. No peace for my fearful soul and no heaven for my future. No frequent prayer trips to his throne of grace, because I'd still be afraid of such a holy God. Then my conclusion would be that he's a cruel God who's all talk and no follow-through.

Knowing what God has done for me in Christ puts new meaning into the word *love.* I may love a cheeseburger and even more so my spouse, but that's nothing compared to God's great love for me. That's like comparing a teaspoon of sand to Mount Everest or the gutter on my street to the Grand Canyon. God's love in Christ is beyond comparison. It's out of this world, and that's where it will take me—out of this world to his heaven.

*Lord, bring me nearer to your Son's cross so that I may
see your love more clearly and enjoy it more completely. Amen.*

> GOD IS LOVE. THIS IS HOW GOD SHOWED HIS LOVE AMONG
> US: HE SENT HIS ONE AND ONLY SON INTO THE WORLD
> THAT WE MIGHT LIVE THROUGH HIM. *1 John 4:8,9*

God Is Love

"If God is love, how can he send people to hell?" asked a person in my adult information class. She wasn't the only one to ask such a question. Many have misunderstood this essential part of God's nature. All should be sweet and happy, they assume. And surely there should be no punishment in a horrible place called hell.

Notice how John in our verse details the close connection between God's love and his holiness. God's holiness demands without exception that every sin be punished. If it didn't, God wouldn't be holy. God's love provided a way to satisfy his holiness. It sent his Son to settle the score, to suffer the punishment for every sin of every sinner in this world. You might say that God's holiness and God's love met at the intersection of his Son's cross.

God's Word is filled with his love. When it speaks of justice, it is justice tempered by his love. When it speaks of righteousness, it is righteousness provided by his love. When it speaks of salvation, it is salvation prepared by his love. When it speaks of resurrection, it is the miracle of his love. When it speaks of his return on the Last Day, it is speaking of the fulfillment of his love.

God is love. If he weren't, I'd have no chance. My sins would still separate me from him forever. Thank God for his love that redeemed me from sin and rescued me from hell.

Lord, help me marvel at your love that would
not let me die but brought me life in Christ. Amen.

<blockquote>
LET US FIX OUR EYES ON JESUS . . . WHO FOR THE JOY SET BEFORE HIM ENDURED THE CROSS, SCORNING ITS SHAME, AND SAT DOWN AT THE RIGHT HAND OF THE THRONE OF GOD. *Hebrews 12:2*
</blockquote>

Worse And Better

"When I can't stand the pain, I think of Jesus on the cross," said the cancer patient. As the waves of searing pain washed over her, she would remind herself how much worse Jesus' pain had been.

None of us likes to endure relentless pain. But if we must, we have an example in Jesus. Our verse reminds us that he "endured" the cross. His cross was not made of smooth, light balsa wood. It was rugged and rough, studded with torture and shrouded with disgrace. But Jesus held up under it. The shame involved was far outweighed by the joy Jesus found in completing the work of salvation and sitting down in triumph at God's right hand. In John 17:4 he told his Father with joy, "I have brought you glory on earth by completing the work you gave me to do."

Jesus endured his cross because he knew what it would mean for sinners like me. He knew that in the serious matter of my salvation, the old saying was true: "No pain—no gain." So he took the pain. With joy he endured even the worst suffering hell could dish out. And I get the gain. Cleansed from my sin by Jesus' blood, I can look up to my Father in peace and joy. Clothed with Jesus' righteousness, I can look forward to standing in his family in heaven.

"Fix [your] eyes on Jesus" is good advice, not just when my body hurts but, above all, when my soul does. His pains were far worse than mine, and I'm far better off because of them.

Lord, fix my heart and soul on you. When I'm hurting, remind me of your pains for me. Amen.

"SHOW ME, O LORD, MY LIFE'S END AND THE NUMBER OF MY DAYS; LET ME KNOW HOW FLEETING IS MY LIFE. . . . MY HOPE IS IN YOU. SAVE ME FROM ALL MY TRANSGRESSIONS." *Psalm 39:4,7,8*

So Soon Sundown

We were in the village of Abak in Nigeria. My first night there taught me how quickly the sun goes down in Africa. One minute it's there in the sky; the next it's gone. What a picture of life.

When we're young, we think we'll live forever. When we hit 40, we start wondering. When we slide past 60, we start feeling our mortality. So soon the sun goes down in life!

Is this some sad lament? Some complaint about how unfair life is? Or is it some "Let's get busy? Let's search feverishly for that elusive fountain of youth?" That's not what the psalmist had in mind. When he writes of life's brevity, he's pointing me to life's purpose. He's trying to remind me to turn to the One on whom time has no claim. He's urging me to take my fleeting life and lay it in his hands for a future that never ends.

Can I do this safely? Don't I hear the psalmist's assurance? "God has saved you from all your transgressions," he reminds me. Death came because of sin. It's the horrible paycheck for sin. Jesus came to pay for all my sins. That means he has also taken care of death. He collected sin's wage for me. It's no longer waiting for me at eternity's pay window. For me the end of life is not something to fear. Each day is another chance to learn more about the Savior whom God has given me and to be reinforced in the sure hope of eternity he offers me.

Gracious Lord, let the sun go down in my life
whenever it's your time. But please don't let the Son
stop shining on me with your forgiveness. Amen.

> "LORD, TO WHOM SHALL WE GO? YOU
> HAVE THE WORDS OF ETERNAL LIFE." *John 6:68*

What's In Your Saddlebag?

The Pony Express was an important part of the early history of the West. Riders rushed the mail 1,900 miles in ten days from St. Joseph, Missouri, to Sacramento, California. They wore light clothing, carried few weapons, sat on skimpy saddles. Mail was written on thin paper and carried in flat pouches. Less weight meant more speed Yet, each rider may have also carried his personal Bible given to him when he was sworn into service. That book was considered standard equipment in the thrilling days of yesteryear.

Life is much like that Pony Express. I hurry through it, facing many dangers, to a distant destination called heaven. To guide me on the way, God has given something precious called his Word. That Word is not some excess weight in the saddlebags of life but necessary equipment.

Where else can I learn the way to heaven? I see my Savior Jesus Christ only on the pages of God's Word. I need to hear that only Jesus has the words of eternal life. God's Word lights the way for me on life's journey to heaven. Through his Word God presents the saving message of what Christ has done to pay for my sins. Through that same message, his Holy Spirit powers my heart to come to faith and continue in it throughout life's journey.

Thank God, his Word is in my saddlebags. Pray God, I don't leave it there but use it as necessary equipment in my life.

"Your Word inspires my heart within; Your Word grants healing from my sin. Your Word has pow'r to guide and bless; Your Word brings peace and happiness." Amen. (CW 282:2 ©1993 by Mark A. Jeske.)

> JUST AS MAN IS DESTINED TO DIE ONCE, AND AFTER THAT TO FACE
> JUDGMENT, SO CHRIST WAS SACRIFICED ONCE TO TAKE AWAY THE
> SINS OF MANY PEOPLE; AND HE WILL APPEAR A SECOND TIME,
> NOT TO BEAR SIN, BUT TO BRING SALVATION TO THOSE
> WHO ARE WAITING FOR HIM. *Hebrews 9:27,28*

Need A Warning Label?

What an odd world we live in. Ever since someone won a lawsuit against a fast-food chain, its Styrofoam coffee cups carry a warning that the contents are hot. On peanut butter jars, we find the notice "May contain peanuts." On a frozen dinner "Defrost before eating." On a milk container "After opening, keep upright." Seems like people need a lot of help protecting themselves from themselves.

Shouldn't we also wear a warning label? Wouldn't it be helpful if we'd see pasted somewhere on us the words "Warning: heading for death and for the judgment." Perhaps, and then again, maybe not. Somehow people try to fool themselves into thinking they'll never die and if they do, there'll be no judge for them to face. I know better. Not only my own conscience but God's Word reminds me that my life will end and judgment will come. Still, a warning label for me to look at each day might be a good reminder.

Better still would be a label about how Jesus has fully paid for my sins and prepared eternal salvation for me. It might read, "Sin's gone, heaven's waiting—through Jesus." Like the renewal date pasted over the old one on my car's license plate, I need this one to cover the warning label about sin and judgment. Come to think of it, I don't really need such labels. Aren't words like our verse enough?

Lord, show me my sin daily and then
show me the Savior who has paid for them. Amen.

"WHEN SHE POURED THIS PERFUME ON MY BODY, SHE DID IT TO PREPARE ME FOR BURIAL. I TELL YOU THE TRUTH, WHEREVER THIS GOSPEL IS PREACHED THROUGHOUT THE WORLD, WHAT SHE HAS DONE WILL ALSO BE TOLD, IN MEMORY OF HER." *Matthew 26:12,13*

A Lasting Fragrance

When that special wedding anniversary came, I splurged and bought my bride a bottle of Chanel No. 5. She loves the fragrance of that perfume and wears it at special times. Unfortunately, the fragrance doesn't last forever and the bottle doesn't stay full.

Mary's perfume was extracted from a plant that grew in India and, as a result, was very expensive. That didn't stop her from splashing it on Jesus. Love for her Savior made her bring that costly gift and made its fragrance sweet to Jesus. We cannot say for sure that Mary realized fully she was anointing Jesus for burial. Yet that's how the Savior viewed her actions. In love she was doing what a few days later a hasty burial would make impossible. And we remember her perfume, though almost two thousand years old, still today.

What perfume have I brought for my Savior? When people are near me, is there a fragrance of love about me? Can they tell that Jesus is something so sweet to me? That without him I'd have no forgiveness of sin, no freedom from fear, no future in heaven? Can they sense that I want them to know about this Jesus too, and that I will do what I can to splash his perfume on them? Like Mary, I want to do this, not to be remembered two thousand years from now but to show Jesus how much his saving love means to me.

Lord Jesus, cover me with the perfume of your salvation and help me share it with others. Amen.

GIVE THANKS TO THE LORD, FOR HE IS GOOD;
HIS LOVE ENDURES FOREVER. *Psalm 118:1*

His Love Never Wears Away

I can still remember the first time I saw Niagara Falls. Blocks away I could hear the roar as 500,000 tons of water a minute rushed over it. What I didn't know was that the same powerful water eats away at the edge of the American Falls, moving it back about six inches each year.

There is no more powerful force than God's love. It is so strong that it has forgiven my sin, not with a Niagara roar but with a stillness out in Calvary's darkness. It is so strong that it brought the Savior back from the grave in the quiet of Easter morning to show that my salvation was complete. It is so strong that it holds open heaven's door for undeserving sinners like me. Now it comes to me through unlikely means like his gospel in Word and sacrament. How quietly God's love operates, but what great things it has done and is doing for me!

What if the passing of time would erode this amazing love of God? What if when my last day comes, I'd find a widening gap between that love and my need? "Impossible," the psalmist reminds me. "His love endures forever." It's not a Niagara that erodes with the passing of time. It's as constant as the God who never changes. It's as eternal as the heaven to which it takes me.

I've been at Niagara Falls several times since that first trip. Each time I stood before the rushing water in amazement. That's nothing compared to the thanks I owe my God each day I stand before his unchanging love.

Lord, help me thank you each day for the
unchanging love you show me in Jesus. Amen.

> COMFORT, COMFORT MY PEOPLE, SAYS YOUR GOD. SPEAK TENDERLY TO
> JERUSALEM, AND PROCLAIM TO HER THAT HER HARD SERVICE HAS BEEN
> COMPLETED, THAT HER SIN HAS BEEN PAID FOR, THAT SHE HAS RECEIVED
> FROM THE LORD'S HAND DOUBLE FOR ALL HER SINS. *Isaiah 40:1,2*

Comfort Food

"Comfort food ahead" offered a billboard on the roadside. It was advertising a well-known restaurant down the road. Immediately my mind started thinking of a smooth mound of mashed potatoes smothered with gravy, and of juicy, crisply fried chicken. Who cares about the calories and bad cholesterol when it comes to comfort food?

Through his prophet Isaiah, the Lord was talking to Israel about comfort food. Not just for their bodies, languishing in captivity in Babylon, but especially for their souls. The time was coming when Israel's separation from God would be over. He would return them to the promised land of Canaan. He would also send the promised Savior to return these wayward people to him. To those who were listening, God's words must have been sweet comfort food.

To me too. I don't stop often enough to assess sin's seriousness. Each of my sins separates me from God more surely than the former wall separated East Berlin from West Berlin in Germany. The Lenten season is a good time for serious thinking about my sins. It's an even better time for joyful hearing of what a gracious God has done about those sins. He's prepared "double payment" for them, so completely has he gotten rid of them. He did this by his wonderful gift on that horrible cross and his undeserved payment through Jesus for my impossible debt. No calories or bad cholesterol in such comfort food, just heavenly nourishment for a sinner like me.

Lord, comfort me with your forgiveness
till in heaven I need it no more. Amen.

WHEN JESUS SAW HER WEEPING, AND THE JEWS WHO HAD
COME ALONG WITH HER ALSO WEEPING, HE WAS DEEPLY
MOVED IN SPIRIT AND TROUBLED. JESUS WEPT. *John 11:33,35*

Tears Of Compassion

Did you know that Jesus cried? On three different occasions Scripture records our Savior's tears. Behind each incident was a different set of circumstances. But each time his tears flowed because of his love.

As Jesus stood before the grave of his dear friend Lazarus and witnessed Mary's and Martha's deep grief, he was visibly distressed. Using a word that indicates anger, the sacred record states that "he was deeply moved in spirit." It also says he was "troubled," indicating agitation. Seldom in Scripture's record does the Savior show such deep emotion. But here in the midst of death's sad scene, he shows his anger over what sin has done to mankind. Physical death is the tragic result of sin. It brings the worst kind of sorrow and suffering with it.

Then came his compassionate tears. The "man of sorrows" is well acquainted with grief. He knows what deep losses death inflicts upon me. He feels the wrenching pain when this monster snatches a loved one from my side. When I cry, so does he! Isn't that sweet comfort for me?

Jesus does more than shed his tears and "feel my pain." He did something about that inescapable enemy called death. On his cross he died in payment for my sins. Because of Jesus, my death will not be a tragic end but a glorious entrance into an eternal existence at his side.

Thank you, loving Savior, for weeping with me and,
even more so, for rescuing me from eternal death. Amen.

DURING THE DAYS OF JESUS' LIFE ON EARTH, HE OFFERED UP
PRAYERS AND PETITIONS WITH LOUD CRIES AND TEARS TO THE
ONE WHO COULD SAVE HIM FROM DEATH, AND HE WAS HEARD
BECAUSE OF HIS REVERENT SUBMISSION. *Hebrews 5:7*

Tears Of Consternation

Sometimes extreme tension and torturing pain can bring tears to our eyes. You can't help it. It hurts so much that your eyes overflow and your heart cries out. Know what I'm talking about?

Jesus did. He had a time just like that in the Garden of Gethsemane. As he lay facedown in the dust, "loud cries" were wrenched from his throat. As he wrestled with the immense load on his shoulders, tears dropped from his eyes. What brought my Savior to such a state? Physical pain and tension were there—more than I can ever imagine. I've never sweat drops of blood or felt such a crushing weight. More than the physical was the spiritual. The weight of the world's sins crushed him into Gethsemane's dust. The bitter cup of suffering he'd have to drink for the world's sins caused him to shudder. And he cried out in consternation to his heavenly Father.

Jesus must surely love me. Why else would he shed his tears in that garden? He must love me enough to carry not just the sins of Adam and Eve, Cain and Abel, David and Absalom, Jew and Gentile, but also all of mine. Facing hellfire, feeling the load, he rose from the dust to walk in love to his cross for all sinners and for me. Oh, Jesus, let your tears of that night fill me with holy awe at the heavy load you had to carry. Let them also fill me with deep gratitude for the love in which you shed them.

*Thank you, Jesus, for the love that took
you to the cross to pay for my sins. Amen.*

> AS HE APPROACHED JERUSALEM AND SAW THE CITY,
> HE WEPT OVER IT AND SAID, "IF YOU, EVEN YOU, HAD ONLY
> KNOWN ON THIS DAY WHAT WOULD BRING YOU PEACE—
> BUT NOW IT IS HIDDEN FROM YOUR EYES." *Luke 19:41,42*

Tears Of Concern

Tears were perhaps the last things we'd have expected from Jesus that first Palm Sunday. He had just ridden triumphantly into Jerusalem and received the homage of the multitudes. Yet, in that moment of triumph, the Savior cries, sobbing out loud as the original word indicates.

Why? Because Jerusalem should have known all about the peace he had come to bring. God had told them often enough, sending prophet after prophet. Finally he had even sent his Son as the Prince of peace into their midst. Foolishly, in unbelief's stupidity, they rejected the only One who could bring them peace with God. Even worse, they rushed him to the cross.

No wonder Jesus wept. Human beings can quickly turn to anger when love is spurned. Not our Savior. He wept when he saw what Jerusalem's rejection would bring it. With divine wisdom Jesus could look ahead and see the beloved city destroyed by Roman legions. With divine concern his tears increased when he looked ahead and saw Jerusalem's unbelieving inhabitants heading into the never-ending destruction of hell.

For me, thank God, Jesus' tears that Palm Sunday have a different message. They tell me he really means his words: "The Son of Man came to seek and to save what was lost" (Luke 19:10). They tell me his love desires the salvation of every sinner, including me.

God, may your tears never be an indictment of me
but serve as an incentive for me to draw ever nearer to you.
God help me, for Jesus' sake. Amen.

> WHEN THEY CAME TO THE PLACE CALLED THE
> SKULL, THERE THEY CRUCIFIED HIM. *Luke 23:33*

How Do You Spell *Cross?*

Draw a line down and another line across near the top and you have it. Shape it like a capital *T* or *X*, and you have other forms of that torture instrument. That's how you draw a cross, but how do you spell it? More than five letters are involved in that Lenten question, you know. Involved is the meaning of the cross for me.

Let's start with that *C.* To do so, I go to a death scene on a skull-shaped hill named Calvary. A death scene is always touching. Those who have watched will know. How much more so with the one out at Calvary. The breath catches in my throat and my heart skips a beat when I realize who's on that cross. That's the everlasting God suffering there, the eternal Christ bleeding and dying. That's God's Son, who took on human flesh and who now as the God-man takes his last breath on that tree. This I must know or else the cross will mean nothing to me.

How do you spell *cross?* I start with a *C* that stands for Christ. I marvel that God would go to such great lengths for a sinner like me. I shake my head in joyful wonder at the thought that he who is eternal took on human flesh and blood to rescue me. He who is immortal even died on that cross so that death could no longer be my mortal enemy. And I mean it when I sing, "Well might the sun in darkness hide And shut its glories in When God, the mighty Maker, died For his own creatures' sin" (CW 129:3).

Lord, take me to the cross of your eternal
Son and show me the love behind his death. Amen.

HE HIMSELF BORE OUR SINS IN HIS BODY ON THE TREE, SO
THAT WE MIGHT DIE TO SINS AND LIVE FOR RIGHTEOUSNESS;
BY HIS WOUNDS YOU HAVE BEEN HEALED. *1 Peter 2:24*

How Do You Spell *CRoss?*

A thing of beauty—that's what we've made of the cross. It dangles smooth and shiny on a chain or stands clean and crisp on an altar. But there was no beauty in that Good Friday cross. Only the sight of Christ's naked body, torn by the worst that man could do to it. Only the sound of his labored breathing, as he anguished under hell's full fury. Hardly a welcomed sight, is it?

No less welcome is the sight of the human heart. How many times a day don't I pause at that bathroom mirror to check my face or pat down a wisp of hair? But how often do I stop to look into my heart? If I did, would I welcome the sight? What about the envy and greed, the gossiping and backbiting, the selfish thoughts that float in my mind and the wounding words that fall off my tongue? The pail of my life is slopping over with sinful thoughts, words, and deeds. Standing before such a mess, I surely have to hold my nose. Even more important I have to confess that those sins nailed my Savior to that accursed tree.

How do you spell *cross?* I add an *R* for revolting, my revolting sins, as I sing in honest penitence, "I smite upon my troubled breast, With deep and conscious guilt oppressed, Christ and his cross my only plea— O God, be merciful to me!" (CW 303:2). On that cross he took the curse my sin deserved and gave me the righteousness his death won.

*Lord, let my sins cause me alarm so that
your payment for them will cheer me. Amen.*

> GOD DEMONSTRATES HIS OWN LOVE FOR
> US IN THIS: WHILE WE WERE STILL SINNERS,
> CHRIST DIED FOR US. *Romans 5:8*

How Do You Spell *CrOss?*

The cross was a diabolical torture instrument. Crucifixion was designed to deliver as much pain as possible to the victim. The Romans crucified only the worst criminals, slaves, and God's Son. As we see Jesus suspended on that cross between heaven and earth, we can only guess at the overwhelming pain he endured.

We do not have to guess at why Jesus was suffering on that cross. God's love put him there for sinners like me. What kind of love is this? It's so far different from the love that I'm used to giving and getting that I can't understand it. A love that delivers what has been earned is how I so often function. A love that demands something in return is what I'm used to. But a love that gives the ultimate for enemies, a love that repays hatred and hostility with pardon and peace, how do I describe it? God help me this Lenten season more fully "to grasp how wide and long and high and deep is the love of Christ, . . . this love that surpasses knowledge" (Ephesians 3:18,19).

How do you spell *cross?* I continue with an *O* for overwhelming, God's overwhelming love for a sinner like me. Watching that love bleed and die for me on the cross, I have to marvel, "See, from his head, his hands, his feet, Sorrow and love flow mingled down. Did e'er such love and sorrow meet Or thorns compose so rich a crown?" (CW 125:3).

Lord, let my worship of you be filled with
amazement and thanksgiving for your love. Amen.

> JESUS SAID, "IT IS FINISHED." *John 19:30*

How Do You Spell *CroSS?*

There can be little question about the fourth and fifth letters in the word *cross*. That double *S* has to stand for salvation. That's what sinners need. That's why God in love came to earth. That's why he was crucified, died, and was buried. With his precious blood and innocent death he came to pay for all sin, from the first one in Eden's garden to the last one that last second when the world ends.

He came to pay for me! When God's Son went to Calvary's cross, the load he carried included also my sins. When hell's punishments washed over him on that cross, my sins added to their sting. When the Savior said from that cross, "It is finished," he was speaking of the payment for my sins too. "God made him who had no sin to be sin for us, so that in him we might become the righteousness of God," Paul wrote (2 Corinthians 5:21). Those words become even sweeter when I know they mean "All my sins on him were laid. All my sins by him were paid." "Finished," that cross says of the payment for my sins. "Open," that cross says of heaven's door when my day comes. "Built," that cross says of the highway there for me, laid and paved with Jesus' atoning blood.

Thank God, I'm "drawn to the cross which you have blessed With healing gifts for souls distressed, To find in you my life, my rest, Christ crucified, I come." (CW 387:1).

*Lord Jesus, thank you for loving
me and paying for my sins. Amen.*

> GRACE AND PEACE TO YOU FROM GOD OUR FATHER AND THE
> LORD JESUS CHRIST, WHO GAVE HIMSELF FOR OUR SINS TO
> RESCUE US FROM THE PRESENT EVIL AGE. *Galatians 1:3,4*

A Time For Rescue

On occasion you read how firefighters rescued a cat stuck high in a tree or a child with a hand caught in a bottle. Such stories may make for interesting reading. Usually though, we think of something much more serious when we hear of firefighters' rescues.

Do Paul's words that Jesus gave himself on the cross to "rescue us" sound serious enough? If not, perhaps the problem is with me. At times sin may not seem so serious to me, and my condition, because of sin, may not seem so desperate. This Lenten season I need the reminder that I was dead in transgression and sin (Ephesians 2:1). I need to be brought up short with the truth that my sins have separated me from my God (Isaiah 59:2). I need to face the horrible reality that the wages of my sin is death here on earth and in hell (Romans 6:23).

Then the news that Jesus came to rescue me will mean more than a firefighter climbing a tree or extracting a fist from a bottle. Hearing how Jesus left his glorious throne on high to hang on Calvary's accursed tree will fill me with amazement. Watching as the eternal God-man breathes his last will cause me to hold my breath in wonder. I will treasure anew the realization that he did all this to rescue me from my sin, though I've heard this blessed news so many times before. My heart will delight in his wondrous love behind my rescue from sin, though this side of heaven I'll never be able to fathom it. What a great rescue! What a greater Savior!

*Help me, Savior, to treasure more deeply
my rescue from sin and your love behind it. Amen.*

> BE KIND AND COMPASSIONATE TO ONE
> ANOTHER, FORGIVING EACH OTHER, JUST AS
> IN CHRIST GOD FORGAVE YOU. *Ephesians 4:32*

A Time For Forgiveness

Isn't the Lenten season a good time for forgiveness? It certainly is the time when I especially think of how much I need God's forgiveness and how freely he offers it. Do I ever stop to think that Lent is also a time for me to forgive those who have sinned against me?

It's not easy to forgive. It's far easier to bear a grudge when someone has sinned against me. I see that person and chafe inside. I think of the wrong done me and speak a silent, "I can never forgive him for that." Perhaps it's my parents who raised me, a relative who has wronged me, a fellow human being who has taken unfair advantage of me. Perhaps I've tried this forgiveness bit only to find that I can't go through with it or the one who needs my forgiveness doesn't want it.

What if God harbored a grudge against me for my sins against him? What if each time I repeated those sins, he turned up the thermostat on his anger? What if he kept score of how often I came and he finally told me, "No more"? But he doesn't! In Christ God forgave me—fully, freely, eternally. Jesus' cross is the plus sign in God's financial ledger, canceling my debt, squaring my account. That's what Lent tells me. That's why the Lenten message is so sweet to me.

Redeemed, restored, forgiven because of Jesus' cross, can I still have problems forgiving my neighbor? Yes, if my eyes stray from the Savior's cross. No, if I draw closer to his forgiveness.

Lord, fill me with your forgiveness
and help me respond with it to others. Amen.

CHRIST REDEEMED US FROM THE CURSE OF THE LAW
BY BECOMING A CURSE FOR US, FOR IT IS WRITTEN:
"CURSED IS EVERYONE WHO IS HUNG ON A TREE." *Galatians 3:13*

A Time For Remembering

Have you heard of the Bermuda Triangle? This area, located off the southeastern Atlantic coast of the United States, is known for a high incidence of unexplained losses of ships and aircraft. Because of this, sailors and aviators have also dubbed this area the "devil's triangle." Questions abound about its reality, but that doesn't change the curse seemingly connected with it.

I don't know about the curse of the Bermuda Triangle, but I know about the one connected with Calvary. That skull-shaped knoll deserves the label of the most cursed spot on earth. Why? Because there God's Son became a "curse for us." The cross, outlined against the sky on Calvary, reminds me that every sin demands God's curse. Because of each of my sins, I'm doomed to the depths of hell. Nor can I extricate myself from the curse. Add to my sins those of every human being in this world, from the first Adam to the last, and I shudder at the seriousness of sin's curse.

Thank God, Calvary for us is not the most cursed but the most blessed spot. Again we ask, "Why?" Because there "Christ redeemed us from the curse of the law." Jesus was cursed for our sins so that we could be blessed with his holiness. He took the wrath of God and suffered the tortures of hell that we deserved. He did this for you. He did it for me. Now instead of being lost in the oceans of God's anger, I'm washed clean in Jesus' cleansing blood. Lent for me is that special time to go to Calvary and remember how a loving Savior removed sin's curse.

Lord, this Lenten season keep my eyes
focused on the Savior dying on the cross for me. Amen.

IT IS BY GRACE YOU HAVE BEEN SAVED, THROUGH FAITH—
AND THIS NOT FROM YOURSELVES, IT IS THE GIFT OF GOD—
NOT BY WORKS, SO THAT NO ONE CAN BOAST. *Ephesians 2:8,9*

A Time For Reflecting

Reaching for the honey jar the other morning, I recalled something I had read. It takes a thousand bees working all their lives to make a single pound of honey. Ever imagine one worker bee buzzing off by itself, sucking up the nectar, making its share of that pound? His smidgen might look impressive to him but rather insignificant to us.

Sometimes my human nature likes to think that I can produce a lot of "honey" by myself. After all, I'm a reasonably good church member. I take care of my spouse and family. I'm reliable on the job. I'm helpful and considerate toward my neighbors. Can't you see the flag going up? Sly as ever, Satan's trying to shift my eyes from Christ's all sufficient salvation to merits of my own.

Paul has it right in our verse. Salvation is God's grace, a gift that is all his. He planned it, prepared it, proclaimed it. He does this for people like me who are totally unworthy. I can't produce even a drop of honey with my own works to make me appealing to God. All I can do is buzz away from him in my ignorance and spite. So he placed that cross on Calvary, pinned his Son to it in payment for sin, powered my heart to believe it. Sweet is the honey of his love.

Now he does look for honey from me. I want to be a good church and family member, worker and neighbor. Not to earn my salvation but to thank my gracious God for giving it to me. As a poet once wrote, "To see the law of Christ fulfilled and hear his pardoning voice changes a slave into a child and duty into choice."

*Lord, help me reflect on your
grace this Lenten season. Amen.*

> "GOD DID NOT SEND HIS SON INTO THE
> WORLD TO CONDEMN THE WORLD, BUT TO
> SAVE THE WORLD THROUGH HIM." *John 3:17*

A Time For Rejoicing

Some of my childhood Lenten memories include somber evening services, hymns in sober minor key, and a certain seriousness about the season. It's true—Lent is a serious time. Reflection on sin and its punishment, death and its judgment ought to slow me down and make me think deeply.

What if that's where my Lenten observance stopped? What if Jesus was no more than a heavenly policeman sent to arrest me, the sinner? What if the heavenly Father was just a hanging judge, more than ready to sentence me, the guilty? Then I might as well put my wrists out for the handcuffs and plead no contest, because there's more than enough evidence to convict me.

But through the Lenten darkness pierces the bright sun of God's love. He sent his Son not to condemn me but to save me. Jesus came so that by his perfect life he could keep all of God's commandments for me. Jesus came so that with his innocent death he could pay for every one of my sins. I can't save myself, nor do I have to. In love God sent Jesus to do what I couldn't do. Through Jesus, God takes me back into his family as a treasured member. Because of Jesus, God will welcome me home when time ends for me in this world.

Lent is a serious time. It's a valuable time to reflect more deeply on my sins. Even more so, it's a blessed time to rejoice more fully in my Savior.

Lord, please use this season to draw me
more closely to your love for me in Jesus. Amen.

> "I WILL SET OUT AND GO BACK TO MY FATHER AND SAY TO HIM,
> 'FATHER, I HAVE SINNED AGAINST HEAVEN AND AGAINST YOU.
> I AM NO LONGER WORTHY TO BE CALLED YOUR SON.'" *Luke 15:18,19*

A Time For Going Home

"You can't go home again," states an old proverb. Most of the time it's true. When I went back to my childhood home, nothing was the same. The house had been torn down, and a sprawling factory covered the acres. In another sense, the saying is not true. Regardless of my age, it feels good to sleep in my familiar bedroom, and when I sit at the old family table, childhood memories come flooding back. For our children, ours is the father's home to which they love to return.

Lent is a time to go home. It's the time for me to recognize myself in that prodigal son in Jesus' parable. He's the symbol for the many times I've done my own thing and wandered from my Father's home. Perhaps my sins are no carbon copy of the prodigal's. Yet selfishness, disrespect for my Father's will, and wasting what I've received from his gracious hand are more than evident in my daily life. Stubborn and stupid, I've walked away from my God, instead of with him.

Lent reminds me that it doesn't have to continue this way. A gracious Father waits for my return. Each day he steps off the porch, scans the horizon, searches for the first glimpse of my return. When I fall in humble repentance before him, he lifts me up, hugs me closely, and returns me to his family. All this he's made possible by sending his Son, Jesus. His obedient Son has paid for my disobedience. Jesus left his Father's house, not to squander some inheritance but to prepare an eternal one for me. Because of Jesus, I can go home again and again and again.

Father, keep my feet, so inclined to stray,
on the path to your heavenly home. Amen.

> IN HIM WE HAVE REDEMPTION THROUGH HIS BLOOD, THE
> FORGIVENESS OF SINS, IN ACCORDANCE WITH THE RICHES
> OF GOD'S GRACE THAT HE LAVISHED ON US WITH ALL
> WISDOM AND UNDERSTANDING. *Ephesians 1:7,8*

A Time For Giving Thanks

"We bring good things to life" was the slogan on an appliance dealer's truck. Would anyone want to go back to scrubbing clothes in a stream or cooking dinner over an open fire? When the electricity goes out, we realize what good things we have in modern appliances.

Lent is a time to consider what good things God has given us in Jesus. "Redemption through his blood" is one of them. The word *redemption* implies that something has a hold on me. How true. Because of sin Satan's made me his captive on earth and his cell mate in a future hell.

"Forgiveness of sins" is another one. The word *forgiveness* implies I've grievously wronged God and deserve some dire consequences. Again, how true. With each sin I've stomped on God's toes and spit in his holy face. When his holiness lashes out at me, it should be no surprise.

In a million years I could never have devised the plan God came up with to redeem me. He used the precious blood of his Son to pay for my sins. He sent Jesus to remove my guilt and bring me peace with him. Not only could I never have planned such salvation, I can't believe in it either. God's love sends his Spirit to work through his powerful gospel to create and continue faith's "wisdom and understanding" in me. Talk about God lavishing riches on me! What would my life be like without God's good things, provided through the Savior, in it?

Lord, help me use the Lenten season to
thank you for your rich gifts to me in Jesus. Amen.

> ALWAYS BE PREPARED TO GIVE AN ANSWER TO
> EVERYONE WHO ASKS YOU TO GIVE THE REASON
> FOR THE HOPE THAT YOU HAVE. *1 Peter 3:15*

A Time For Telling

An old story tells of a heavenly debate about who had received the most forgiveness. One person told of his wasted life till Christ came to him on his deathbed. Another cataloged his many grievous sins. Just before the vote was taken, another man stepped forward. "I have known Jesus my whole life," he said, "but never once did I tell anyone else." And this man won the debate.

When I popped the question to the young lady who became my wife, I couldn't keep the good news a secret. When our babies were born, we didn't keep the news of their arrival to ourselves. When surgery took care of a problem, we didn't sit on the results. Good news is for telling!

If good news begs to be shared, how about the best news I've ever received? How about the sure hope for heaven that Jesus has earned for me? His cross with its full payment for my sins and his empty tomb with its full assurance of my redemption are just too good to hoard. God, in his grace, has brought salvation to me. Now, in that same grace, he wants to bring that salvation to others through me. "Be ready to tell others of this best news," Peter urges me.

Lent is a special time for telling. May the Lord open my eyes to those around me who need to hear about the sure hope Jesus has prepared for sinners. May the Lord use me to tell them what they so desperately need to hear.

*Lord, the more I see of your saving love this
Lenten season, the more I have to tell others. Amen.*

THE LORD TURNED AND LOOKED STRAIGHT AT PETER. THEN PETER REMEMBERED THE WORD THE LORD HAD SPOKEN TO HIM: "BEFORE THE ROOSTER CROWS TODAY, YOU WILL DISOWN ME THREE TIMES." AND HE WENT OUTSIDE AND WEPT BITTERLY. *Luke 22:61,62*

Weeping Because I've Failed

I was catching a few hours sleep in an airport hotel in Miami. I had a 7:00 A.M. flight to Colombia. All at once I woke up and checked the clock. It was 6:00 A.M. The wake-up call had never come.

Lent is a time for wake-up calls, especially one for repentance. When I recognize more fully what I deserve because of my sins, will I appreciate the wonder of God's forgiving love for me in Christ?

Peter needed such a wake-up call. Remember how he stood in the shadows that night to warm his hands and ended up singeing his soul? It wasn't that the Lord had forgotten about Peter. Earlier Jesus had told him, "Simon, Simon, Satan has asked to sift you as wheat. But I have prayed for you, Simon, that your faith may not fail" (Luke 22:31,32). Jesus had prayed for Peter, and God was ready to supply suitable strength. But Peter thought he didn't need it. So the rooster crowed, and Peter cried that night. His tears of repentance said, "I've failed."

Peter denied the Lord with his lips. To deny him with my life is no better. Have I ever run with the world and warmed my hands over its fires? Been silent when someone ridiculed Christ or his Word? Tried telling the world, "Look, fellows, I'm one of you"? If so, it's time for Lent's wake-up call. Time to join Peter, and with tears in my heart, if not in my eyes, to confess, "I've failed."

Lord, too many times I've forgotten you in the pressures of this world. Please, receive my confession and again assure me of your forgiveness through Jesus, who never forgets me. Amen.

THE LORD TURNED AND LOOKED STRAIGHT AT PETER. THEN
PETER REMEMBERED THE WORD THE LORD HAD SPOKEN TO HIM:
"BEFORE THE ROOSTER CROWS TODAY, YOU WILL DISOWN ME THREE
TIMES." AND HE WENT OUTSIDE AND WEPT BITTERLY. *Luke 22:61,62*

Weeping Because I'm Sorry

Jesus' look at Peter that night must have spoken volumes. It must have said, "Peter, I saw it all. I know what happened." That look must also have said, "Peter, how could you hurt me so?" That look pierced right to Peter's heart. Out of that courtyard he stumbled, tears of remorse scalding his cheeks. "What have I done?" those tears said. "How could I do this to him who has always shown love to me? I'm sorry, so sorry for what I've done."

If only I could see the hurt in Jesus' eyes each time I choose sin. You see, there is no such thing as cheap grace. It's just not enough to say, "So I've sinned. So what? Jesus paid for those sins." Of course, he did, but remember that my sins, each one of them cost him dearly. Each of them made him shudder in the garden, struggle on the cross, sigh his last breath in death. Sin is no light matter nor was its payment.

Nor is repentance! True repentance is not just the mechanical mouthing of words like "I'm by nature sinful and unclean and have sinned against you by thought, word, and deed." It's rather my heart's shuddering sigh, "Against you, you only, have I sinned and done what is evil in your sight" (Psalm 51:4) It's my gulping in shame when I see the sorrow on my Savior's face. It's saying in true repentance, "I'm sorry, Lord, so sorry that I've sinned against you."

*Lord, teach me to sorrow over my sins and
then to appreciate your forgiving love in Jesus. Amen.*

THE LORD TURNED AND LOOKED STRAIGHT AT PETER. THEN
PETER REMEMBERED THE WORD THE LORD HAD SPOKEN TO HIM:
"BEFORE THE ROOSTER CROWS TODAY, YOU WILL DISOWN ME THREE
TIMES." AND HE WENT OUTSIDE AND WEPT BITTERLY. *Luke 22:61,62*

Weeping Because I'm Grateful

A little boy had invited his friend to stay for supper. "We're having spaghetti," he said, "but first mama has to bend it before we can eat it." When Jesus bends me in true sorrow over sin, I'll know, appreciate, and respond to his forgiveness.

That's what happened to Peter. When the Savior looked at Peter that night, it wasn't "I warned you about this. You got yourself into it; now get yourself out." Instead there had to be love in that look. The same love that caused Jesus to exchange his throne of glory for one of pain on Calvary. The same love that later petitioned forgiveness for his enemies and promised a place in heaven to a penitent criminal. That look had to say, "Peter, I love you and I forgive you." That look of love melted Peter's heart to tears of gratitude and moved him to a life of grateful service.

This holy season can I leave the cross with its message of God's love for sinners like me without tears of gratitude? Jesus still loves me. Jesus has forgiven me fully. He knows my daily defeats and denials. He's well aware of all my sins and shortcomings. And he forgives me! Can it be? Oh, thank God that it is!

Yes, time for a wake-up call. Time to check God's loving heart and shed my tears of gratitude.

*Lord, help me look at your loving forgiveness
and then devote my life to you in thanks. Amen.*

> HE WAS DESPISED AND REJECTED BY MEN, A MAN OF SORROWS, AND FAMILIAR WITH SUFFERING. LIKE ONE FROM WHOM MEN HIDE THEIR FACES HE WAS DESPISED, AND WE ESTEEMED HIM NOT. *Isaiah 53:3*

The Savior Rejected By People

"The Old Testament Evangelist" is what some call Isaiah. Though he lived and wrote seven hundred years before Calvary, yet in his 53rd chapter, it's as if Isaiah were kneeling before the Good Friday scene.

What did Isaiah see as he wrote by inspiration of the Holy Spirit? On the cross he foresaw One who "was despised and rejected by men." How true in that Calvary scene. A lowly carpenter, who came not to be served but to serve, was not to their liking. They wanted a conqueror and a caretaker who would make life easy for them. A Savior from sin irritated them. After all, to admit their need for a Savior meant exposing their sins.

Jesus was so repulsive to them that they turned away in disgust from him. What could this Galilean, without any earthly goods and with only a ragtag bunch of disciples, offer them? "Away with him," they said, "the sooner the better." So they helped hang him on a cross.

What kind of a Christ do I want? The answer helps determine what I will do with him. Do I want a Jesus who will give me heaven here on earth? Who will keep all trouble and trial away from me or make it all magically disappear? Who will lead me to success in the marketplace and in daily life? Or do I want a Jesus who came to suffer for me? To die for me? To pour out his blood for my sins? To prepare and promise heaven for me?

God of grace, let my answer show that he's my beautiful Savior to whom I want to draw ever closer. Amen.

> HE WAS PIERCED FOR OUR TRANSGRESSIONS, HE WAS CRUSHED FOR OUR INIQUITIES; THE PUNISHMENT THAT BROUGHT US PEACE WAS UPON HIM, AND BY HIS WOUNDS WE ARE HEALED." *Isaiah 53:5*

The Savior Substituting For Sinners

What's your definition for a substitute? To me that's someone who takes your place but is not quite as capable. When the starting quarterback is injured, a second stringer comes in. Not so with Jesus. When Isaiah says he substituted for sinners, I learn that Jesus not only was better but did something that I couldn't do.

Isaiah foresaw Jesus being "pierced" and "crushed." In the Hebrew original, both are very strong words for describing violent and painful death. The prophet also saw "punishment" and "wounds" coming for this man of sorrows, this Son of God. Not only was Isaiah referring to the excruciating pain of crucifixion but to hell's more painful punishment that hit Jesus on the cross.

Why would this happen to Jesus? Wasn't he the sinless Son of God who did all things well? Isaiah has the answer for this question. "Ours," "us," and "we" he wrote. Jesus was there as our substitute. He carried the world's sins to the cross, suffered every ounce of punishment for them. Because he did, sinners have the full healing of God's forgiveness. The prophet's words are just as clear as those written later by Paul, "God made him who had no sin to be sin for us so that in him we might become the righteousness of God" (2 Corinthians 5:21). That's the glorious, beautiful, comforting truth of the gospel.

It's not enough to say that Jesus substituted for sinners. God help me say, "Jesus substituted for me. With his wounds I am healed." Please, gracious Lord, for Jesus' sake. Amen.

> HE WAS OPPRESSED AND AFFLICTED, YET HE DID NOT OPEN
> HIS MOUTH; HE WAS LED LIKE A LAMB TO THE SLAUGHTER,
> AND AS A SHEEP BEFORE HER SHEARERS IS SILENT,
> SO HE DID NOT OPEN HIS MOUTH. *Isaiah 53:7*

The Savior Suffering In Silence

"[There is] a time to be silent and a time to speak," wrote a wise king (Ecclesiastes 3:7). My problem at times is mixing the two up. Not so with Jesus. With his disciples, the time to speak was during three years of instruction, as they walked the length and breadth of the Promised Land. With Nicodemus, it was a night spent in conversation about being born again through the work of the Spirit. With the woman at the well in Samaria, it was a talk about the water that quenches the soul's thirst. Whenever Jesus had a soul before him that was searching for the truth, he was ready and willing to speak.

So why was he silent on Good Friday? When the soldiers whipped him, wove a spiny crown for his brow, wrapped a royal robe in mockery around him, he opened not his mouth. When the weight of the cross pressed his face into the dirt of Jerusalem's street, again he was silent. Like some passive lamb, he let them impale him on the cross without speaking in his own defense.

Did he keep silent because he was powerless? Earlier in the garden, his words had knocked the arresting mob flat on their backs before he let them tie his hands. Now just by lifting one omnipotent finger he could have avoided the cross. But something very powerful wouldn't let him. It was his love for sinners like me. God's eternal Lamb suffered in silence so that I could be made holy by him and nestle in peaceful silence in his loving arm.

Lord Jesus, speak to me through your Word
that I might know you as my loving Shepherd. Amen.

BY OPPRESSION AND JUDGMENT HE WAS TAKEN AWAY.
AND WHO CAN SPEAK OF HIS DESCENDANTS? FOR HE
WAS CUT OFF FROM THE LAND OF THE LIVING; FOR THE
TRANSGRESSION OF MY PEOPLE HE WAS STRICKEN. *Isaiah 53:8*

The Savior Judged Unjustly

I wasn't guilty. The boy sitting ahead of me had done the whispering. But my seventh-grade teacher judged us both guilty of cheating. Sometimes it happens that we are judged unjustly. But never has there been and never will there be a case like the unjust judging of my Savior.

Isaiah wrote of "oppression" and "judgment." Both words in the Hebrew refer to a courtroom. Both speak of a prisoner being held under restraint and a verdict being rendered. The guilty verdict cut the Savior off "from the land of the living." But few among his generation paid much attention. Only a handful of loyal women and one disciple huddled at the foot of his cross.

Jesus wasn't guilty! This was a travesty of justice like none other. Listen in wonder as Isaiah explains, "For the transgression of my people he was stricken." The word *transgression* means rebellion. Each of my sins is a rebellion against God. I may try to minimize my sins by comparing them with someone else's. I may try to marginalize them by rationalizing that everyone else is doing them. That doesn't reduce, much less remove, a single one of them. Each of my sins helped lash my Savior's back and nail his limbs to the cross. Yet a righteous God has pronounced me not guilty. He could do this because his innocent Son took on all my guilt and paid for it completely. By sentencing his Son, God's love took care of his justice. And all this he did for me!

*Lord, fix my heart in wonder on the Savior
who took my guilt and gave me his holiness. Amen.*

HE WAS ASSIGNED A GRAVE WITH THE WICKED, AND
WITH THE RICH IN HIS DEATH, THOUGH HE HAD DONE NO
VIOLENCE, NOR WAS ANY DECEIT IN HIS MOUTH. *Isaiah 53:9*

The Savior Buried With The Rich

When I vicared in Tucson, Arizona, I invited our chaplain from the state prison in Yuma to speak to the young people's group. He told of serving men on death row with God's law and gospel. One teenager asked about the burial of prisoners who were executed. "A pauper's grave," the chaplain answered, "unless relatives offer something better."

Those who crucified Jesus had a pauper's grave in mind for him. They would have stuck him away in some obscure spot with others like him. Such a dishonorable burial was part of the punishment for the wicked. Instead, rich men, Joseph of Arimathea and Nicodemus, stepped forward to lift Jesus' lifeless body from the cross and lay it lovingly in a fitting tomb.

Was Jesus' burial with the rich just mere coincidence? Again listen as Isaiah explains, "He had done no violence, nor was any deceit in his mouth." Jesus' burial was God's way of emphasizing the innocence of his Son. Though he was put to death like a criminal, he was not to be buried like one. The Lamb who was slain was truly without spot and blemish as his burial indicates.

What comfort for me! "Precious in the sight of the LORD is the death of his saints," the psalmist reminds me (116:15). Because of Jesus' innocent suffering and death as my substitute, I am one of God's saints, cleansed whiter than snow. Because Jesus died to pay for my sins, I can be buried with the riches of divine forgiveness.

Please, Lord, when my day comes, grant
me such a death through my Savior Jesus. Amen.

> THOUGH THE LORD MAKES HIS LIFE A GUILT OFFERING, HE WILL SEE HIS OFFSPRING AND PROLONG HIS DAYS, AND THE WILL OF THE LORD WILL PROSPER IN HIS HAND. AFTER THE SUFFERING OF HIS SOUL, HE WILL SEE THE LIGHT OF LIFE, AND BE SATISFIED. *Isaiah 53:10,11*

The Savior Fully Satisfied

Can you remember a time when you were completely satisfied? When things were just as you wanted them? Even in our most positive times can lurk a bit of the negative.

Not for Jesus. Good Friday was not some ignoble last day for him, but the glorious prelude to the rest of his life. "It is finished," the Son had said of sin's payment on Good Friday. "That's right, my Son," his Father now responded on Easter Sunday. Jesus' resurrection is proof positive that his holy Father had accepted his guilt offering for the world's sin. What could be more satisfying for the One whose desire was always to do his Father's will?

Also what can be more satisfying than for the risen Savior to "see his offspring"? He who never married or fathered children has more descendants than we can even imagine. Among them are the women that first Easter, the three thousand on Pentecost, the many who have gone before and will come after us. Among them also am I. What satisfaction Jesus receives when people are brought to faith in him. How fully satisfied he is when he can hold me in his living arm.

Can anything be more satisfying for me than knowing I am one of Jesus' own? How about the satisfaction that comes from my telling others about him?

Lord, thank you for making me one of your own.
Use me in some small way to tell others. Amen.

> AFTER THAT, HE POURED WATER INTO A BASIN
> AND BEGAN TO WASH HIS DISCIPLES' FEET, DRYING THEM
> WITH THE TOWEL THAT WAS WRAPPED AROUND HIM. *John 13:5*

Loving Hands
Washing Me Clean

We use hands to express love. With them I caress my spouse, hold close my children, comfort my loved ones in distress. What would I do if I couldn't touch those nearest and dearest to me?

Jesus also used his hands to express love. In the upper room at Jerusalem the night before his death, his hands picked up the basin of water and proceeded to wash his disciples' feet. Shouldn't it have been turned around? Shouldn't they have been washing the feet of their Lord and master? He whom the holy angels serve now serves sinful men. He who came to seek and save the lost stoops to the work of the lowest slave.

Why? To give me an example of humble service, of course. He wants to remind me that he gave me hands to wipe away tears, watch over a soul, forgive a fault, bear with an injustice, invite a sinner, encourage a saint. Loving hands change diapers, scrub floors, prepare meals, do homework, carry out the garbage, bring home the paycheck, fill offering envelopes.

Even more, he wants me to remember how deep his love for me really is. That night his hands washed feet with water. The next day they washed souls with his blood on Calvary's cross. That night the Savior in love handled his disciples' feet. The next, in a far greater display of love, he handled the world's sins. From such wondrous love comes wonderful cleansing for my soul.

Lord, help me, the sinner, to pray daily,
"Wash me, Savior, or I die." Amen.

GOING A LITTLE FARTHER, HE FELL WITH HIS FACE TO THE GROUND AND PRAYED, "MY FATHER, IF IT IS POSSIBLE, MAY THIS CUP BE TAKEN FROM ME. YET NOT AS I WILL, BUT AS YOU WILL." *Matthew 26:39*

Loving Hands Petitioning His Father

What do you do with your hands when you pray? Usually I fold mine. With those folded hands I'm humbly and confidently telling my Father, "It's all up to you. You answer as you think best."

I don't know about Jesus' hands the night he prayed in Gethsemane. I do, however, know how extreme anguish drove him face down into the dirt. Before him stood a cup filled to the brim with the poison of the whole world's sins. Its every drop would be bitter right down to the dregs. This horrendous cup was his to drink if he would save mankind's souls. And he would have to empty it alone. No wonder the Savior fell with his face to the ground in prayer that night.

Note carefully. Jesus deeply felt sin's weight but did not refuse to bear it. He prayed earnestly with tears but did not turn away from the Father's will. "It's up to you," he was humbly telling his Father. He also was confidently telling his Father, "You answer as you think best." Or to use his own words, "Not as I will, but as you will." My Savior trusted a Father who loved him.

How could Jesus do it? The answer has to be divine love. Out of love for his Father he came to this ball of mud where I live. Out of love for me, the sinner, he stained Calvary's dirt with his precious blood. Because of his saving work, I can fold my hands in humble, confident prayer to his and my Father. Even more so, I can live with him forever in his and my Father's eternal home.

Lord, teach me so to pray. Amen.

> HE APPROACHED JESUS TO KISS HIM, BUT JESUS
> ASKED HIM, "JUDAS, ARE YOU BETRAYING THE
> SON OF MAN WITH A KISS?" LUKE 22:47,48

Loving Hands Reaching For A Sinner

From a person's hands, I can learn something about his occupation. If they're calloused, he's used to manual labor. If they're somewhat softer, he might be an office worker, a professional, a pastor. Hands tell much about people and what they do.

I'm so used to zeroing in on Judas in the scene before us. "Judas, how could you?" I feel like shouting. "What a way to be remembered. Every time people hear the words 'Our Lord Jesus Christ on the night he was betrayed,' they'll think of you and your hypocritical kiss."

Far better that I concentrate on the One whom Judas kissed. Even as the traitor steps forward, the Savior still calls him friend (Matthew 26:50). Did you hear that? I might have shoved Judas roughly away or blasted him with explosive words. But to the one who fingered him for death, the Savior offers friendship and forgiveness. Judas turned away from Jesus' loving hands, but that didn't make them any less real.

Each of us has sold the Savior for our own "30 pieces of silver," more times than we care to admit. Yet in love Jesus warns me. In love he wants me. In love he reaches for me. Through his sweet gospel his hands of tender love reach for me, reminding me no matter what hypocrisy I have practiced, he still calls me friend. His reaching hands speak to me of his immense love.

Please, Savior, never stop reaching
for me with your powerful love. Amen.

> THEN THE DETACHMENT OF SOLDIERS WITH
> ITS COMMANDER AND THE JEWISH OFFICIALS
> ARRESTED JESUS. THEY BOUND HIM. *John 18:12*

Loving Hands Bound For Me

Today police use metal or plastic handcuffs. In Jesus' day they were made of rope. But the purpose was the same—to restrain the criminal. So why were the authorities handling Jesus like some common criminal? What was the crime listed on the warrant issued for his arrest? There wasn't any. Those hands, bound by twine, belonged to the holy Son of God. His loving hands had done only good and bestowed only blessings. The lepers who were cleansed, the lame who could walk, the blind who could see, the sinners who were forgiven would quickly attest to this fact.

"Why?" I have to ask then. "Why were his hands bound if he was so innocent?" I should know the answer. I've heard it often enough, but I need to hear it again this Lenten season. Earlier Jesus said, "Everyone who sins is a slave to sin. . . . If the Son sets you free, you will be free indeed" (John 8:34,36). He's telling me to look at my hands. Not cuffs of rope but sin's heavy chains immobilized them. From such restraints there was no escape for me. Each sin doomed me to a maximum security cell in hell with an iron door that once shut would never clank open again.

They secured Jesus' hands with rope in Gethsemane and later with nails on Calvary. And Jesus in his love for me let them. "Don't you see," he says, "I let them tie me that I might untie you." "Don't you see," he says, "with the crimson blade of my blood I've cut through the cords of sin that bound you hand and foot for hell." "Don't you see," his bound hands shout out to me, "you're free—free from sin, free from Satan, free from death, free to serve me, free to live with me forever!"

Thank you, Jesus, for freeing me
from my sin and for your service. Amen.

> "IF I SAID SOMETHING WRONG," JESUS REPLIED,
> "TESTIFY AS TO WHAT IS WRONG. BUT IF I SPOKE
> THE TRUTH, WHY DID YOU STRIKE ME?" *John 18:23*

Loving Hands
Making Mine Clean

We try to get to as many of our granddaughters' basketball games as we can. At the payment window, they stamp our hands so that we can leave and reenter at will. Did you ever try to get that ink off the back of your hand? It takes a lot of rubbing with soap.

Many people that Maundy Thursday evening thought Jesus' hands were dirty. At least they wanted them to be, so much so that they were willing to bend and break their own laws. Yet, when all was said and done in their trial of Jesus, they could come up with nothing. We're not surprised. We know who Jesus is—the holy, sinless Son of God. He had no sin of thought, word, or deed.

In the courts of men—that is. Look deeper at the other trial going on that night. The court in heaven was in session. God, the righteous judge, was on the bench. He examined the totally innocent One before him and pronounced him horribly guilty. The verdict was just, because God saw on his Son the sins of the world. "We all, like sheep, have gone astray," yes, "and the LORD has laid on him the iniquity of us all" (Isaiah 53:6).

Where can I find a scale strong enough to weigh such a burden? Even more, how do I explain the love that moved Jesus to dirty his clean hands with my sins? I can't explain it, but I can thank God it happened. In his clean hands made dirty by my sins lies the supreme truth of my salvation.

Lord, be merciful to me and
cleanse me with Jesus' holy blood. Amen.

> THEY PUT A STAFF IN HIS RIGHT HAND AND KNELT IN FRONT OF HIM AND MOCKED HIM. "HAIL, KING OF THE JEWS!" THEY SAID. THEY SPIT ON HIM, AND TOOK THE STAFF AND STRUCK HIM ON THE HEAD AGAIN AND AGAIN. *Matthew 27:29,30*

Loving Hands Holding A Scepter

On his torn back the soldiers placed a tattered robe. On his tender scalp, a thorny crown. Now in their coarse humor it occurred to them that this "king" needed a scepter. One of them hurried forward with a hollow, weedlike reed and thrust it into Jesus' right hand. Such a scepter seemed suitable for a king who was rejected by his own people and who stood so helpless before them.

Wasn't that reedlike scepter a good one for my heavenly King? He doesn't use guided missiles or megaton bombs to cow people into submission, compel allegiance, or control opposition. He doesn't draft people into his service with his power but enlists them with his love. With the gospel message of his love, he accomplishes what the coercion of crowbars and the force of dynamite cannot do. Through the still, small voice of Word and sacrament, which to many appear as worthless as that hollow reed, he has drawn my heart and life to him.

Like the soldiers that day, many see no power in my King and give only mockery to him. I know better. I know he rules not only my heart but also the world. Though wicked men seem to prosper and unrighteousness to prevail, my King still rules. Evil can prosper only as far as he permits it. Finally he will destroy it. In Jesus' almighty power, we also believe, we who have felt the saving power of his humble gospel.

King of kings and Lord of lords,
rule over my heart with your saving love. Amen.

THEY CRUCIFIED HIM. *Mark 15:24*

Loving Hands Crucified For Me

Every tool has its purpose. I cut with a knife, eat with a fork, and write with a pen. And a nail? A nail is used to fasten. Though the crucifixion accounts don't mention nails by name, Thomas would tell us they were there. He saw their imprint on his risen Savior's limbs.

The gospels simply record, "They crucified him." But there was nothing simple about it. Splintery wood and sharp nails, torn flesh and screaming nerve endings, constant pain and slow death, and more were involved in this form of execution. Far worse were the tortures of hell. All of hell's acid waves that were the wages for the world's sins washed over God's Son. I can only guess at what this involved for Jesus as he hung fastened by those nails to that cross.

There's no guessing, though, as to who pounded those nails through his hands and feet. Calloused soldiers, a spineless judge, a turncoat disciple, hateful country men, all took a swing at the nails with sin's hammer. So did I! This Lenten season is not going to be what it should until I change the *they* to *I* crucified him. I and my many sins did it!

This Lenten season won't be what it should until I also realize why Jesus let my sins nail him to the tree. It was because he loves me. One of his disciples, after standing beneath Jesus' cross, wrote later, "This is how we know what love is: Jesus Christ laid down his life for us" (1 John 3:16). How Jesus must love me! How strong must be the love that held him to that cross for me!

"O all-atoning Sacrifice, You died to make me free."
Thank you, Jesus. Amen. (CW 138:5)

> THERE WAS A WRITTEN NOTICE ABOVE
> HIM, WHICH READ: THIS IS THE
> KING OF THE JEWS. *Luke 23:38*

Our Matchless King—
The Virgin's Son

Would you like to see a king? I mean a real King, a heavenly one. Then shift with me from your comfortable chair to one of the crosses out at Calvary. When we look at Jesus the way the penitent thief did on Good Friday, we'll be ready to hail Jesus as our matchless King.

What did the thief see when he looked at that center cross? A fellow human being, bleeding and dying as he was? That was all too obvious. Even the sign up on Jesus' cross said it. John's gospel relates that it read, "JESUS OF NAZARETH, THE KING OF THE JEWS" (19:19). His name was Jesus. Nazareth was his home. His mother was standing weeping beneath his cross.

The thief saw more. So must I. He asked Jesus for things only God could grant. He spoke of heaven where only God could be. Every Sunday I claim that I have seen what that thief did and more. I confess that I believe in "Jesus Christ, his only Son, our Lord, who was conceived by the Holy Spirit, born of the virgin Mary." I claim that he is God come into human flesh, born of a virgin mother through the miracle of the Holy Spirit. Born without sin to do what I could not do, to pay for every sin. Not to worry that I can't explain the miracle behind Jesus' virgin birth. I can't really explain the miracle behind my own children's births. But I do need to marvel at the love behind the birth of my King. A love that brought him into my flesh, onto that cross, to set me free. Then I'll be ready to hail him as my matchless King this holy season and always.

Lord, give me a heart of faith to see my
matchless King and to thank him for his love. Amen.

> THE OTHER CRIMINAL REBUKED HIM. "DON'T YOU FEAR GOD,"
> HE SAID, "SINCE YOU ARE UNDER THE SAME SENTENCE? WE ARE
> PUNISHED JUSTLY, FOR WE ARE GETTING WHAT OUR DEEDS DESERVE.
> BUT THIS MAN HAS DONE NOTHING WRONG." *Luke 23:40,41*

Our Matchless King– The Lord Of Love

What did the penitent thief see when he looked at the center cross? He knew what he saw when he looked at himself and the other thief crucified with him. "We are getting what our deeds deserve," he had to admit. But not the One on the center cross. Here was a matchless King whose every thought had been right, every word pure, and every deed proper.

How much like that dying thief I am. In God's eyes I'm a criminal who deserves the due reward for my sins. The more I recognize this horrible truth the better the One on the center cross will appear to me. Unfortunately, I'm often inclined to downplay my sins. I try to set up a "sinometer" on which murder and muggings get a 10 and immorality and idolatry only a 1. I'm tempted to think that God only winks at gossip and greed while lowering the boom on adultery and abortion. Lent is that serious time in which I need to look honestly at my heart, my words, my actions, and admit my heavy guilt.

To stop with this dismal look at myself would be tragic. Lent is also the blessed time for me, like that thief, to look at the King of love on the center cross. He who had no sin became sin for me. He who was eternal came to die for me. He who was righteous came to make me righteous. He who died rose again as living proof that my sins were gone and his heaven is open for me.

Lord of love, bend me down with my sinfulness,
and then lift me up with your forgiveness. Amen.

THEN HE SAID, "JESUS, REMEMBER ME WHEN YOU COME INTO YOUR KINGDOM." *Luke 23:42*

Our Matchless King— The Lord Of Life

The whole scene on Calvary can be summed up with one word—*death*. Death was ruling and three men were dying. But look what one of those three saw in Jesus on the center cross. He saw a source of life that would last forever. And he just had to have this life for himself.

Don't ask how the penitent thief received his eyes of faith. We aren't specifically told nor is it important. Faith is always the Spirit's working. With eyes of faith the thief now looked at Jesus and prayed, "Jesus, remember me when you come into your kingdom." Usually we try to do favors for dying people not ask them for favors. Yet that's what the penitent thief did with Jesus. And look for what he asked. No, not the top position on the highest throne in heaven, just a thought of remembrance from Jesus. Alone, this man had to be deathly afraid to enter eternity. But with the Lord of life remembering him, he would dare to face his God.

My life smells of death just as Calvary did. Life is a one-way street. Not much straight thinking is needed to determine where the street is leading. Where can I turn? At whom should I look? Let that dying thief remind me. There is One who has conquered death and now offers me life. He's my Jesus, who left his glorious throne on high to bleed and die for my sins. He's my Jesus, who deposited his soul for safekeeping in his Father's hands when he breathed his last. He's my Jesus, whom a stone sepulcher couldn't hold and whose resurrection promises no cement vault will hold my body captive forever either. He's my matchless King in whose heaven I will live forever.

Lord of life, keep me in faith
till in heaven I see your face. Amen.

JESUS ANSWERED HIM, "I TELL YOU THE TRUTH,
TODAY YOU WILL BE WITH ME IN PARADISE." *Luke 23:43*

Our Matchless King– The Lord Of Salvation

What did the penitent thief see as he looked at the center cross? Perhaps the question needs rewording. Let's ask, "What did he hear from the One on that cross?" The thief had asked for eternal life, and the Lord of salvation gave it to him.

"I tell you the truth," the Savior said. When he who owns heaven and earth speaks this way, it's as good as done. "Today," the Savior commented. Three or four more hours the thief would draw his ragged breath in pain on his cross. But then—that very day—not years down the road, his soul would be lifted up to heaven's glory. "With me," the Savior continued. All heaven is in those two words. What do I really know about heaven except that it is to be with Jesus and share eternally in his love? "In paradise," Jesus concluded. That very morning had seen the thief led from his prison cell to pay his final debt to society. That afternoon saw him dying on a cross and fast approaching hell's yawning jaws. But that evening saw him enjoying heaven with his Savior.

If he could talk to me today, what might that thief say? Surely he'd bubble over with the joys of heaven. Surely he'd breathe word after word of praise for the Lord of heaven. Might he not also speak rather wistfully about what his life might have been if he had only met the Lord of his salvation sooner? What treasures he could have enjoyed longer? What opportunities he could have had to praise his matchless King with both his lips and his life?

Lord, help me to hail you as my
matchless King today and always. Amen.

> WHEN HE HAD RECEIVED THE DRINK,
> JESUS SAID, "IT IS FINISHED." *John 19:30*

No Unfinished Symphony

In 1822 the great composer Franz Schubert began working on his "Eighth Symphony in B-minor." Two years later he had completed the first two movements. But for some unknown reason he never finished it. As a result, today we know his masterwork as "The Unfinished Symphony."

Early in his ministry the Savior told his disciples, "My food . . . is to do the will of him who sent me and to finish his work" (John 4:34). For me the Good Friday question has to be, Did he finish the work of salvation for which his Father had sent him? What if Jesus had left just one requirement of God's holy law undone? What if he put his holy obedience into my hands and said, "See, I have just about done what God wants you to do. Now you have only to add this little bit by yourself"? Or, what if Jesus had paid for all my sins, except for one or two? What if he put his almost complete payment into my hands and said, "See, I have covered 99 percent of your guilt. Now it's up to you somehow to pay for the rest"? Then his salvation would be no masterwork of love. It would be useless, and I would still be lost in my sins.

How sweet is my Savior's shout of triumph from his Good Friday cross! "Finished," he said, not "almost finished" or "just about done." "Paid in full!" he shouted for the whole world to hear, using a word stamped on tax bills when payment was complete. My Savior has kept God's holy law perfectly. My Savior has totally paid for each of my sins. Because of his finished work, I can stand cleansed from sin and clothed in holiness before his Father.

Lord, thank you for the sweet music of
Jesus' completed work of salvation. Amen.

> JOSEPH TOOK THE BODY, WRAPPED IT IN A CLEAN
> LINEN CLOTH, AND PLACED IT IN HIS OWN NEW TOMB
> THAT HE HAD CUT OUT OF THE ROCK. *Matthew 27:59,60*

Thoughts From A Cemetery

Cemeteries! Who wants to go to them, much less think about them? A cemetery is not one of the places I prefer to visit. But when I must, what are my thoughts?

Are they thoughts of sadness and loss? Beneath those gravestones lie my father and my mother. What hurt there is in losing loved ones! What wounds that time never seems to heal! Are there thoughts about the flight of time? How soon it really is all over with me. How frail life truly is. How much like the flower of the field and the breath of my mouth. Are they thoughts tinged with fear? What will death be like for me? Where will it find me? What will it do to me? Though the artificial green grass is draped over that hole, yet how deep and dark it appears! And how final!

Those early believers carried the Savior's lifeless clay to a rocky tomb on Good Friday. I can imagine their thoughts as they did their last labor of love for one so dear to them. I've been there too, out in the cemetery with morbid thoughts flooding my heart.

I've also been with them back in the cemetery on Easter Sunday. Jesus' body is no longer cold but gloriously warm with life. His tomb is no longer filled but wonderfully emptied. Death no longer is something to fear but the necessary step between earth and heaven. My Savior lives triumphant. So shall I! How this glorious truth changes my thinking about the cemeteries of life!

Lord, when I have to walk to the cemetery,
go with me and remind me of your victory. Amen.

IF CHRIST HAS NOT BEEN RAISED, YOUR FAITH IS FUTILE; YOU ARE STILL IN YOUR SINS. IF ONLY FOR THIS LIFE WE HAVE HOPE IN CHRIST, WE ARE TO BE PITIED MORE THAN ALL MEN. *1 Corinthians 15:17,19*

The World's Most Miserable Sinners?

The best-dressed people, the most-admired citizens, the players who made all-American are a few of the lists about which we read. Sometimes I may even catch myself wishing my name were on one or more of these lists. How about another category, one to which I surely would not want to belong, the one labeled "The World's Most Miserable Sinners"?

Paul details very clearly what a Christ still dead in the tomb would mean. "Your faith is futile," he writes, "you are still in your sins." Then the penitent crucified thief might scream in terror, "Jesus lied," as hell's fire licks at his heels. "He said, 'Today with me in paradise,' but look at me now." Then Simon Peter might moan from hell's prison, "Jesus looked at me that night, but his look meant nothing." "Still in your sins." How horrible! How miserable!

What about me, a sinner just like them? What if I've based my faith on something that doesn't exist? What if the plank I'm trying to walk from earth to heaven is rotten wood? If Christ has not been raised, then I'm to be pitied more than all people because my sins condemn me.

Thank God, that's not how it is. Christ has been raised. His empty grave shows he has paid for all my sins. The resurrection was the Father's loud "Amen" to his Son's words about sin's payment being finished. Because of his resurrection I'm one of the world's most joyful people.

Thank you, Lord, for your resurrection and
its joyful assurance of my forgiveness. Amen.

IF CHRIST HAS NOT BEEN RAISED . . . THEN THOSE ALSO
WHO HAVE FALLEN ASLEEP IN CHRIST ARE LOST. IF ONLY
FOR THIS LIFE WE HAVE HOPE IN CHRIST, WE ARE TO
BE PITIED MORE THAN ALL MEN. *1 Corinthians 15:17-19*

The World's Most Miserable Mourners?

Each of us is going to die. In our youth we don't stop to think about this. In our old age we try not to. But the drum beat of death goes on without pause.

What if Christ has not been raised? Can I even bear to ask that question? If Christ has not been raised, then only one word would fit our tombstones, that terrifying word *lost*. "Lost" it would have to say over Abraham's grave and Jacob's bones. "Lost" over John the Baptist's headless corpse and the dead believers at Corinth. "Lost" over my loved ones wherever they lie buried and over me too, wherever I might end up.

Then I'd belong on that list of the world's most miserable mourners. I'd have nothing to dry my scalding tears or soothe my aching heart when I lay a loved one to rest in the cold ground. Nothing to quiet my own thudding heart when death comes knocking on my door. Then the grave would be a dark prison and death the dismal door leading to eternal destruction in hell.

Thank God, that's not how it is! Christ has been raised. His emptied grave is a preview of what will happen to mine. His living presence is proof positive that all believers, including me, will live with him etenally. Because of his resurrection I'm one of the world's most joyful people.

*Thank you, Lord, for your resurrection and
its joyful assurance of eternal life for me. Amen.*

IF CHRIST HAS NOT BEEN RAISED, OUR PREACHING IS USELESS. . . .
IF ONLY FOR THIS LIFE WE HAVE HOPE IN CHRIST,
WE ARE TO BE PITIED MORE THAN ALL MEN. *1 Corinthians 15:14,19*

The World's Most Miserable Preachers?

Contrary to what some might think, being a preacher is not an easy job. There's much involved. Much that, if he would let it, could make a preacher feel miserable. The half-filled pews at worship, the critical nature of people, the selfishness that can show so easily—all these can bring misery into a preacher's life on occasion. But there is one thing, above all, that would make him most miserable. That is, as Paul put it, "If Christ has not been raised."

Who then would want to preach? All the phrases designed to edify and instruct, warn and strengthen, comfort and inspire would be just so many empty words. All the instruction classes and all the counseling would be just so much time wasted. All the baptisms and all the burials would be just so much hollow ritual and sham hope. Then a preacher, besides being miserable, might as well quit and look for something else to do. What would he have to say, and who would want to listen?

Thank God, that's not how it is! Christ has indeed been raised from the dead. He lives and reigns to all eternity as a loving, forgiving, helping Jesus. At the heart and center of all a preacher's work is this glorious message. The truth of Christ's resurrection turns a preacher from most miserable to most joyful. It makes him fairly shout out to the young men in the congregation, "Come, join the ranks. Become a preacher of the risen Savior and share the joy."

Thank you, Lord, for your resurrection and
the joyful message it gives me to tell others. Amen.

> JESUS SAID TO HER, "I AM THE RESURRECTION AND
> THE LIFE. HE WHO BELIEVES IN ME WILL LIVE EVEN
> THOUGH HE DIES. AND WHOEVER LIVES AND
> BELIEVES IN ME WILL NEVER DIE." *John 11:25,26*

Not The End,
But The Beginning

How's this for voices from the grave? A California inventor has come up with a talking tombstone on which video messages from the dearly departed can be viewed. You can even get a signal blocker so that only approved viewers can access the messages on the screen set into those headstones. There's just no end to man's inquisitiveness about what happens after death.

Do I want to know what happens after I take my last breath? Then listen I must to Jesus as he comforts Martha grieving over the death of her brother Lazarus. "Death is not the end," the Savior promised her. The physical death that terminates my earthly existence leads to the beginning of full enjoyment of the eternal life in heaven. From the moment a gracious Lord brings me to faith in Jesus, eternal life is mine. Not fully, though, because it is still marred and marked by sin and sorrow. But on my last day on this earth, my soul will go to a heaven where there is only joy forevermore. On the last day of this earth my body will be raised from its grave and rejoined in perfect form with my soul for eternal joy at my Savior's side.

Can I be sure? Martha was sure that day after Jesus raised her brother Lazarus from his grave. So can I be when I look at Jesus' empty grave. He lives and I shall live also. He truly is the Resurrection and the Life. I don't need talking tombstones, for I know what death brings because I know Jesus.

Lord, increase my confidence that
because you live, I shall live also. Amen.

> SHE [MARY MAGDALENE] TURNED AROUND AND SAW JESUS STANDING THERE, BUT SHE DID NOT REALIZE THAT IT WAS JESUS. "WOMAN," HE SAID, "WHY ARE YOU CRYING?" . . . JESUS SAID TO HER, "MARY." *John 20:14-16*

A Question From The Risen Savior

What a question to ask! Imagine how Mary must have felt when first the angels and now this stranger inquired about her tears. The One on whom she had pinned her hopes for salvation was a corpse—or so she thought. Then had come his hurried burial, leaving no time for friends like her to take care of his corpse properly. And now the final indignity—his body was missing or so it seemed, stolen by grave robbers or the unrelenting authorities. No wonder she was crying.

But Mary cries no longer. Behind her that first Easter stood the risen Savior. And he had a fitting question for her. "Why are you crying?" he asked in love. Then he spoke just one word. "Mary," he said, but, oh, how he said it! The love with which the risen Savior spoke her name brought an end to her tears and hope to her future.

I have my tears too. Tears shed in the hospitals and cemeteries of life. Helpless sobs that the problems and pains of daily living wrench out of me. Sorrow over sin that makes my heart cry out looking for relief. Like Mary, I need to hear the risen Savior's question, "Why are you crying?" I need to hear him call out my name. I need the assurance that his tomb is empty and he is gloriously alive. He is my Savior from all sin. He is my helper in life's problems. He is the conqueror of death. "He lives to silence all my fears; He lives to wipe away my tears. He lives to calm my troubled heart; He lives all blessings to impart" (CW 152:5).

Risen Savior, remind me daily that you are the answer for all my tears. Amen.

> AS THEY TALKED AND DISCUSSED THOSE THINGS WITH EACH OTHER,
> JESUS HIMSELF CAME UP AND WALKED ALONG WITH THEM; BUT
> THEY WERE KEPT FROM RECOGNIZING HIM. *Luke 24:15,16*

Walking With The Risen Savior

If a time machine could turn back the clock and permit us to share one scene with Jesus, which would you pick? His birthday when angels sang and shepherds adored? His crucifixion when divine blood ran and the sun was darkened? Or the beautiful, familiar scene of our verses?

It was Easter Sunday, and two disciples were on the way to Emmaus. They had walked this way before, but never with such heavy hearts. Back and forth they talked as they trudged along. We can well imagine how often Jesus' name came up in their conversation. "We hoped that he was the one who was going to redeem Israel," they lamented. But now Jesus was dead and so were their hopes. Oh, sure, they knew the promises from the Old Testament about the Savior's death and resurrection. But obviously they did not understand them until the risen Savior joined them and opened their eyes to see and their hearts to believe that first Easter afternoon.

Ever trudged along like those Emmaus disciples? I have, more times than I care to admit. When my daily and oft-repeated sins weigh heavy upon me, I come close to kicking the dust in despair. Can he really forgive me? When the problems in life weary me, I come close to trudging along head down as if there were nothing or no one to look up to. Far too often, I put the question mark of doubt behind my risen Savior instead of the exclamation mark of confidence. How I need that risen Savior to walk with me through his Word and set me straight!

Walk with me, risen Savior, and show me from your Word how real you are. Amen.

> BEGINNING WITH MOSES AND ALL THE PROPHETS,
> HE EXPLAINED TO THEM WHAT WAS SAID IN ALL
> THE SCRIPTURES CONCERNING HIMSELF. *Luke 24:27*

Studying Under The Risen Savior

What would I have done if I had been in Jesus' shoes? Would I have opened the eyes of those Emmaus disciples immediately so that they could see me alive and then just as quickly left them? Would I have reminded them of all my promises about rising again the third day and then asked condescendingly why they hadn't believed them? Or would I have left them trudge along in their ignorant despair?

Not so for the risen Savior. What a loving Shepherd he is! He seeks the heavy hearted and perplexed. He clears up their misunderstandings and clears out their doubts. And he does this by leading them into the green pastures of his Word. He who is the living Word sent by the Father shows the importance of the written Word given by the Spirit. If only I could have been there, soaking in the words that Easter afternoon as my risen Savior explained how the humility of Christmas, the pain of Good Friday, the victory of Easter had been conceived in eternity, foretold in Scripture, and now carried out in time so that I might be redeemed.

I don't need to go back in time to that Emmaus road in order to study under the risen Savior. He stands ready to feed me anytime. All I need to do is remember where the green grass grows. In the words and promises of Holy Scripture! Doesn't this truth make my church and Bible class attendance something important? Doesn't it make my daily grazing in his Word valuable? I can never learn enough about how Jesus was conceived, born, suffered, died, and rose again to save me from my sins.

So, teach me, risen Savior, I need your Word so much. Amen.

AS THEY APPROACHED THE VILLAGE TO WHICH THEY WERE GOING, JESUS ACTED AS IF HE WERE GOING FARTHER. BUT THEY URGED HIM STRONGLY, "STAY WITH US, FOR IT IS NEARLY EVENING; THE DAY IS ALMOST OVER." SO HE WENT IN TO STAY WITH THEM. *Luke 24:28,29*

Inviting The Risen Savior

Who's the most important person you've ever invited to your house? Most of us would have a hard time answering that question. We're not all that well acquainted with the rich and famous or into the world of important people. Yet aren't my family members and close friends important to me? Don't they light up my home and cheer me with their presence? And what about my dearest friend, the risen Savior? My home is simply not complete without him. Turn it around—when he is there, all is well.

So also with those Emmaus disciples. Though they still didn't recognize the risen Savior, they didn't want to part with him. Nor did Jesus want to leave them. He saw how much they needed his heartwarming and soul-comforting presence. But the risen Savior doesn't stay where he's not wanted. Wouldn't it have been a pity had those disciples not invited him in? How much they would have missed! And their home would still have been incomplete.

"Come, Lord Jesus, be our guest," I invite at mealtimes. "I pray the Lord my soul to keep," I petition at bedtime. But not just at those brief moments. Morning, noon, and night I need the risen Savior. I need his forgiveness for my sins, his strength for my temptations, his comfort for my sorrows, his heaven for my future. And I know where to find him— in his Word. When I live in his Word, I have the risen Savior at my side.

Risen Savior, I need you, I want you.
Keep me in your Word so that I have you. Amen.

> JESUS . . . STOOD AMONG THEM AND SAID, "PEACE BE WITH YOU!"
> AFTER HE SAID THIS, HE SHOWED THEM HIS HANDS AND SIDE. THE
> DISCIPLES WERE OVERJOYED WHEN THEY SAW THE LORD. *John 20:19,20*

Peace From The Risen Savior

I could speculate about much that first Easter evening. How securely bolted the door to that upper room must have been. How filled with despair the disciples' hearts must have felt. How miraculously Jesus' glorified body must have swept through those locked doors. How startled the group must have been when the risen Savior stood suddenly before them.

There's no speculation, however, about the risen Savior's first words to them. "Peace be with you!" he said. How necessary that word was! In the Garden of Eden my first parents, fallen into sin, told their holy Maker, "I heard you in the garden and I was afraid." (Genesis 3:10). In that upper room my risen Savior told his followers, "There's no more need to be afraid."

Let me not minimize or underestimate the peace of which Jesus spoke. His peace is far more valuable than earthborn peace that men never reach in the shuffling of papers on conference tables. His peace comes not from setting up homeland security measures and rooting out terrorists. Jesus' peace is spelled with capital letters. It's peace with God. Peace knowing sins are all forgiven. Peace being assured that heaven is open and eternal life is waiting.

It's a peace I can be sure of. The wounds in his hands and side show me where and how he earned it. Those wounds are not found on a dead Jesus but a living One. Now he stands before me, and through his Word, he tells me, "Peace be with you."

*Please, Lord, let my reaction be the same kind of
joy the disciples had that first Easter evening. Amen.*

AGAIN JESUS SAID, "PEACE BE WITH YOU! AS THE FATHER HAS SENT ME, I AM SENDING YOU." *John 20:21*

Sent By The Risen Savior

"Use me, O Lord, use me," prayed the new church member, "but only in an advisory capacity." He didn't want to be in the front lines slugging away, but in a rear pew where sluggish faith could relax. Such advisory Christianity is not what the risen Savior had in mind for his followers.

"I am sending you," he told them. Nor did he leave them clueless as to what they were to do. "Peace be with you!" he told them again. God had sent Jesus to prepare this peace. Now Jesus was sending them to publish it. They were to march out into the world with the cross of their risen Savior held high. The peace of sin's forgiveness, won by the Savior on the cross, was to be their message as they reached out to those around them.

Do you think they relocked the doors in that upper room after Jesus' left? Or looked around and complained about the odds? Those first followers didn't need any prodding. They had something the world desperately needed and with joy went about distributing it. When you read again the book of Acts, you'll sense their joy in carrying out the mission the risen Savior had given them.

Do I see my risen Savior standing before me? Do I feel his hand on my shoulder? Do I hear him say, "As the Father has sent me, I am sending you"? He has work for me to do. I not only have his peace to hold in my heart but to hand on to others who need it as much as I do.

Please, risen Lord, let it not be an advisory capacity for me but a joyful witnessing about you. Amen.

> THEN HE SAID TO THOMAS, "PUT YOUR FINGER HERE;
> SEE MY HANDS. REACH OUT YOUR HAND AND PUT IT
> INTO MY SIDE. STOP DOUBTING AND BELIEVE." THOMAS
> SAID TO HIM, "MY LORD AND MY GOD!" *John 20:27,28*

Reassured By
The Risen Savior

It's not wrong to ask questions. Of course, sometimes they can be superfluous. Like when I've already put out the garbage, but my wife still has to ask if I did. How about matters like death, cemeteries, heaven? Do you think questions are in place here and even more so their answers?

Thomas did. His problem was that he asked for the wrong reason. When Thomas said that he wouldn't be satisfied till he examined the risen Savior's wounds, he was not just making a statement. He was questioning in doubt, "You don't expect me to believe Jesus is alive, do you?" A week later Thomas got the reassurance he was demanding. Almost before the gentle voice had stopped, the doubter was on his knees at the nail-pierced feet of his risen Savior. "My Lord and my God!" was all he could say, but it was enough. He had seen and now believed.

Two ten-year-old cousins were at their first funeral. Riding home, one asked the other, "Is that what happens when you die? They put you in a hole in the ground?" "Yeah," replied the other, "but don't worry. Jesus is strong enough to get you out of that hole."

Do I have questions about death, cemeteries, and heaven? Jesus wants me to know where to go with my questions and whom to ask. The risen Savior invites me to listen, and not to doubt, as he speaks to me through his Word.

*Risen Savior, reassure me through
your Word that eternal life is mine. Amen.*

> NONE OF THE DISCIPLES DARED ASK HIM, "WHO ARE YOU?" THEY
> KNEW IT WAS THE LORD. JESUS CAME, TOOK THE BREAD AND GAVE
> IT TO THEM, AND DID THE SAME WITH THE FISH. *John 21:12,13*

Breakfast With The Risen Savior

How ordinary life can seem at times. We wake up, clean up, eat up. We hurry off to our place of business, hurry home for dinner, hurry to the television. We smile, snap, and snarl at others. We get tired, go to bed, and wonder what it's all about. There has to be more to life than this.

What a strange account to include in the appearances of the risen Savior. Why this story of Jesus preparing breakfast for his disciples that morning on the shore of the Sea of Galilee? Among other lessons, do you think he was trying to teach them that life would never be ordinary for them again? That there was more to their days than going fishing? Could it be that he wants me to realize that once I have seen the risen Savior, life becomes something special for me too?

"Come to me," he says and "I'll give you more than a fish breakfast. I'll put meaning into your life, such as the world can't even imagine or ever rob you of. I'll put peace and hope into your life that passes all understanding. I'll have waiting for you a life that defies description in my Father's house in heaven. And on the way to my Father's house, I have work for you to do. I'll help you as you work to feed my sheep and lambs and I'll bless your efforts."

When the risen Savior enters my life, "ordinary" goes out of the window. Life becomes a time to live in his Word, learn more about him, and look for opportunities to tell others about him.

*Risen Savior, fill my life with your presence
through your Word and with work for you. Amen.*

> PETER WAS HURT BECAUSE JESUS ASKED HIM THE THIRD TIME,
> "DO YOU LOVE ME?" HE SAID, "LORD, YOU KNOW ALL
> THINGS; YOU KNOW THAT I LOVE YOU." *John 21:17*

Loved By The Risen Savior

Do you notice how the risen Lord dealt with the disciple who had deserted him and denied him three times? Jesus didn't ask Peter, "What have you done?" He didn't urge, "Repent." He didn't command, "Trust my grace and forgiveness." He simply asked, "Do you love me?"

With that question, repeated three times, Jesus dealt with the present. He didn't want Peter to answer with a yes that confessed the sins of the past but with the yes of present love. The risen Savior had already forgiven Peter for his threefold denial. So he asked about Peter's present love to assure him of that full forgiveness and to certify him by grace for the work of feeding precious sheep and lambs.

Notice also how Peter answered? "Lord, you know all things; you know that I love you," was his humble reply. No longer did the penitent disciple boast about his great love for his risen Savior. Peter had nothing to point to as proof for his love. Instead, he pointed to the knowledge of Jesus. Peter relied on the loving understanding of the risen Savior, who had lived and died for his sins of denial. Jesus would know how Peter longed to love him and would help him do so.

What a lesson for me! Like Peter, I need to know that the risen Savior has forgiven me for my past denials. I need also to know that he can see my heart and fill it with love for him.

Risen Savior, you know I love you.
Help me love you more and more each day. Amen.

THEN JESUS CAME TO THEM AND SAID, "ALL AUTHORITY IN HEAVEN AND ON EARTH HAS BEEN GIVEN TO ME. THEREFORE GO AND MAKE DISCIPLES OF ALL NATIONS, BAPTIZING THEM IN THE NAME OF THE FATHER AND OF THE SON AND OF THE HOLY SPIRIT, AND TEACHING THEM TO OBEY EVERYTHING I HAVE COMMANDED YOU. AND SURELY I AM WITH YOU ALWAYS, TO THE VERY END OF THE AGE." *Matthew 28:18-20*

The Risen Savior Says "ALL"

In our devotions we've been looking at the appearances and statements of the risen Savior. What better way to conclude than with his appearance on that mountaintop in Galilee. What better word to summarize his statements than his own three *alls*.

"All authority," the risen Savior begins. In his hands is power over everything with no exceptions. Storms and sunshine, simple ants and complex human beings, the destiny of each individual and every nation are alike in his power. And that includes also me, his child!

"All nations," Jesus continues. He who died for all nations wants them to be his own. In the work of reaching them with his salvation, he gives me a part. I don't have to ask how to reach the nations. "By baptizing and teaching," he says. Nor does he leave me wondering how much to tell them. "Everything," he says. "If it's in my Word, it's important, and it needs to be taught."

"With you always," he promised. I can't see him or touch him. But he sees me and goes with me. He powers me for witnessing about him. He protects me in the problems of daily life. He pardons me when I stumble. And he preserves me in faith till I am with him always in heaven.

Risen Savior, you are all to me.
Oh, make me all for you. Amen.

> FOR THE WAGES OF SIN IS DEATH,
> BUT THE GIFT OF GOD IS ETERNAL LIFE
> IN CHRIST JESUS OUR LORD. *Romans 6:23*

Ready For The Tax Man?

In a December issue of a news magazine was the article "Get Ready for the Tax Man." Forget the elves and sugarplum fairies, it suggested, because the Internal Revenue Service was going to crack down with increased audits and forced collections in the next round of tax filings.

I try to keep my records in order so that my income tax filing will be accurate. I don't want to receive a notice from the IRS about having my return audited. But if it comes, I hope to be ready.

There is another tax man for whom I had better be ready. That's God, the holy judge of all. He audits everyone, not just selected individuals. His audit is accurate with no discussion about what's owed or not. And he does enforce the collection of the tax. Need I explain? God says that every one of my sins has a payment attached to it. The amount I owe for each sin is not calculated in dollars but in a horrible death. The wage for my sins is not just ending up in some cemetery but in the dungeons of hell. Nor are there any loopholes I can use to avoid sin's tax.

Thank God, I don't have to pay this tax. Why not? Because God's love has paid it for me. Good Friday was God's tax collection day. On the cross, his Son with his holy, precious blood wrote out the check that paid for my sins in full. God's justice was satisfied by his love. And I am the recipient of what that love has done. When my time comes to step before the eternal judge, my tax return will say, "Paid in full by Jesus' precious blood."

Thank you, Lord, for Jesus' blood that pays for
all my sins so I can stand holy before you. Amen.

THE LORD IS MY SHEPHERD. *Psalm 23:1*

Look Who's My Shepherd

Little ones sing it. Young couples request it as their wedding text. Old saints die with it on their lips. Countless hearts have treasured it; countless lips have sung it. The words of Psalm 23 flow endlessly with rich comfort. Not just for David, not just for others, but for me too!

"Shepherd," David calls his God. This aged believer knew from experience how important a shepherd is. He holds the flock together. He leads and feeds it. He protects and provides for it. He carries the newly born lamb in his arm and cares for the wounded sheep. Without their trusty guide, the sheep would scatter aimlessly and scamper away in fear.

"The LORD," David calls him, using the Old Testament term for the God of all grace and mercy, the God who always keeps his promise. Certainly he is an almighty God, but always as a Shepherd he directs his power with his love for me. Surely he is an all-knowing God, but always as a Shepherd he uses his wisdom with goals of love in mind for me. Absolutely he is an ever-present God, but always his presence at my side speaks of loving comfort, not anxious dread. Such a loving Shepherd David had, and so do I. A Lord who lays down his life to save the sheep. A Lord who cares all through life for his sheep. A Lord who has heaven prepared for his sheep.

The conclusion is obvious, isn't it? With such a Shepherd I'm safe. The world may flare up with bombs and hatred. Earthquakes of massive force may toss my life back and forth. But my loving Shepherd is still leading me, and I'm safe when I trustingly follow him.

Lord, help me never to
forget who my Shepherd is. Amen.

> THE LORD IS MY SHEPHERD. *Psalm 23:1*

"I Am Jesus' Little Lamb"

When her friends give birth, our daughter makes a bib with a lamb cross-stitched on it. That's her way of reminding parents whose child their little one really is. Regardless of my age, I also need the reminder of whose lamb I am.

David knew. All through his psalm he speaks not of "they" and "theirs" but "me" and "my." Jesus was his Shepherd, and he was Jesus' sheep. As an ex-shepherd David knew how weak and helpless a sheep is. It can't find green pasture by itself. It can't like a camel scent water from a distance. It can't find its way home like a dog or a dove. It can't defend itself when attacked. When lost, it runs aimlessly, getting farther and farther away from the fold.

How much like me! I've got sin's thistles in my wool because I've lagged behind my Shepherd. Stubborn pride blinds me to my Shepherd's leading. The world's call dulls my ears so that I don't always hear my Shepherd's voice. He's still the Good Shepherd, but I forget that he's *mine*.

But sheep are also one of the most trusting of animals. When the shepherd picks up a lamb, it's content in his powerful arm. Whenever the shepherd calls out, the sheep crowd around and follow. How much I want to be like them. I want to nestle securely in his strong arm. I want to stay close to his heels and never stray. My days for wearing a bib with a lamb on it are long gone. Yet, hopefully, all my days, words like Psalm 23 will remind me whose lamb I am.

Lord, help me ever sing, "Who so happy
as I am? Even now the Shepherd's lamb." Amen.

I SHALL NOT BE IN WANT. *Psalm 23:1*

Well Cared For

Is that how it really works? Those who follow the Shepherd will never be in want? At times my heart objects, "But I do want. I have troubles that don't go away. Bills that aren't paid. Illnesses that aren't healed. Sorrows that aren't stopped. If you only knew, you wouldn't expect me to say with David, 'I shall not be in want.'"

The Good Shepherd does indeed know my needs. In his own way, at his own time, and with his own measure he will take care of them. Or else he could hardly be my Good Shepherd. But I need to know him better. I need to look back and see how often he has supplied my needs in the past. I need to look forward and see how he will set me free from all my needs in that glorious future called heaven. Then I can look at today and entrust to him whatever lays heavily upon me.

Even more important, I need to look at his cross. My greatest need in this world is not measured in dollars and cents, health and well-being. It's the salvation of my soul. And there my Shepherd has well supplied me. On the cross he paid his precious blood for me. Through his Word and sacraments he makes his forgiveness my very own. In heaven he has eternal happiness waiting for me. "Well taken care of" fits completely when I see my Shepherd on his cross. At times life's troubled tears may blur faith's eyes. Then it's time for me to step closer to his cross and be reminded that "He who did not spare his own Son, but gave him up for us all—how will he not also, along with him, graciously give us all things?" (Romans 8:32).

Lord, give me the assurance that when you
are mine and I am yours, I am well supplied. Amen.

> HE MAKES ME LIE DOWN IN GREEN PASTURES,
> HE LEADS ME BESIDE QUIET WATERS. *Psalm 23:2*

Quiet Contentment

One of my jobs on the farm was to feed the calves. When I entered their pen, pail in hand, they would come running. Just look how much better the Good Shepherd feeds his sheep.

"He makes me lie down in *green* pastures," David says. Not all pastures are the same. Some are brown with dried up grass and little nourishment. My Shepherd leads me to pastures that are like the fresh, tender grass of springtime. In them I can "lie down," that is, stretch out in complete relaxation. "He leads me beside *quiet* waters," David also says. Of course. No shepherd worth his salt leads his sheep with their heavy wool to swift currents that could sweep them away. See what rest and contentment the Shepherd wants his sheep to have.

I live in a world that runs around, often in circles. It chases it knows not what and is not content to catch it. Sometimes I get tired just watching. More often I weary myself because I've joined in its mad chase. See what my Good Shepherd has for me. He wants me to be content with his leading. He wants me to trust that he will supply what I need and in a measure good for me.

He also wants me to feed regularly in the green pastures of his Word and drink deeply of the refreshing waters of his sacraments. When he tells me, a sinner, "Go in peace, your sins are forgiven," that's more relaxing for me than if I were some sheep stretched out in the shade. When he promises, "Never will I leave you; never will I forsake you" (Hebrews 13:5), that brings more contentment to me than any sheep ever found in the best pasture and sweetest stream.

Good Shepherd, let me find quiet
contentment in you and your promises. Amen.

HE RESTORES MY SOUL. *Psalm 23:3*

Soul Restoration

Working with old pieces of furniture can be fun. You find that old table, covered with dark varnish, pockmarked with dents, scarred by past neglect. Tender, loving care can restore it to a piece of furniture you'd be proud to have in your house.

What a faint picture of the loving restoring the Shepherd does for my soul. Like a sheep I at times just put my head down and start grazing. Before I know it, I have strayed from my Shepherd. I'm dented by sin. Satan's brush has spread sin's dark varnish over me. My neglect of God's Word has left its scars on me. I'm in danger and need the restoring work of Jesus.

So the Good Shepherd goes to work on me. With the wire brush of his law, he makes me feel my sin. His commandments make me cry "ouch," not just in sorrow over sin but in regret that I have wronged my loving Lord. Then he follows up with his gospel of forgiveness. My sins cannot be masked with some paint over. They need sanding away with the blood of Jesus.

"You were like sheep going astray," the apostle reminds me, "but now you have returned to the Shepherd and Overseer of your souls" (1 Peter 2:25). How well I know this blessed truth! Often as I've strayed, my Shepherd has found me. Though marked and marred by sin, he has taken me and restored me into a child fit to stand in his Father's house above. I pray my Shepherd never grows weary in his work of restoring my soul.

Good Shepherd, when I stray, bring me back.
Make me clean and precious in your sight. Amen.

> HE GUIDES ME IN PATHS OF RIGHTEOUSNESS
> FOR HIS NAME'S SAKE. *Psalm 23:3*

The Right Guide

When people go fishing in northern Ontario, they usually hire a guide. They want someone who knows where to take them. They're even ready to pay a fair amount of money for such service.

When David called Jesus his guide, he had more in mind than fishing. He was referring to walking the paths of righteousness. "I run in the path of your commands, for you have set my heart free," he explained in Psalm 119:32. As God's sheep, he didn't want to run off by himself or follow his own course. He wanted to walk where he could see the Shepherd's footprints. He wanted to do what his Shepherd wanted and follow what his Shepherd willed. "Paths of righteousness," he called it. "Being a faithful sheep" would be another way of putting it.

How easy it is to fall into the ruts of sin. How hard to follow the right paths where sheep are to walk. Nor does the world help me either. It keeps temptation's road looking green. It makes the lines on sin's highway seem so straight off into the horizon. When sin's potholes give me a sprain or plunge me off the path, I wake up and realize my need for a guide.

And I have One, the best One. Jesus not only shows me by example what my Father wants, he empowers me to walk that blessed road. He also has prepared the pardon I need for the many times I slide into the ditch of disobedience. He picks me up, picks out the burrs, and puts me back on the right track. Best of all, it doesn't cost me a cent because it cost him everything.

Guide me, Good Shepherd, in
your path and into your heaven. Amen.

Not Spooked By The Shadows

The wind was blowing. The tree branches were swaying. Waking up suddenly, I was spooked by the threatening shadows on my bedroom window. That was as a child. Now I'm an adult, and there still are shadows on my windows of life.

How about life's most threatening shadow—the one cast by death? There's no deeper valley, no darker shadow than death. If I pretend otherwise, I'm only fooling myself. If I claim I'm not afraid, I'm blowing hot air. Whistling in the cemetery makes noise but can't make death go away.

Yet I can say with David, "I will fear no evil." Five short words sum up my confidence—"for you are with me." When the Good Shepherd walks with me through death's dark valley, I'm safe. Notice he doesn't tell me, "Here's another valley for you to walk through. Good luck on your trip. I'll wait for you on the other end." Instead he walks with me. He knows the way. He's walked it before. His own walk through this valley has changed death from a monster into an empty shadow. His nail-pierced hands will hold mine tightly as we make this journey together. He'll even hold me close to his spear-pierced side when my legs give out. And with him as my Shepherd, I'll end up safely on the other side.

Death's shadows aren't real. They may be spooky, but they can't hurt me. What is real is Jesus. With his suffering, death, and resurrection he reminds me that sin has been paid for and death is nothing to fear.

Lord, walk with me when my
time comes to face death's shadows. Amen.

YOUR ROD AND YOUR STAFF,
THEY COMFORT ME. *Psalm 23:4*

Breathing Easier

I was holding my breath. The road had become suddenly icy. The car started skidding. When it finally ended up safely on the shoulder, I could unclench the steering wheel and breathe again.

Life is filled with incidents that cause me to hold my breath. Trouble like some black ice coats the road and makes it treacherous. Sin like some debris punctures a tire and sends me veering toward the ditch. Death looms before me like some car running a stoplight and smashes my existence. What am I going to do? How long can I hold my breath in apprehension, not to mention fear?

Like David, I need to remember something important. The Shepherd's rod and staff are always there to comfort me. With his staff a shepherd would hold enemies at bay. The wolf learned to fear its lethal swing. With his staff a shepherd also corrected his sheep. When they started straying, he would snag their legs and pull them back.

Any lesson here for me? Sin, death, and the devil are my bitterest enemies. They hound me regularly, but they had better fear my Good Shepherd's staff. More than occasionally do I in my ignorance begin to stray. I need the correcting yank of my Good Shepherd's staff. And I have it. Protection and correction are mine as a sheep in his flock. The result is "comfort," or as the word means "breathing easier." I can unclench the steering wheel in life and breathe again because of my Good Shepherd.

Lord Jesus, pull me closer and protect me
as we travel together toward your heaven. Amen.

> YOU PREPARE A TABLE BEFORE ME IN
> THE PRESENCE OF MY ENEMIES. *Psalm 23:5*

A Peaceful Table

Mealtimes don't mean much anymore these days. They are often snuffed out as the pressures of life and the pursuit of who-knows-what has people scrambling about. Relaxed dining has given way to grab-and-gobble at the fast-food window. No wonder antacids are a hot seller at the discount store.

That's not the picture David sets before me. I'm inside a gorgeous castle, seated at a finely appointed table. I can take my time enjoying a splendid meal without distraction. Even my greatest fears can't get at me. While I feast inside, they can only grind their teeth outside.

"That's not how it goes in life," you say? True, at times life's pace can be hectic and I can do little to slow it down. At times life's problems sit down with me at the table and keep my stomach acid flowing. But just imagine what it would be like if I didn't have the Shepherd. What if I had to carry the pounds of temptation, sorrow, disappointment alone? Would I ever get a chance to grab a bite?

And what if I couldn't sit in my church bench on Sunday? Outside my church the world rages and life wearies. But inside a feast is going on. The table of God's grace is spread. He himself stands ready to serve me, to offer me the life-restoring, life-invigorating food of his forgiveness for all my sins. No antacids for me when I sit at his table. Just food that nourishes for life amidst my enemies and eventually life without enemies in his heaven.

Good Shepherd, through your Word and sacraments,
feed me till in heaven I want no more. Amen.

> YOU ANOINT MY HEAD WITH OIL;
> MY CUP OVERFLOWS. *Psalm 23:5*

Tender, Loving Care
And Then Some

David's words bring two pictures to mind. The first is how good the right lotion can feel on sunburned cheeks. I should have worn a hat. I should have put on sunscreen. But I didn't, and now I need relief. The second is how our son used to fill his glass. He wouldn't stop till the orange juice ran over the top. He wanted as much as he could get.

Sheep didn't have an easy time in Palestine. Briars would scratch their faces. The hot sun would sap their strength. What a relief when at the end of the day their shepherd would move among them with his vial of oil. Can't you just imagine them nuzzling against his leg as he gently spread the soothing oil on their heads. Do I need explanation for this picture? Like the sun's hot rays, life's troubles beat down on me, searing my faith, sapping my spiritual strength. I can name my troubles; you can name yours. I need the Shepherd's tender, loving care. I need daily rubbing with his soothing Word to take the sting out and assure me all is well.

The second picture also speaks of my Shepherd's tender, loving care. When I hold faith's cup out for refilling, he doesn't just wet the bottom. He fills it right up to and over the top. "I want you to have as much comfort as you can get," he tells me. And I need it. Life's cup overflows with my sins. Even more so does his cup of forgiveness. Life's cup runs over with trouble. Even more so does his cup of comfort. Life's end seems to empty the cup. But he reminds me that he has prepared for me a life that keeps running over the top, all the way to his heaven.

Good Shepherd, soothe me with your promises.
Fill me with their comfort. Amen.

> SURELY GOODNESS AND LOVE WILL FOLLOW
> ME ALL THE DAYS OF MY LIFE. *Psalm 23:6*

In Hot Pursuit

Want to know the best way to see the future? The best way to be sure what tomorrow will bring? Then I need to do as David did. He looked at today. He wrote how his Good Shepherd leads, feeds, restores, and guides. He trained faith's binoculars on today in order to be assured of what tomorrow would bring. As it was for him in the present, so he was sure it would be in the future.

What did David see in the present? Twin traveling companions who would surely follow him into each tomorrow. In fact, in the Hebrew original, David said those companions would pursue him. They would chase after him, catch him, clutch him close. Who were these relentless companions? God's "goodness and love," David said. *Goodness* refers to God's providing what is needed for earthly life each day. *Love* refers to God's providing forgiveness, strength, comfort for the soul. With such companions David could step safely into each tomorrow that life might bring.

To preview the future I need to look at today and yesterday. What do I see when I do? Isn't it those same two traveling companions? On some days storm clouds gathered, thunder sounded, and lightning flashed. But the resulting rain refreshed my soul. Eyes washed by tears end up seeing the Lord more clearly. Faith tested by trial learns to trust more fully. The Shepherd knows what he is doing. He knows what I need even if I don't. And his love sends it. When I take my eyes off my Good Shepherd, tomorrow looks dark. When I see him leading me as his beloved sheep, I can know that my tomorrow will be just like today, filled with his goodness and love.

Good Shepherd, let your goodness
and love pursue me all my days. Amen.

AND I WILL DWELL IN THE HOUSE
OF THE LORD FOREVER. *Psalm 23:6*

My Forever Home

Where would you like to live? In the Southwest where beautiful sunsets light up the saguaro and overcoats are seldom needed? In northern Wisconsin where the pine trees stand tall and the big fish beckon? Each of us has his or her own preference, though we may not achieve it.

Now let's change the question just a bit. Where would you like to live forever? David has the answer. "In the house of the LORD," he said. David was referring to heaven, where he would stand with all believers before the Savior's throne. This was not just some preference for him that might or might not be realized. "I *will* dwell in the house of the LORD," he said with the confidence of one who trusts the Good Shepherd's leading.

How wonderful my forever home will be! There I'll be freed from all sin and temptation, all trouble and sorrow that keeps chipping away at my soul. There my body will on the Last Day rejoin my soul in perfect form. There I'll be in some wonderful company. I can hardly wait to sit down with people like Paul and Peter who gloried in the cross of Christ. And think about my first glimpse of Jesus, the Shepherd who gave his life for sinners like me. Heaven won't be a vacation place for me, but a home where I will be overjoyed to live forever.

"What's wrong?" a cabbie asked his fare. "My mother died today," replied the sobbing woman. "Was she a Christian?" asked the driver. "Yes," the woman answered. "Then why are you crying as if everything were over?" was the cabby's query. Say it with me, "I will dwell in the house of the LORD forever."

Please, Good Shepherd, make
it possible, for only you can. Amen.

> YOU ARE ALL SONS OF GOD THROUGH FAITH IN CHRIST JESUS,
> FOR ALL OF YOU WHO WERE BAPTIZED INTO CHRIST HAVE
> CLOTHED YOURSELVES WITH CHRIST. *Galatians 3:26,27*

Famous Names

I just spent a few moments browsing through the greater Milwaukee area phone book. Do you know that George Bush, James Carter, and John Kennedy are listed there? I find it interesting, when I travel, to look for "famous" names in phone books.

I have a famous name too. Not Lauersdorf. There aren't too many of them listed in phone books across the country. I'm referring to the name Christian. That name was given me at my baptism. When the Spirit worked faith in my heart through water and the Word, Christ's cross was put upon my breast and better still upon my heart. God wrote my name in his Book of Life in heaven. He clothed me with Christ as with a garment that covered me more tightly and completely than my skin. He claimed me as a treasured member of his heavenly family. All the treasures of salvation—all the perks of his family became mine.

I sign my checks, Richard Lauersdorf. God wants me to sign my life with Richard Lauersdorf, Christian. He wants me to be rightly proud of my family name. He doesn't want me to bring dishonor on such a famous name or cause others to think lightly of it. Nor do I. I want others to know what it means to belong to God's family. The best way I have is being a "little Christ," walking in love toward my Father and toward all those around me in life. People don't need to see my name in phone books. They do need to see Christ's name in my life.

Lord, help me use my life to bring
honor to the family name of Christian. Amen.

> THERE IS NEITHER JEW NOR GREEK, SLAVE
> NOR FREE, MALE NOR FEMALE, FOR YOU
> ARE ALL ONE IN CHRIST JESUS. *Galatians 3:28*

Being First

Who ran the first four-minute mile? Who was the first to hit 60 home runs in a season? Who took the first step on the moon? Maybe you remember the names. Maybe you don't. Others more recently have accomplished similar feats and more. Wonder about those names, though? They were Roger Banister, Babe Ruth, and Neil Armstrong.

Some people think being first is important. Even in the church. Jesus' disciples did too that day when they asked about being greatest in his kingdom (Matthew 18:1). For their selfish ambition the Lord Jesus had a strong answer. In one sense, though, each of us is first in God's eyes, as Paul reminds us. Regardless of nationality, gender, or social status, each believer is on the same level in God's kingdom. Each shares equally in an awesome inheritance. Each has forgiveness through Jesus, membership in God's family, and a future home in their Father's heaven.

So I can say, "I'm first," not in pride but in gratitude. God has made me into something special. His love made his only Son into a child so that I could become his child. His grace scrubbed out sin's dirt from my soul so that I could stand holy in his sight. His Spirit worked in my heart the faith to believe in the Savior so that I could stand beside him in heaven. I and others like me have no cause for patting ourselves on the back. Instead, I have every reason to praise the God of love.

Lord, keep me as one whom your love
through Jesus has made your very own. Amen.

IF YOU BELONG TO CHRIST, THEN YOU ARE
ABRAHAM'S SEED, AND HEIRS ACCORDING
TO THE PROMISE. *Galatians 3:29*

What An Inheritance!

I tease my wife at times that she didn't bring much dowry into our marriage. As a parochial school teacher, she was rich in many ways, but not in dollars and cents. Her answer is that she married a poor preacher. I always hope she meant poor in income, not preaching.

But both of us are rich in Christ. As believers we are "heirs according to the promise." After years of marriage, we marvel often about the riches God has showered on us. What joy to kneel together at Christ's manger bed and pray, "O holy Child of Bethlehem, Descend to us, we pray; Cast out our sin And enter in; Be born in us today" (CW 65:4).

What peace to kneel together before his Calvary cross and pray, "Sweet the moments, rich in blessing, Which before the cross we spend, Life and health and peace possessing From the sinner's dying friend" (CW 111:1).

What victory to shout together before his open tomb, "Oh, where is your sting, death? We fear you no more; Christ rose, and now open is fair Eden's door. For all our transgressions his blood does atone; Redeemed and forgiven, we now are his own" (CW 143:4).

Certainly faith is an individual matter. But never do I want to discount the richness of being able to walk through life with one who has the same inheritance I do. That's God's gracious gift too, for which I thank him daily.

Thanks, Lord, for making us rich together. Amen.

THOUGH YOUR RICHES INCREASE, DO NOT
SET YOUR HEART ON THEM. *Psalm 62:10*

Rich The Right Way

In a novel I read recently, one character asks, "Why is it that so many people think that all the answers are in their wallets?" Good question.

People usually look at money in two ways. They worry about not having enough of it. Or they dream about having huge amounts of it. The first one keeps people awake at night worrying about paying their monthly bills. Being unemployed or having only a small balance in the checking account are not easy matters. They require prayer, perspiration gained from working hard to get ahead, and patient waiting for the Lord's help.

What about the second category—those wanting huge amounts of money? There's nothing wrong with being wealthy. Abraham, David, and Joseph of Arimathea were rich and yet true believers. It's the wanting that gets people into trouble. Wealth has a way of making fingers sticky—fingers wanting to have it all, hanging on to it all, hoarding it all. If only the wealthy would stop to think that when God gives much, he also requires much. I'd rather be a steward of limited income than of millions. There's much less temptation involved.

And I'd rather be rich the right way—in Jesus. All in God's kingdom are millionaires. No, not always in terms of money but always in spiritual riches. What can compare to the riches of God's pardon, his love, his promises, his heaven? In Jesus I'm rich beyond imagination and measure.

Lord, give me what I need to live. Above all,
give me the riches of salvation in Jesus. Amen.

> YET THE LORD LONGS TO BE GRACIOUS TO YOU; HE RISES TO SHOW YOU COMPASSION. FOR THE LORD IS A GOD OF JUSTICE. BLESSED ARE ALL WHO WAIT FOR HIM! *Isaiah 30:18*

Wait For Him

Somewhere I read that God is never in a hurry, but that he is always on time. Just a little looking proves these words. The seasons come and go at the time the Creator has set. Nations rise and fall according to God's design. His Son entered a stable when his time had fully come. So also with my life. How much happier life would be if I could just remember to wait for God's time. Sometimes I find myself fidgeting because I forget God sets his own schedule.

The same truth applies in the matter of salvation. God wants all to be saved. He wants all in his eternal kingdom. He sent his Son to pay for everyone's sins. He wrote his Word so that everyone could know. He delays his Son's return on the Last Day till the news of salvation has reached to the ends of the earth. Then all who believe will be saved and all who do not will be damned.

Sometimes I forget to wait for the Lord. Like with Sig whose wife was terminally ill with cancer. For years she had invited, urged, even begged her husband to come with her to church. But he was too stubborn. After her death he came. Finally he was instructed and confirmed. Almost every Sunday he would say to me at the door, "Why did I wait so long? I missed so much." My answer, "Sig, you finally have what you need and just in time."

When it comes to my life, my salvation, my efforts to witness, the end of my world, I can do nothing better than wait for the Lord. His timing is always right.

Come, Lord Jesus, I wait for you. Amen.

LET US RUN WITH PERSEVERANCE THE RACE MARKED OUT FOR US. LET US FIX OUR EYES ON JESUS, THE AUTHOR AND PERFECTER OF OUR FAITH. *Hebrews 12:1,2*

In It For The Long Haul

Ever hear of the Iditarod Trail Race? When we visited in Alaska, I was intrigued by this dog sled race. It runs over a thousand miles across frozen terrain from Anchorage to Nome and lasts about 11 days. To win, the dogs need good training, and they need good care at the end of each hard day on the trail.

That Alaskan Trail Race is nothing compared to the one I'm in. "Race" the author calls it, using a Greek word from which our word *agony* comes. He's talking about a contest involving exertion and struggle. He's also talking about a constant contest, for in the Greek he wrote, "Let us keep on running." And he's talking about an extremely difficult contest, one that requires "perseverance." That word means holding out under stress, not slowing down or stopping for any reason. Faith's race is not some 11-day dash but a lifelong marathon. On faith's track I dare not slow down after a mile or two but need to be in it for the long haul.

Where can I find the stamina and strength I need for such a grueling race? "Fix [your] eyes on Jesus," the author directs me. Again in the Greek, he says, "Keep your eyes fixed on Jesus." Why? Because Jesus is "the author and perfecter of our faith." He's the one who authored and worked out my salvation. He's the one who has given me faith's feet to run the track to heaven. He's the only one who can strengthen my feet so that I end up a winner in heaven. At the end of each hard day on heaven's trail, I need the strength my Jesus provides through his Word.

Lord, thank you for putting me into heaven's race. Keep me going till I win. Amen.

"ANYONE WHO WILL NOT RECEIVE THE KINGDOM OF GOD LIKE A LITTLE CHILD WILL NEVER ENTER IT." AND HE TOOK THE CHILDREN IN HIS ARMS, PUT HIS HANDS ON THEM AND BLESSED THEM. *Mark 10:15,16*

Make Me Your Little Child

What did Jesus know firsthand about children? He never experienced the unique feelings that a child's birth brings a parent's heart. Nor did he taste the special joys of being a grandparent.

Or did he? As the Savior, he loves children more deeply than parents or grandparents ever can. He reaches for our children, wants them on his knee and in his kingdom. He even instituted the Sacrament of Holy Baptism so our children could be brought to faith and become his very own.

Unfortunately, Adam and Eve's sin blighted the hearts of our little ones also. From sinful parents can come only sinful children. But the Savior washes that original sin away with the promises connected with Baptism's water. The simple faith he grants them is a model for me. Little ones believe whatever you tell them. They don't question why or hesitate when the promises appear impossible. Going under a railroad or highway overpass, I would say to our children, "Put your hands up so the bridge won't fall." How long they believed me I don't know. But they did and up would go the hands.

Jesus doesn't ask me to put my hands up or to believe that the moon is made of cheese. He does, however, ask me to trust that his blood has paid for all my sins. That all things are possible for him, even in the most severe circumstances in my life. That he will never leave me and that nothing can separate me from him. That he has prepared a room for me in his Father's house and will take me safely there. The prayer is in place, isn't it?

Lord Jesus, make me a little child, your simple trusting child who believes your every word. Amen.

> WHEN HE HAD LED THEM OUT TO THE
> VICINITY OF BETHANY, HE LIFTED UP HIS
> HANDS AND BLESSED THEM. *Luke 24:50*

A Reminder
Of What He Has Done

What did those disciples see when they looked at Jesus that first Ascension Day? How could they miss the nail prints in his hands stretched out over them? At once they must have recalled Calvary's cross with its agony. At once they must have remembered the cause behind his cross. In love the almighty One had come to earth to serve. In love the sinless One had come to be defiled by man's sin. In love the eternal One had come to face mankind's death and fill mankind's grave.

But look! Those nail prints were not found on dead hands locked in rigor mortis on his lifeless chest. Again and again they had seen their risen Savior during the 40 days since his resurrection. Again and again he had assured them of full forgiveness, perfect peace, and heaven's home. Now he was about to leave them with his work of salvation done. And those hands lifted in blessing over them plainly reminded them of his completed mission.

"Why does Jesus still have the nail marks?" asked a confirmation class student. We were studying the resurrection of the body and how our raised bodies will be like "his glorious body" (Philippians 3:21). That prompted the question. Why does Jesus' glorious body still have the marks of the cross? Imagine my surprise when another student answered, "They show that he paid for our sins." For Jesus those nail marks are medals of honor speaking visibly of his distinguished service. For me they are sweet assurance of something most vital—my salvation.

*Ascended Savior, through your Word remind
me of what you in love have done for me. Amen.*

> WHILE HE WAS BLESSING THEM, HE LEFT THEM
> AND WAS TAKEN UP INTO HEAVEN. *Luke 24:51*

A Reminder
Of What He Still Does

What was the last view those disciples had of their ascending Lord? Wasn't it his hands lifted in blessing over them? How that sight must have stuck with them. When troubles arose, they needed only to recall his hands stretched over them in blessing. When temptations came, those same hands were there, always ready to strengthen them. The same was true with sorrow and suffering, danger and even death. Jesus was not off in a secluded heaven, unaware and unconcerned about them. He was holding his loving, living hands in blessing over them. No wonder they returned to Jerusalem with great joy. They knew what Jesus would still do for them.

It's easy for me to see his hands lifted in blessing when the sun shines brightly and my step is sprightly. In fact, in such days I may not even see his hands, to my shame, and may forget where my thanks belongs. But then come other days when his arms are extra visible and I cannot exist without them. Do you know of any days like that too?

Did you think about those arms when you were wheeled into that operating room? When the lab report came back with news about cells not normal? When you've had to walk to the grave behind a loved one's casket? When you rise to loneliness each day? What would I do without his blessing arms? Who else can hold me close and wipe away both my tears and my fears?

> *What confidence to be able to pray, "Lord Jesus, since you love me,*
> *Oh, spread your wings above me And shield me from alarm.*
> *Though Satan would assail me, Your mercy will not fail me;*
> *I rest in your protecting arm." Amen.* (CW 587:3)

AFTER HE SAID THIS, HE WAS TAKEN UP
BEFORE THEIR VERY EYES, AND A CLOUD
HID HIM FROM THEIR SIGHT. *Acts 1:9*

A Ruling Lord

Facing the marine and his 1,800 buddies on the front lines in Korea were 100,000 communist troops. In the 42° below zero weather, his uniform was frozen board solid on him. With hands blue from the weather, he was trying to eat cold beans with his trench knife. The war correspondent asked him, "If I were God and could give you anything, what would you ask for?" Without hesitation the marine answered, "I'd ask you to give me tomorrow." That's what the ascending Lord Jesus offers his followers. At his ascension he had so much to say to his followers and so much of it is about our tomorrows.

We look at those young people who this month will be confirmed or will graduate. Their spiritual wings have been growing. But are they strong enough to fly above the storms of our sinful world? Will the heat of temptation singe their wings of faith? Do they have a chance at a tomorrow? We look at them because we also look at ourselves with the same question.

Time to look again at the ascending Lord Jesus. That's no mere mortal. He's the God-man who came to earth to save us. He's no fake, no pushover. He's the almighty Lord, who rules over everything. Nor does he rule arbitrarily or according to whim. The ascended Savior rules always with the interests of his church in mind. God has put all things in his hands, and his hands are strong enough to hold them. With such a ruling Lord, those graduates and I have a tomorrow.

Lord, help me believe that you are giving me
a good tomorrow, even when I can't see it. Amen.

"YOU WILL BE MY WITNESSES IN JERUSALEM,
AND IN ALL JUDEA AND SAMARIA, AND
TO THE ENDS OF THE EARTH." *Acts 1:8*

A Gigantic Task

Jesus had finished his work. He had accomplished what he had come to do. With his perfect life, he had fulfilled all of God's commandments. With his innocent sufferings and death, he had completely paid for all our breaking of those commandments. Salvation was complete as his return to his Father in heaven indicated. Now it's our turn. The tomorrow Jesus gives me is not to be an empty one. I'm to fill it with witnessing about Jesus. That's what witnesses do. They simply tell others what they have seen and heard. And for me as a witness the topic is Jesus my Savior, Jesus who is the world's Savior too.

Perhaps this task of witnessing doesn't seem so gigantic to me because I don't see the Savior's finger pointing right at me. I hear him say, "You will be my witnesses," and I think he means others like my pastor or my child's teacher or those missionaries in far-off places. *You* means other people, I think, not me.

Time to think again. His finger still points directly at me. The ascended Savior reminds me that I'm to light up the little corner of the world where I live. Let the words I speak, the life I lead, the goals for which I live, the way I treat others show that I know what each tomorrow is for. It's to share with them what has been given me—salvation that's complete and the Savior who prepared it.

Lord, thank you for telling me about salvation.
Help me tell others. Amen.

> "YOU WILL RECEIVE POWER WHEN THE
> HOLY SPIRIT COMES ON YOU." *Acts 1:8*

A Reassuring Promise

Can you imagine the disciples' reaction? "Jerusalem? Well, Lord, we'll try." "Judea and Samaria? We don't know, Lord, that might be stretching it." "But the ends of the earth? Come on, Lord, what do you expect?" How were they going to take on the whole world?

Imagine then the reassurance they received from their ascending Savior. "You will receive power," he promised them, "when the Holy Spirit comes on you." For them this promise was fulfilled at Pentecost as the Spirit was poured out on them in special measure. Empowered by that Spirit, the disciples went out into the world and changed the course of history. The rest of the book of Acts describes the Holy Spirit's activity as he built Christ's church through them.

"We can't do it alone," we too tell Jesus. "We can't survive alone in this hostile world, much less preach to it about you." "You don't have to," the Savior replies. "I will send my Spirit and he will be your power." One day at the South Pole, Admiral Byrd, while out for a walk, got caught in a blinding snowstorm. Suddenly he realized he could no longer see the chimney of his hut. Fighting back panic, he drove a stake where he was standing. Fastening a rope to that stake, he moved out in ever widening circles around it until he ended up right at the door of his little hut. Can we learn from him? My stake is Christ. The rope that connects me to him is faith as the Spirit works it through Word and sacrament. His Spirit powers me to live in this sin-swept world and to witness to it about its only refuge in the storm.

Keep me close to your Word, Lord.
Strengthen me through it. Use me to spread it. Amen.

> THEY WERE LOOKING INTENTLY UP INTO THE SKY AS HE WAS
> GOING, WHEN TWO MEN DRESSED IN WHITE STOOD BESIDE THEM.
> "MEN OF GALILEE," THEY SAID, "WHY DO YOU STAND HERE
> LOOKING INTO THE SKY? THIS SAME JESUS, WHO HAS BEEN
> TAKEN FROM YOU INTO HEAVEN, WILL COME BACK IN THE
> SAME WAY YOU HAVE SEEN HIM GO INTO HEAVEN." *Acts 1:10,11*

An Eye-Lifting Hope

Their eyes were glued on their ascending Savior. Slowly he rose until a cloud covered him. Jesus' actual entrance into heaven's glory was not a sight for sinful eyes. They couldn't watch as the Father welcomed his beloved Son home. They couldn't listen as the angels sang his eternal praises. They could, however, receive one more promise from their Lord, this time delivered through his angels. "He's coming again," the angels told them and us. "And when he does, it will be that glorious Last Day when he'll take all his own to live with him in that eternal tomorrow."

Those young confirmands and graduates before us this month will make the same mistakes we often have. They'll think they'll have many tomorrows ahead of them. They'll assume that they'll have plenty of time in which to think about the eternal tomorrow. Believe me, how quickly life flashes by. It seemed like only yesterday when we were young like those confirmands. Now, here we are with only God knows how few tomorrows left.

It's time to look again at my ascending Savior. Time to hear his angels remind me that he's coming again. Time to pray that when he does, he'll find me ready with eyes of faith fastened on him. A glorious tomorrow is waiting, but only for those who wait for their Savior's return.

Lord Jesus, keep my eyes of faith fastened
on you so that I'm ready when you return. Amen.

> BLESSED IS THE MAN WHO DOES NOT WALK IN THE COUNSEL OF
> THE WICKED OR STAND IN THE WAY OF SINNERS OR SIT IN THE SEAT
> OF MOCKERS. BUT HIS DELIGHT IS IN THE LAW OF THE LORD,
> AND ON HIS LAW HE MEDITATES DAY AND NIGHT. *Psalm 1:1,2*

Trees Rooted In The Soil Of God's Word

God's trees, like all good trees, must be rooted in the right soil. Believers cannot grow, much less stay alive, if planted in the wrong place. Look what happens to those in the wrong soil. Light brushes with sin can so quickly lead to close contact and finally complete saturation with sin. The walk with the wicked soon becomes the standing in the way of sinners and ultimately leads to sitting down with mockers. Sin is like that. Like the little live coal of a cigarette, it smolders and in the end burns down the whole forest. It can and does happen. Looking back at the picture of my confirmation class, I see what appears to be some dead trees. Looking at the young confirmands kneeling before the altar of my church this month, I pray it doesn't happen to them.

The psalmist knew good soil. So do I. There's only one soil for Christian trees, the "law of the LORD." In the Hebrew that word meant the whole instruction or Word of God. God's Word is the only soil in which Christian trees can be rooted. Lovingly, tenderly, carefully the heavenly gardener has done his planting. Only he can. Through Holy Baptism he planted me like some tender seedling in his precious promises of salvation. Through his Word as heard in my home, instruction classes, and weekly services, he has worked the roots of faith deeper.

*This confirmation season, as I look at myself and
then at those young confirmands in my church, I pray humbly,
"Lord, keep us rooted in your Word. Keep us as your trees." Amen.*

HE IS LIKE A TREE PLANTED
BY STREAMS OF WATER. *Psalm 1:3*

Trees Watered With God's Grace

When we purchased our house, the young trees in our landscaped backyard were almost dead. Because ours was a model home, built to showcase the builder's skills, no one had lived in it. Neither had anyone bothered to water those tender trees.

God's trees, like all trees, need moisture. Without it trees can only die. The Lord himself has provided the streams of water beside which he plants his trees. The gospel of his forgiveness in Christ, as channeled through Word and sacrament, is the only life-giving water for the soul. This blessed gospel—with the news of a God who loved the world so that he gave his only Son the lost to save; of a God who regardless how often I come will pardon, cleanse, relieve; of a God who will finally bear me safe above, a ransomed soul—is the water the Spirit uses to soak my roots, keep me alive as his tree, and cause me to grow.

The builder had positioned faucets in strategic places on the outside of our house. All I had to do was connect the hose, run it to each tree, and let the water do its work. Today those trees are all alive and growing nicely. Get the point? If I'm to grow as one of God's trees, I need to be connected to the faucet of his gospel. I need close linkage with his Word. The life-giving stream of God's love for me in Christ will do its work when its hose is laid close to the trunk of my faith. For myself and for those young confirmands in my church, so much depends on how we use that precious and powerful gospel message.

Lord, keep us watered regularly with your Word. Amen.

> HE IS LIKE A TREE WHICH YIELDS ITS FRUIT
> IN SEASON AND WHOSE LEAF DOES NOT WITHER.
> WHATEVER HE DOES PROSPERS. *Psalm 1:3*

Trees Green In Leaf And Abundant In Fruit

God's trees, like all good trees, when planted in the right soil and watered properly, will be productive. Down one street from our church stood some stately maples, leafed out and alive with beautiful green. Interspersed with them were some splintered, weather-beaten utility poles. Those poles stood tall and were made of the same material but were merely lifeless wood sunk into the ground. Those maple trees were green and productive only because of daily nourishment from the soil.

What will I, or those young confirmands in my church, have to face in the future? I don't know. But of this much I am sure. When they and I remain rooted in God's Word and watered by his grace, our leaves will not wither. That's what God has promised. What will those young confirmands become? Pastor or teacher, professional person or assembly line worker, husband and father or wife and mother, church council or other church group member? I don't know any more than I could see ahead as to what would happen with my life. But again, of this much I am sure—in a world where "utility poles" are rapidly on the increase, they will be trees green in leaf and abundant in fruit. Again, that's what a gracious God has promised.

This confirmation season as I look at those young confirmands in my church and myself, I pray humbly, "Lord, cause us to remain constant in every condition and consecrated in every service to you. Lord, keep us alive and flourishing as your trees." Amen.

> SEEK FIRST HIS KINGDOM AND HIS RIGHTEOUSNESS,
> AND ALL THESE THINGS WILL BE GIVEN
> TO YOU AS WELL. *Matthew 6:32,33*

Shatterproof

My wife decorates eggs as a hobby. She turns hen's eggs, goose eggs, even ostrich eggs into beautiful works of art. She has shown me how tough the shell of an egg can be. It takes a strong cutting tool to bite through the shell of an ostrich egg. If you try to crush a hen's egg by pushing the two ends together, you'll find out how strong its shell can be.

The Creator has designed the egg to protect tiny birds. The heavenly Father shows concern about the very least of his creatures. Now what about me? I'm not just one of his creatures. I'm his child. He chose me in eternal love to be his very own. He sacrificed his own Son on Calvary's cross to pay for my sins. He sent his Holy Spirit into my heart through Baptism to add my name to his family register. That's how much he loves me!

Since my heavenly Father cares so deeply for me, won't he take care of my earthly life? Doesn't his love do better than put some tough egg shell around me? Won't he provide what I need for my bodily existence? Won't he defend me against all danger and guard and protect me from all evil? When life's troubles, pushing on the shell of his love around me, seem so strong at times, I may wonder. I may even foolishly worry that his love will crack and I'll be exposed to harm. But my Father knows better than I. And through his Word he reminds me how shatterproof his love for me in Christ really is.

Heavenly Father, help me trust your
love and cast all my cares on you. Amen.

> BY FAITH WE EAGERLY AWAIT THROUGH
> THE SPIRIT THE RIGHTEOUSNESS
> FOR WHICH WE HOPE. *Galatians 5:5*

How Homesick Are You?

When our children were small, we left them for about a week with grandpa and grandma. Our youngest boy became so homesick that he ended up ill. Grandma had to take him to the hospital. One of the first things he said when we drove into the yard was "I got sick."

Christians know something about homesickness. Strange though, we are homesick for a place we've never been or seen. As Paul put it, we "eagerly await through the Spirit the righteousness for which we hope." Of course, the apostle is referring to heaven. When I finally arrive home in heaven, just think what will be mine. No longer will I have to hope through faith for freedom from pain and problems, sickness and suffering. Those former things, brought into my world by sin, will be gone.

Best of all, I'll be free from sin. Here on earth I battle daily with the old evil foe. In heaven there will be no trace of his temptations. Here on earth I wrestle every waking hour with my sinful heart. In heaven my heart will be pure. Here on earth I rub shoulders with the world's temptations. In heaven the world's trash is swept away. I'll be holy just as my Savior is holy.

I've never been there. I can't even imagine what heaven will be like. But I'm homesick for it. When the Spirit brings me to faith, he fills my heart with a longing for my Father's home.

Lord, thank you for the hope of heaven.
Come and turn my hope into glorious reality. Amen.

> WE KNOW THAT WHEN HE APPEARS,
> WE SHALL BE LIKE HIM, FOR WE
> SHALL SEE HIM AS HE IS. *1 John 3:2*

Just Like Him

Often I took my wife with me when visiting prospects for our little mission in Sault Ste. Marie, Canada. One of these people, an immigrant lady from Germany, invited us to supper. During the course of the evening, she looked at us and commented, "You look so much alike." Then she observed, "Did you ever notice how after a while married people begin to look like each other?"

Check it out! My wife and I have. Often it's true. After a time people in love begin to look like one another. Perhaps it's a shared taste in styles. Or the way they speak. Even the way they smile and respond. If true of loved ones, how about the One we love the most? How much do I look like my heavenly bridegroom? How much do I reflect his character, his speech, his love? When people look at me, do they see some of my Savior's beauty? Do they catch a glimpse of his grace shining in my life? How much I want to be like him already here on earth.

How much I want to be like him in heaven. I don't know what my Savior looks like. But I do know what he is like. And I want to be like him. Already here on earth my prayer is, "I long to be like Jesus: Meek, lowly, loving, mild; I long to be like Jesus, The Father's holy child. I long to be with Jesus Amid the heav'nly throng To sing with saints his praises, To learn the angels' song" (CW 372:4). And in heaven I shall. By God's grace I'll be just like him.

Lord Jesus, thank you for the love that made me your very own. Help me reflect your love more fully each day till in heaven I see you face-to-face. Amen.

> THE BREAD OF GOD IS HE WHO COMES DOWN FROM HEAVEN AND GIVES LIFE TO THE WORLD. *John 6:33*

Don't Throw Away This Bread

In my mission travels I've seen children with stomachs swollen because of protein deficiency. I've seen 40-year-olds looking like 70 with shriveled arms and legs because of lack of food. Yet last year each US household, it is estimated, tossed out $590 worth of food.

When people starve, don't point the finger at God. He's promised that he will "open [his] hand and satisfy the desires of every living thing" (Psalm 145:16). He can provide more than enough for the world's burgeoning population. Point the finger rather at mankind. People's sinfulness makes them too selfish to share the abundance of their fields. Their stubbornness and superstition also prevent them from doing all they can to harness the acres.

When Jesus described himself as the "bread of God," he didn't have loaves made with flour in mind. When he spoke of giving "life to the world," he meant more than keeping bodies alive with regular meals. He was referring to mankind's spiritual needs. He meant satisfying sin's hunger that eats away at the soul, death's pangs that rumble throughout life. Jesus with his payment for sin and his victory over death is the bread that every human being needs.

That includes me! Strange, isn't it? I know what to do when my stomach rumbles. How come I at times think I can live without Jesus, the Bread of Life? I donate for the needy when tragedy strikes. How come I'm not so concerned about reaching them with the bread that sustains their souls?

Jesus, Bread of Life, feed me and help me
feed others with your soul-sustaining Word. Amen.

> WHATEVER YOU DO, WHETHER IN WORD OR DEED, DO IT
> ALL IN THE NAME OF THE LORD JESUS, GIVING THANKS
> TO GOD THE FATHER THROUGH HIM. *Colossians 3:17*

Thanks In Every Detail

Want a detail-minded job? Try being an Arlington National Cemetery honor guard. Recently I saw a PBS special about them. From it I learned that a guard spends four hours polishing his shoes. He also carries a lighter to burn loose threads off his uniform. And after marching stone-faced at the Tomb of the Unknown Soldier, he has to practice smiling again.

Doesn't the apostle talk about details too? He asks more of me than the service does of honor guards. I'm to reflect the Lord Jesus in all my words and all my deeds. Everything in my life, from the littlest to the largest, is to give thanks to the Father, who sent Jesus to be my Savior. Sounds like a lot of detail to me.

I don't know if honor guards ever get bounced from their job for not attending to details. I do know how often I mess up. How often sin's dust spots my shoes! How often the world hangs like snagged threads on my coat of life. How often I forget to smile because I don't recall how much my Savior loves me. How often I look like some shabby would-be guard of my Savior's honor. God forgive me when I forget what his love has done for me and fail to love him back. God also help me pay more attention to my life of thanksgiving. That means I need to pay more attention to his Word with its details about his saving love for me. When that Word fills me with his love, I will also be filled with thanksgiving for him.

Lord, fill my heart with your great love for me in Jesus.
Power my life to love you back. Amen.

> "THE KINGDOM OF HEAVEN IS LIKE A MERCHANT LOOKING FOR FINE
> PEARLS. WHEN HE FOUND ONE OF GREAT VALUE, HE WENT AWAY
> AND SOLD EVERYTHING HE HAD AND BOUGHT IT." *Matthew 13:45,46*

The Priceless Pearl

Are you sure your diamond is real? Several years ago an inventor came up with a process that makes imitation stones almost as good as the real. His process places carbon seeds into a special high-pressure chamber that turns them into nearly perfect fakes.

The world is always looking for diamonds. It pursues education, science, and philosophy as ways of making mankind better. It piles up good works as currency that should count in heaven. Worst of all, it doesn't recognize that such pursuit is chasing after fake diamonds.

There is only one diamond that is priceless. That's Jesus. In our verse he uses a priceless pearl to describe his kingdom. We could say that with that pearl he's describing himself as the Savior. For it was his blood that established his eternal kingdom and his love that rules over it. He also uses the picture of a merchant who sells all in order to purchase the pearl of great price. Again that merchant is a picture of our Savior. No one could ever possibly pay for this pearl. The whole world wouldn't be payment enough for just one soul. My own righteousness, tainted by sin, wouldn't even make a down payment. Only God's holy Son, with his precious blood and innocent death, could meet the price. With this price he bought the kingdom, not for himself but for me. Now Jesus is mine. And he's no fake. He's the true diamond that is mine now and will be mine in heaven.

*Jesus, priceless treasure, wrap my hand of
faith around you and be mine to all eternity. Amen.*

> YOU ARE NO LONGER FOREIGNERS AND ALIENS,
> BUT FELLOW CITIZENS WITH GOD'S PEOPLE
> AND MEMBERS OF GOD'S HOUSEHOLD. *Ephesians 2:19*

From Outsiders To Citizens

We were traveling the plateaus outside of Medellin, looking for expansion room in our Colombian mission field. As we walked around the town square in one village, people stopped talking and stared at us. After we had passed by, they started talking again, this time about us. We were foreigners, outsiders. We didn't belong. And we knew it.

I didn't belong either when it came to God's kingdom. How could I? By nature I was "separate from Christ, excluded from citizenship in Israel and [a foreigner] to the covenants of the promise, without hope and without God in the world" (2:12). Born a sinner, I had no salvation, no hope for heaven, no knowledge of faith in Christ, no nothing! Talk about being an outsider. Why, I had no hope on my own of ever becoming an insider or "citizen" of heaven. Till God the Holy Spirit stepped in. He's the power behind the extreme makeover in my life, from foreigner to citizen, from unbeliever to believer. Through Word and sacrament, he works faith in my heart so that I am a citizen in God's kingdom. Thanks to his gift of faith, I enjoy all the privileges that citizenship brings me—pardon, peace, and the promise of heaven are mine.

Many members in our first congregation in Canada were immigrants who later became Canadian citizens. They didn't just want to live in Canada; they wanted to belong. Often in our visits they would proudly show their citizenship papers to us. When's the last time I thought about my heavenly citizenship and about the Holy Spirit behind it?

Thank you, Holy Spirit, for making me
a citizen of God's wonderful country. Amen.

> YOU ARE NO LONGER FOREIGNERS AND ALIENS,
> BUT FELLOW CITIZENS WITH GOD'S PEOPLE
> AND MEMBERS OF GOD'S HOUSEHOLD. *Ephesians 2:19*

From Aliens To Family Members

Family is such a rich word. It reminds us of mom and dad, of home, of love and care. Do you get a warm glow inside when you think of the family to which you belong? Now think of God's family and of yourself as a member of that "household," as Paul calls it. Think of standing alongside Jesus, Abraham, Paul, John. Think of the advantages to be enjoyed in that family, the sure forgiveness of all sins, the strength for daily living, the surety of heaven. In such a wonderful family, words like *sinners* and *aliens* are no longer heard. Instead, *sons* and *daughters* apply. Instead, it's titles like "member of God's household" and "heir of his heaven" for me.

How come? Who changed me from a sinner to a saint? From God's enemy to his favored son? From one rejected by his holiness to one received by his love? Time for me this Pentecost season to think of the Holy Spirit again. Without his miraculous working of faith in my heart, I'd still be on the outside looking in. My Father's house would be off-limits. His family would be something to which I could never belong. The devil would be my father; and his hell, my eternal dungeon. Think what kinds of thoughts such a home would raise in my unbelieving heart!

Time to get my baptismal certificate out again. Time to reread passages like the verse before me. Time to treasure Christ's Holy Supper. Through these powerful means, the Spirit works not only to bring me by faith into God's family but also to keep me there.

Holy Spirit, thank you for making me
God's child and an heir of his heaven. Amen.

> [YOU ARE] BUILT ON THE FOUNDATION OF THE APOSTLES AND
> PROPHETS, WITH CHRIST JESUS HIMSELF THE CHIEF CORNERSTONE.
> IN HIM THE WHOLE BUILDING IS JOINED TOGETHER AND RISES
> TO BECOME A HOLY TEMPLE IN THE LORD. *Ephesians 2:20,21*

A Trowel In His Hand

A building's going up—one that keeps rising throughout all time. One that will not be complete till Jesus returns. One that cannot be seen with the naked eye. What's this building? We call it God's church. It's composed only of believers. Believers not in just anything or everything, but believers in Christ Jesus as their only Savior. Like living stones they are cemented on this one foundation. The apostles and prophets knew of only one Savior. All their teachings revolve around the central truth that Jesus is God's Son sent from heaven as the world's Savior. In this church of God, the Lord Jesus is the cornerstone. He's like the stone laid at the corner from which all measurements were taken. Without him there simply is no salvation, no believers, no foundation for God's holy temple.

Without the Holy Spirit no blocks would be laid on this sure foundation. The Spirit holds a trowel in his hand. He's the mason who mortars people in by bringing them to faith in their only Savior. His work of mortaring is a constant one. Not only did he create faith in me at my baptism, fitting me in as a stone in God's temple. He also, throughout my days, has to use the trowel of the gospel to clean out the cracks and strengthen the joints in my faith. As Martin Luther put it, "I believe that I cannot by my own thinking or choosing believe in Jesus Christ, my Lord, or come to him. But the Holy Spirit has called me by the gospel, enlightened me with his gifts, sanctified and kept me in the true faith." That sounds like a lot of mortaring to me.

Thank you, Holy Spirit,
for working faith in me. Amen.

> IN HIM YOU TOO ARE BEING BUILT TOGETHER
> TO BECOME A DWELLING IN WHICH GOD
> LIVES BY HIS SPIRIT. *Ephesians 2:22*

My Heart–His Home

"My home is your home," members in Latin America would say, only in Spanish. Graciously they would invite us in. Our presence in their often humble abodes was a joy to them.

Paul says something like this in our verse, only much greater. He reminds me that when the Spirit creates faith in my heart, he makes it a dwelling place for my loving God. My heart becomes his home. Theologians call this dwelling of God in the believer's heart the *mystical union.* I can't explain all this, but Scripture assures me it's true. In John 14:23, Jesus promises those who love him, "We will come to him and make our home with him." In 1 Corinthians 3:16, Paul reminds believers, "Don't you know that you yourselves are God's temple and that God's Spirit lives in you?" In Galatians 2:20, Paul declares, "I no longer live, but Christ lives in me."

What joy God's dwelling in me brings! When the enemies of faith swarm around me, I can answer, "If God is for me, who can be against me?" When my faith seeks to bloom in daily life, the triune God is there with his power to aid me. With Martin Luther I can say, "If somebody raps at my heart, its door opens and I say, 'Luther is gone out. The Holy Spirit is now at home.'"

And all because of the work of the Spirit. He makes my heart into a bed, soft, undefiled, a quiet chamber kept for my loving God.

*"Holy Spirit, Pow'r divine, Dwell within
this heart of mine." Amen.* (CW 183:4)

> SING PSALMS, HYMNS AND SPIRITUAL
> SONGS WITH GRATITUDE IN YOUR
> HEARTS TO GOD. *Colossians 3:16*

Let The Song Be Heard

Can you name some sounds not heard much anymore? How about the sound of rotary dialing, replaced by touch tones on the telephone? Or the scratch of chalk on a blackboard, exiled by the squeak of dry-erase markers on a white board? Or the clink of pull-chain light switches, extinguished by motion-sensing ones? You can name your own examples. These are some that came to my mind.

Hopefully on our lists will not be singing praise to God. I'm not much of a singer. Even after being married to my musically talented wife for over 40 years, I can hardly carry a tune. But that doesn't stop me. My wife correctly reminds me that to God's ears my bullfrog croaking sounds like the sweetest music. It tells him that I appreciate what he has done for me. My singing is the sound of gratitude to his ears. He enjoys hearing it, and I need to send it.

Luther put it this way, "God has cleared our hearts and minds through his dear Son whom he gave to redeem us from sin, death, and the devil. He who believes this earnestly cannot be quiet about it. But he must gladly and willingly sing and speak about it so that others also may come and hear it." "People, sing," the Reformer urged. "You are God's choir on earth." If the angels who didn't need the Savior sang at his birth, how about me for whom he came and for whom he has done so much? Gratitude for his saving love makes me sing in my heart and with my lips. To the God of all grace such singing is always in tune.

Lord, accept my songs of thanksgiving and
keep me till I sing them perfectly in heaven. Amen.

> HE WHO WATCHES OVER YOU
> WILL NOT SLUMBER. *Psalm 121:3*

No Need To Lose Sleep

What does sleep do for us? Experts can't fully explain why we need sleep. They can detail how necessary it is, like food and water, for our survival. Tests have shown that after five days without sleep people begin to hallucinate. After more days they behave as if they were mad.

All of us have lost sleep at one time or another. Perhaps it was because of travel or work or even celebration. More often, though, it's because of concern. As a pastor I've spent nights tossing, weighed down with some problem in the parish. As a parent I know what it's like waiting for a grown-up child to come safely home. As an individual, many things may keep my eyes wide open regardless how much warm milk I drink or soothing music I listen to. Lab reports from the doctor, bills lying unpaid on the counter, loneliness because I have lost a loved one. And sin! What a sleep depriver sin can be for a serious child of God! Can God forgive me again? Won't he get sick of me when I come with the same old problems again and again? Won't he slam heaven's door in my face when I, in shameful repentance, carry that special sin to him?

Time for me to hear the psalmist's words again. My loving Lord never slumbers. His pardon covers my sin—morning, noon, and night. His power handles all my problems 24 hours a day. His wisdom leads my earthly steps 1,440 minutes each day and always in the heavenly direction. Because he never slumbers, I can. Because he's always watching, I can sleep in peace.

"Now the light has gone away; Father, listen while I pray, Asking you to watch and keep And to send me quiet sleep." Amen. (CW 593:1)

PRAISE THE LORD, O MY SOUL, AND
FORGET NOT ALL HIS BENEFITS. *Psalm 103:2*

More Than Fringe Benefits

With most jobs come some fringe benefits. Health insurance is one of them. So are contributions by the company to a retirement fund. Other benefits are paid holidays and a certain number of paid sick days. And then there's the matter of paid vacation. Such fringe benefits count up, both in cost to the company and in benefit to the employee.

When the psalmist says, "Forget not all his benefits," he's not talking about extras or incidentals. The word David used is deeper than this. It means treatments that are kind and generous. Note also the plural *benefits*. Could be that the psalmist is trying to tell me something about how generously the Lord deals with me. And that word *LORD*—that's the name for the God of love, the faithful God who makes and keeps all his promises, especially his promise of salvation.

So far David hasn't identified a single benefit. Yet, by using the words *LORD* and *benefits*, he has given me more than enough reason for praise. Just think how that Lord deals with me. When I wake up each morning, I can expect from him even better care than an earthly father provides his children. When I fall into sin during the day, I can expect from him even better discipline and more wondrous forgiveness than an earthly father offers his children. When I lay my head on the pillow at night, I can expect from him never-ending care and wide open eyes over me unlike what comes from a sleeping earthly father. That's my Lord, and that's the treatment he guarantees me. Sounds like much more than fringe benefits to me!

Lord, just to know you and your kindness
gives me reason to praise you. Help me do so. Amen.

[HE] FORGIVES ALL YOUR SINS. *Psalm 103:3*

Five Big Words

Name some words that really make a difference. How about "I love you." Or how about "I missed you." When lovers or family members talk this way, their simple words speak volumes. What about the words David puts before me? Can I ever find bigger words than "[He] forgives all your sins"?

"All your sins," David said. I know something about sin, more than I care to admit. I know, though I tend to forget, about my habitual sins. Each day I fall into the same ruts—the indecent thoughts, the unkind words, the spiteful actions that are almost second nature to me. Some days it can happen that some "special" sin rocks me like some earthquake and leaves me behind in the rubble. Such sins I have no trouble remembering. They rattle around in the closet of my conscience like some skeleton causing me dread. "Sin"? Yes, indeed, of this I'm well aware.

"[He] forgives," David also wrote. I desperately need forgiveness for all my sins. I need the assurance that they are canceled out completely in God's account books. That when I one day stand before his judgment seat, the entry behind my name will be blank. David reminds me how this can be. The Lord, my Savior-God, has done it. He can't just erase my sins as if they didn't matter. He can't just sweep them under the carpet like some indulgent grandpa. He had to pay for my sins. And he did, with his Son's precious blood. Are there any bigger words in the whole world than those five: "[He] forgives all your sins"?

Lord, each day let me thrill to these blessed words:
"I have forgiven all your sins." Amen.

[HE] HEALS ALL YOUR DISEASES. *Psalm 103:3*

The Lord Is My Doctor

Often I have read the first verses of Psalm 103 to members going home from the hospital. "You're more fortunate than other members of St. John," I'd tell them. When they'd look at me in puzzlement, I'd explain. "Now you know from experience what the psalmist said. No longer is it trust in God's promises but trust strengthened by God's keeping his promises."

Some reading this devotion know from experience about the Divine Physician's healing. He was behind a surgeon's skill, a doctor's knowledge, nurses' care, pills, and medicines. Without his blessing hand, there would have been no healing. Others will learn about his loving care in the future. Some of us know also about the divine physician's continued care. When he doesn't heal, he helps me endure. When he doesn't remove a burden, he helps me carry it. When he asks me to walk with limping steps into the future, he assures me he's at my side. That too is healing from his hand, as only a child of God can appreciate.

There's also the healing of the heart. "He heals the brokenhearted and binds up their wounds," assures the psalmist (147:3). All of us know something about such healing. Lack of or loss of a mate inflicts wounds that never seem to heal. Temptation and trouble bring headaches that no pills seem to relieve. Sin etches scars on my soul, and I wonder where to find relief. Where would I be without the heavenly physician? Thank God, I know what he can do for my heart. Thank God, I have experienced, above all, the healing his love brings my sin-sick soul.

Lord Jesus, cradle me in your arms as you
take care of my physical and spiritual needs. Amen.

[HE] REDEEMS YOUR LIFE FROM THE PIT. *Psalm 103:4*

"I Walk In Danger All The Way"

One of our elderly members often asked for this hymn. She was well aware of the dangers for both her body and soul as she traveled the road to heaven. "Pastor," she would say at the church door, "why don't we sing 'I Walk in Danger All the Way' more often?"

She was right about the dangers along the way. The psalmist spoke of "the pit," using a word that meant "grave" or "destruction." I can hardly back out of the garage and pull onto the freeway without a sense of danger. I leave for work in the morning, not knowing if my heart will keep beating till I return. I go to bed at night without assurance that I will rise in the morning. Dangers to life are all around me. Death seems to be waiting for me at every corner. Could the psalmist also be referring to the worst destruction possible? Could it be that he meant also a pit called hell and a death that's worse than destruction? It's true. I do walk in danger all the way, danger both for my body and my soul.

But I have the Redeemer. If only I could see how often Jesus sends his angels to keep me safe on the highway. How often his angels keep harm and danger away during the day. How often they guard and protect me on my pillow. Better still, if only I would stop to consider more frequently how my Savior stepped in to rescue me from hell. Redeeming me was no easy task. Jesus had to face the punishment my sins had earned. He had to suffer the pains of hell my guilt had piled up. I do walk in danger all the way, but Jesus will never fail me. He redeems my life from the pit.

Jesus, walk with me. In your love,
preserve my life from danger and my soul from hell. Amen.

> AND CROWNS YOU WITH LOVE
> AND COMPASSION. *Psalm 103:4*

What A Crown!

While in England, we had to visit the Tower of London. Its damp dungeons in the past held many famous prisoners securely until their execution. Another part of this strong structure today safeguards the crowns, scepters, and other glittering royal treasures. That's what we went to see behind the glass cases in the Tower. We wanted to ooh and aah at the crown with diamonds, rubies, and precious jewels that the queen wears on special occasions.

I too wear a crown. To the world the jewels in my crown may not seem very valuable. Compared to diamonds and rubies, God's "love and compassion" don't even make the chart. But to me, they are everything. God's love is his steadfast concern for my soul. His love neither leaves me nor forsakes me. Day by day it covers me in Jesus. It provides, through his Word and sacraments, all that my soul needs for eternity. His compassion is his concern and then resulting care for my body. Covered by his compassion, I can walk with contentment through each day.

Wouldn't it be something if each morning I could look into the mirror and see my crown? If I could run faith's fingers over the diamonds of God's forgiveness, there for me when I sin? If I could hold in faith's hand the rubies of God's compassion, there for me in the necessities of life? I'd want to do more than ooh and aah at that precious crown. I'd want to thank my gracious God for such a treasure.

*Lord, you were once crowned with thorns so that I
could be crowned with your righteousness. Help me wear
with thanksgiving the precious crown you have given me. Amen.*

> [HE] SATISFIES YOUR DESIRES WITH
> GOOD THINGS SO THAT YOUR YOUTH IS
> RENEWED LIKE THE EAGLE'S. *Psalm 103:5*

Satisfaction And Strength

Are people ever really satisfied? They eat only to eat again. They reach for the world's baubles only to want more. They experience thrills only to desire something more exhilarating. For so many, if there is any sense of satisfaction, it's only momentary.

How different with God's children. The psalmist says that God satisfies my desires with good things. Or as it could also be stated that God fills my soul with good things. I can never be satisfied until my soul is. I can never be content until my soul is at rest. And my good Lord is the great satisfier. He offers no meaningless toys or empty pleasures for my soul. He extends instead the good things of forgiveness, peace, and heaven. For me as a child of God such treasures are not just "good things" but the only good things with which God keeps satisfying my soul. It's not some one-shot deal with him, but daily, generous giving through his blessed Word.

Filled with forgiveness for all my sins, I can fly like an eagle, regardless how grey my hair may be. Sure of his presence at my side, I can soar through the valley of trouble and over the mountain of temptation without losing a feather. Guaranteed a home with him in heaven, I can keep flapping my wings till I finally get there. To be able to fly out of the wilderness and up beyond the stars is enough to make anyone cry, "Praise the Lord, O my soul!"

Lord Jesus, keep me close to your Word with its good things for my soul so that I may fly like an eagle with your strength. Amen.

> PRAISE THE LORD, O MY SOUL; ALL MY INMOST
> BEING, PRAISE HIS HOLY NAME. *Psalm 103:1*

"With Hearts And Hands And Voices"

"You never say you love me," complained the wife to her husband of 42 years. "Why should I?" was his taciturn response. "After all these years you should know I do." Does that sound somewhat familiar—not just about taking my spouse for granted, but my God? How often do I praise his holy name? How often do I stop to thank him for all he has done and continues to do for me?

The psalmist urges wholehearted praise. I'm to praise my gracious God with "my soul" and "all my inmost being." Such comprehensive praise germinates in my heart. I need to think before I can properly thank. I need to be aware that without God opening his gracious hand, I would have nothing and need everything. Thanksgiving begins in a heart that bows before a gracious God.

Then it proceeds to my voice. Around the family table, it means joining in words like "O give thanks unto the Lord, for he is good." In the worship service it's singing words like "Oh, bless the Lord, my soul! Let all within me join And aid my tongue to bless his name Whose favors are divine" (CW 238:1). On the streets of life it's telling others, "Look what he has done for me. Look at what he can do for you also."

Then come my hands. I'm to use them not only to receive from a gracious God but also to give to him and to my neighbor. When I fold them in prayer and worship, I should be able to see calluses on them from working in and for God's kingdom. May God never have to say to me, "You never say you love me." May my heart and hands and voice praise his holy name daily.

God, grant it for Jesus' sake. Amen.

THE EYES OF THE LORD ARE ON
THE RIGHTEOUS AND HIS EARS ARE
ATTENTIVE TO THEIR CRY. *Psalm 34:15*

The Prayer Button

The hospital elevator stopped at the main floor. Getting on with me were several people whom I knew and with whom I had been visiting. The elevator door closed behind us as we continued our conversation. Finally someone noticed that we hadn't moved. Someone else asked, "Did you push the button?" Chuckling, I reached for it and up we all went.

Praying is something like pressing that elevator button. God's eyes are always on me. His love ever watches over me. He doesn't need my prayers to tell him what I need and when I need it. Like that hospital elevator, he's there. But he does want me to push the button. When I turn to him in prayer, I'm telling him that I know he's there. I'm indicating to him that I need his help and trust his love. When I press the prayer button, my faith lifts my needs to his open ears.

So why do I have to be reminded to push the button? Turning to my loving Father in prayer should be my first response, not a last-ditch effort. It should be my confident response, not some it-doesn't-hurt-to-try reaction. Hasn't he told me that his eyes have me always in sight? Hasn't he promised that his ears are always within hearing distance of my requests? Hasn't he, better still, assured me this is true because of what he is and has done for me? He's my loving Father who has already taken care of my greatest need. He's sent his own Son to pay for my sins. Now he waits for me to press the button and lift my lesser needs up to him too.

Father, thank you for making me your child and
for making it possible for me to talk with you. Amen.

"I TELL YOU THE TRUTH, MY FATHER WILL GIVE YOU WHATEVER YOU ASK IN MY NAME." *John 16:23*

Always He Answers

"You keep telling me to pray, but I don't think God hears. At least he never seems to answer me," complained a needy Christian. Sound familiar? Have I reacted in similar fashion to what seemed to be unanswered prayer? Have I had my doubts about my Savior's promise: "My Father will give you whatever you ask in my name"?

When my request isn't granted, then it's time to take a critical look not at God but at my prayer. Is it a prayer I send heavenward with the trust that my Father's loving wisdom will answer as he sees best? Or is it more like a crowbar with which I try to pry loose from God my own predetermined answer. In prayer, believers don't dictate answers to God. They lay their troubles in his lap. Then they wait patiently and confidently for whatever answer he will send. "Whatever you ask," Jesus promises, but he means asking as God's child. If I still don't quite understand, a related passage can help me, "This is the confidence we have in approaching God: that if we ask anything *according to his will*, he hears us" (1 John 5:14).

Out in the garage my five-year-old son begged for a chance to help paint the bedside stand for his room. Smilingly, I let him dip the brush in the paint can and spread it on the wood. But when he wanted to help cut a board with my saber saw, I refused. Even his tears didn't change my loving wisdom. Who knows better how to answer my prayers than my heavenly Father? Sometimes he answers yes; sometimes, no. But always his answers fit, and my good is the result.

Lord, thank you for the privilege of prayer.
Give me the confidence to trust that you always hear. Amen.

THE LORD IS YOUR SHADE AT YOUR
RIGHT HAND; THE SUN WILL NOT
HARM YOU BY DAY. *Psalm 121:5,6*

Better Than Sunscreen

In the Midwest we're seeing more of the sun these days. And it feels good. It's time to get rid of winter's pallor and soak up some rays. My wife warns me to be careful, though. With my fair complexion, I'm a good candidate for skin cancer. "Wear your cap," she reminds me. "And don't forget the sunscreen."

Isn't that what the psalmist is telling me too? While in this world, I face something far more dangerous than the sun in the sky. The devil beats down on me with temptation's rays, seeking to burn my faith. The world invites me to get some sinful exposure and build up a "tan." My sinful nature is all too ready to oblige, telling me that sin's rays won't hurt me. Before I know it, I've been burned. Sometimes I don't even know it. If I continue without any sin-screen, the result will not be skin cancer but the eating away of my faith and the burning fires of hell ahead.

What's the answer? "Wear your hat," the psalmist says. Or to use his words, "The LORD is your shade." When Jesus spreads his wings over me, sin's harmful rays can't reach me. He who stretched his nail-pierced hands wide on the cross to pay for my sins now shields me with those same loving arms. "Use your sin-screen," I can also imagine the psalmist saying. There's no better lotion to protect me from the dangers threatening my faith than God's Word. There's no better way to use that Word than to apply it liberally every day.

Lord, draw me deeper into your Word
and shield me from temptation's harm. Amen.

"SURELY THEN YOU WILL COUNT MY STEPS BUT NOT KEEP
TRACK OF MY SIN. MY OFFENSES WILL BE SEALED UP IN
A BAG; YOU WILL COVER OVER MY SIN." *Job 14:16,17*

Steps And Missteps

What an exhilarating sight to see little ones take their first steps!
Parents let go of tiny fingers and laugh with joy when their baby takes
those faltering steps. It's almost as exhilarating to watch a patient who's
had hip or knee replacement surgery take first steps.

Do you ever think of the Lord as watching your steps? How he must
rejoice when he sees me trying to walk according to his will. My steps
may be wobbly at times like those of a baby. My attempts may
falter like that surgery patient. But God hugs me in joy when I try to
match my little steps of faith to his steps of love. He works also at
strengthening my feet through his Word.

Sometimes my feet fail me as if I were a little baby. I fall on my nose in
sin. Sometimes, like some surgery patient I think the pain is too much.
Walking according to his will in this wayward world is not exercise for
sissies. Sometimes, though I hope not, I may just not care and use my
feet to walk away from the Savior who loves me as no one else ever can.

What then? Will the Lord pull his outstretched arms back? Will he let
me fall on my nose in this world and even worse, to the floor in hell?
No, Job tells me. My Savior doesn't keep track of my sins, my missteps,
but bundles them up out of sight in the bag of his forgiveness. That's
what his cross reminds me. That's what his love assures me.

Savior, I long to walk closer to you.
Keep me close to your Word so I can. Amen.

"THEREFORE DO NOT WORRY ABOUT TOMORROW, FOR TOMORROW WILL WORRY ABOUT ITSELF. EACH DAY HAS ENOUGH TROUBLE OF ITS OWN." *Matthew 6:34*

Day By Day

Some people have backs bent low with worry. They worry about what yesterday has brought, what today brings, and what tomorrow might bring. Far better, Jesus reminds me, is to live day by day in him.

As young people in love, would we have been afraid to marry if we could have seen all the problems of the years ahead? Wouldn't I have missed out on the even more numerous joys the days have brought with my life's companion at my side? Or if all the burdens in my work over the years had been visible, like some massive mountain, would I have thrown up my hands without taking the first step? Day by day, Jesus reminds me, is the only way to face life.

Even better, Jesus reminds me, is to deal with yesterday, today, and tomorrow with him at my side. I can't change yesterday. Only my Savior's blood can cover what went wrong. I can't even handle today. Only my divine guide knows where to lead. Tomorrow will bring whatever, in spite of all my worrying. Only my steadfast helper can handle all of those whatevers.

"Each day has enough trouble of its own," my Savior reminds me. May he also remind me that I never have to bear those troubles by myself. His almighty arm will always be there to get me through.

Jesus, keep me safe in your loving arm today, tomorrow, and always. Amen.

> "EVERYONE WHO HEARS THESE WORDS OF MINE AND PUTS THEM INTO PRACTICE IS LIKE A WISE MAN WHO BUILT HIS HOUSE ON THE ROCK. THE RAIN CAME DOWN, THE STREAMS ROSE, AND THE WINDS BLEW AND BEAT AGAINST THAT HOUSE; YET IT DID NOT FALL, BECAUSE IT HAD ITS FOUNDATION ON THE ROCK." *Matthew 7:24,25*

Safe In Any Storm

Sooner or later everyone faces storms in life. Perhaps only a few for the young, more for the middle aged, and seemingly endless for the elderly. What to do when the winds rattle the shutters and the rain gathers in the basement of the house called life?

Perhaps it's the storm of sickness. Sometimes pain comes and passes. Sometimes it stays or returns even stronger. Sometimes it leads to a hospital room and surgery. Sometimes it lingers for the rest of our lives. Nobody likes this storm. But just think what the days would be like if our lives weren't built on Christ—if we didn't have his promise never to leave or forsake us.

Often it's the storm of sin. As I write this, a snowstorm is blanketing our area. About ten inches are piling up and making our roads dangerous. So my sins keep piling up, blocking the road to God. But just think how the roof would cave in under sin's weight if my life weren't built on Christ—if I didn't have his promise: "Go in peace, your sins are forgiven."

Finally comes the storm of death. I can't dodge it. Sooner or later I must face it. Yet it can't carry me away if I'm standing on my living Redeemer. He has conquered death, and in him so shall I. Built on Christ, I'm safe in this and any storm.

Savior, put the rock foundation of your Word under my feet that I may stand in any storm. Amen.

"BE FAITHFUL, EVEN TO THE POINT OF DEATH, AND I WILL GIVE YOU THE CROWN OF LIFE." *Revelation 2:10*

Faithful To God

June is no longer famous as the wedding month. Now weddings are spread out over the year. But one thing has not changed. Faithfulness is still a vital ingredient in marriage. Both groom and bride still properly promise to be faithful to each other as long as they both shall live.

Behind that important promise is a still more important faithfulness, the one our Lord commands. "Be faithful" he commands. When I read the Greek, I notice that my Savior is talking to me individually. "*You* be faithful," he urges. I'm to be loyal and true, attached to him, filled with constant love for him. He who died for me is to be the Rock on which I set my trust and the ruler for whom I live my life. "Even to the point of death," he goes on. From the day he called me to faith till the hour of my death, I'm to be his. This is what life's all about: believing, loving, never leaving my beautiful Savior.

When my Savior commands something, he also makes it possible. That's why he promised, "I will give you the crown of life." He who cannot lie or change his mind is the One making the promise. When he gives, it's a pure gift with no strings attached. And look at what he offers so full and free—"the crown of life," or as it reads in the original: "the crown of *the* life." Only one life counts, the one in heaven, which never ends.

Faithfulness in marriage is important. As a believer I realize that such faithfulness begins with my connection to my Savior.

Lord, thank you for a spouse
who shares that faithfulness. Amen.

> "BE FAITHFUL, EVEN TO THE POINT
> OF DEATH, AND I WILL GIVE YOU
> THE CROWN OF LIFE." *Revelation 2:10*

Faithful To Each Other

Recently I read again that among Christians divorce figures are lower. The article even stated that among conservative Christians, the incident of divorce was the lowest. I'm not equipped to analyze such statistics, but I do know what God's Word says. When both husband and wife are faithful to the Lord that will have an effect on their life together. Faithful to God, they will be faithful to each other.

When success enters our life together, faithfulness to Christ helps us not to boast self-centeredly about such things. Instead, we thank our gracious Lord for what he has granted. When we sin against each other, faithfulness to Christ helps us not to tally up the score and nurse grudges. Rather, we work at forgiving each other just as Christ has forgiven us. When sorrow and suffering cast their shadow over our marriage, faithfulness to Christ helps us to support each other and step forward. When God blesses our union with children, faithfulness to Christ enables us to raise them as souls bound for eternity. When death parts the two of us, faithfulness to Christ quiets grief with the sure hope of reunion at the side of the heavenly Bridegroom.

Need I go on? How fortunate I am to have a Christian mate! God's greatest gift to me is bringing me to faith in my Savior. His second greatest is bringing me a spouse who is faithful to the Savior. Faithful to our God, we can work at being faithful to each other.

Lord, keep both me and my spouse faithful to you and
bless us with faithfulness to each other all our days. Amen.

LEAD ME TO THE ROCK THAT
IS HIGHER THAN I. *Psalm 61:2*

Hang On To The Rock

I wonder how often I've used this little verse with a Christian in trouble. Impending surgery, family catastrophe, temptation's pressure, and sin's guilt have a way of knocking God's children to the ground. Many of us can relate how helpless the sins and sorrows of life can make us feel.

Time then for David's prayer. "Lead me to the rock," he cried out to the only One who could. I need him to lead me too. Helpless, hopeless, false, and full of sin, I can't plant faith's feet on the Rock of ages any more than David could. My feet are feeble; I need God's strength to carry me. My troubles are massive; I need his never-failing power to lift me. My sins are numerous; I need his ever-cleansing blood to cover me. "Lead me," I cry out to my ever-listening Lord.

"To the rock that is higher than I"—there's the comfort. The Lord is a solid rock. Those whose feet the Spirit plants in faith on him are safe. Life's hurricanes may sway me back and forth, but they can't sweep me away. Life's sins may drench me, but they can't wash me loose. Death's bony finger will one day point at me, but I'll still be safe on Jesus, the rock that is higher than I.

One day two brothers were walking along some railroad tracks. Halfway through a tunnel they heard the whistle of a freight train bearing down on them. All they could do was throw themselves up against the rocky wall of the tunnel and hold on for dear life. As the train rumbled past them, the older brother kept shouting to the other, "Hang on to the rock. Hang on to the rock."

"Rock of Ages, cleft for me, Let me
hide myself in thee." Amen. (CW 389:1)

> "BUT I, WHEN I AM LIFTED UP FROM THE EARTH,
> WILL DRAW ALL MEN TO MYSELF." *John 12:32*

The Magnetism Of His Cross

A writer pictured Pilate's wife and the centurion conversing out on Calvary. "What do you think of Jesus' claim?" asked the wife of the man who had tried the Savior. The centurion who had crucified Jesus replied, "If a man believes something so much that he is ready to die for it, then he is going to get others to believe it too." Looking up at the cross, Pilate's wife asked, "Is he dead?" "No, lady, he is not dead," came the reply. "What is he then?" she asks. "Let loose in the world, lady, where neither Roman nor Jew can stop his truth" was the insightful answer.

Isn't that what the Savior said even before his crucifixion? His cross would be like a magnet drawing all men to him. Some, thank God and his grace, are drawn in faith to the One lifted up in payment for the world's sins. Nicodemus and Joseph, who helped bury him; the three thousand on Pentecost, who believed Peter's sermon; the treasurer of Ethiopia in his chariot, who read about him; Paul the persecutor, who was stopped in his tracks by him on the Damascus road; and you and I are among those who have been drawn to the crucified and risen Savior in faith.

Many reject him. At the cross all must invariably stand, either in faith or unbelief. For those who disregard or disbelieve the truth of "Jesus crucified for me," the cross is a dividing point. Those who reject Jesus as Savior will have to face him as judge. The Savior's cross is empty and so is his tomb. He's loose in the world with the truth of salvation only through him. Thank God, I'm not among those who reject him. Thank God, I can kneel in faith before my Savior, lifted up on that cross for me.

Yes, thank you, Lord, for drawing me to my Savior's cross. Amen.

WE ARE GOD'S FELLOW WORKERS. *1 Corinthians 3:9*

The Lord And I Working Together

I remember the story a successful farmer in the congregation once told me. It was about another farmer who had purchased a run-down farm. Its acres had been neglected, and its buildings left untended. With hard work, he put the acres back into production and the buildings back to snuff. One day his pastor commented, "The Lord has certainly blessed you." "That's true," replied the farmer, "but you should have seen this farm when God had it alone."

The farmer meant no irreverence. He wanted in all sincerity to voice an important truth. The Lord works through people, including me. He gives me ability, wants me to use it, and then wait for him to bless our joint efforts. In all the affairs of life, it's the Lord and me working together.

Nowhere is this more true than in building his kingdom. He sent his Son to die for sinners. Now he sends me to tell them. His Son, with his perfect payment for sin, is the foundation. Now he sends me to handle the Word and sacraments so that his Spirit can cement people by faith onto that foundation. When I realize with whom I'm working, can I hold back or grow tired? Or do I rather accept every opportunity and cherish the privilege of working together with my Lord?

I don't know who wrote it, but the thoughts hit home: "Christ has no hands but our hands to do his work today. He has no feet but our feet to lead men in his way. He has no tongue but our tongue to tell men how he died. He has no help but our help to bring them to his side."

Lord, thank you for using me.
Bless all my labors together with you. Amen.

> YOU TURNED MY WAILING INTO DANCING; YOU REMOVED MY
> SACKCLOTH AND CLOTHED ME WITH JOY, THAT MY HEART
> MAY SING TO YOU AND NOT BE SILENT. *Psalm 30:11,12*

Why The Long Face?

Among things remembered from my visits to the African mission fields is the singing of the Christians. They raised their voices in beautiful songs of praise to their Savior-God. The joy in their hearts found loud expression in their harmonious singing and rhythmic clapping. I found myself thinking, "If only we back home were more like them."

Why don't I, not only in the worship service but throughout life, wear a smile on my face more often? Or why do the artists so often portray the Savior as somber and serious instead of smiling? Don't I have plenty to smile about because of the Savior? Wasn't his birth announced as "good news of great joy" (Luke 2:10)? Didn't his apostle urge me, "Rejoice in the Lord always" (Philippians 4:4)? So why the long face?

My Savior wants me to smile. He paints the rainbow and the sunset. He gives songs to birds and unmatched beauty to wildflowers. All this is of little use to me except to make my soul smile. My Savior does even more. He delivers me from my sin with its accompanying fear of death. Coarse sackcloth worn in mourning and intense wailing caused by the loss of a loved one have been replaced by dark colors and silent tears today. But when the Lord of life touches a believer's casket, a wonderful transformation takes place. The believer's heart sings for joy because of Christ's victory over death. In life and death I have reason to smile because of Jesus.

Lord, help me walk through life smiling because
I know you live and I too shall conquer death. Amen.

> CALLING HIS DISCIPLES TO HIM, JESUS SAID, "I TELL
> YOU THE TRUTH, THIS POOR WIDOW HAS PUT MORE
> INTO THE TREASURY THAN ALL THE OTHERS." *Mark 12:43*

Love And Dandelions

This spring our little granddaughter while visiting came in from the backyard with a fistful of dandelions. "Look," she said proudly, "I picked them for you, Grandma." My wife quickly filled a vase with water, placed those blossoming weeds into it, and positioned it in a prominent spot. Laura's love made those dandelions precious to my wife.

How great love is! It takes a widow's pennies and expands them into the most expensive offering given. It turns a cup of cold water offered to the needy into a deed of faith done to my Savior. It transforms everyday acts of kindness toward my spouse, my family, my fellow workers, even people I don't know, into offerings for my heavenly King. My "dandelions" become "roses" when my acts are done out of thankful love for him who loves me.

I'd do no dandelion picking without Jesus' love for me. I can only love him because he first loved me. My love seeks to give to him only because he first gave his all to me. His love for me on Calvary's cross lights the fire of love in my heart. The deeper his Spirit, through Word and sacrament, leads me into his love, the more I'll want to bring not just my dandelions to him but roses too. As with the widow, my concern will be not "how little" but "how much" for the One who loved me so much. I'll want to live my daily life, work in my congregation, fill my offering envelopes, knowing that my loving God doesn't see weeds when my love brings flowers.

Lord, help me dedicate my life, my
soul, my all to you. For Jesus' sake. Amen.

> COMMAND THOSE WHO ARE RICH IN THIS PRESENT WORLD NOT
> TO BE ARROGANT NOR TO PUT THEIR HOPE IN WEALTH, WHICH IS
> SO UNCERTAIN, BUT TO PUT THEIR HOPE IN GOD, WHO RICHLY
> PROVIDES US WITH EVERYTHING FOR OUR ENJOYMENT. *1 Timothy 6:17*

What's Wrong With Wealth?

There's nothing wrong with money. In fact, it is one of life's necessities. With it I put food on the table, pump gasoline into the car, place down another payment on the mortgage. Nor is there anything wrong with having a lot or a little of money. God in his own wisdom decides how much he will give to each individual. With the psalmist I pray that God give me neither too much nor too little of earthly wealth. If too much, then I might be tempted to forget about God. If too little, I might be tempted not to trust him. Whatever God gives me is for my use and enjoyment.

There may be something wrong with my attitude toward money. If I have abundance, I may become arrogant. I may think the size of my bank account determines my standing in this world and gives me the right to look down my nose at others. Or I may fall into the trap of setting myself even above God. How quickly Satan can seduce me into thinking a fat wallet guarantees anything and everything. People call it the almighty dollar, but it really is so feeble. It can bring food but not appetite. Medicine but not health. Joy but not happiness. Earthly tidbits but not heaven's treasures. Only God can bring me the treasures of salvation. Only his Son's cross provides the currency that has already paid for heaven. Only when I have a heart filled with Jesus am I rich in this world and the next.

Lord, help me use whatever earthly riches you have granted me for you, my fellowman, and then myself. Help me put my hope for salvation only in the riches you provide in my Savior. Amen.

> "I TELL YOU, USE WORLDLY WEALTH TO GAIN FRIENDS
> FOR YOURSELVES, SO THAT WHEN IT IS GONE, YOU WILL
> BE WELCOMED INTO ETERNAL DWELLINGS." *Luke 16:9*

Investing Wisely

"Why should I give my money away to the church?" grumbled a coworker during lunch break. On Sunday both persons had been in the worship service and heard a presentation on the budget for the coming year.

Actually the person's complaint revealed several wrong thoughts. It wasn't really *his* money. Whatever he had came from God to whom everything belongs. If I have trouble at times believing this, I ought to follow a hearse out to the cemetery. Never yet has a hearse pulled behind it a U-Haul filled with the deceased's so-called belongings. Or I ought to look around and see how quickly the changing winds in life can take away what has been given.

Nor is giving to the Lord wasting my money. It's not some "giving away" as if I'm throwing it into a hole. When I give my dollars to help preach the gospel in my congregation and the world, I'm making a wise investment. I'm using them for heavenly gain. Someday in heaven people will stand next to me because my gifts helped bring the gospel to them.

No U-Haul trailer will be hooked to the hearse that carries me out to God's acre. Hopefully, though, what I have "given away" for the Lord's work will result in others joining me in the eternal riches at my and their Savior's side.

*Savior, help me use what you have
given to make others rich in you. Amen.*

> SO HE RAN AHEAD AND CLIMBED A
> SYCAMORE-FIG TREE TO SEE HIM, SINCE
> JESUS WAS COMING THAT WAY. *Luke 19:4*

Water That Tree!

Remember the name of the tax collector who climbed the tree when Jesus traveled through Jericho? It was Zacchaeus, a name meaning "pure" or "innocent." Remember why he climbed that tree? Because he wasn't tall enough to see Jesus above the heads of the crowd. Remember what he received from Jesus that day? Forgiveness of sins that he so desperately needed and that really made him "innocent."

An old story, and of course it is only a story, relates that as Zacchaeus grew older, each morning he would leave his house at sunrise. An hour or so later he would return, his face lit up with joy. One morning his wife followed to see where he went each day. To her surprise she watched as he walked directly to that sycamore tree. Quietly she watched as her husband poured jar after jar of water on its roots, pulled whatever weeds were growing around its base, and then patted its rough trunk. When Zacchaeus reached home, she asked him why. His quiet answer was "Because it lifted me up to see him who brought me what my soul needed."

My church is like that sycamore tree. Every week it lifts me up to see my Savior. It brings me the Word through which the Savior speaks of my forgiveness just as surely as he did to the tax collector. And my church needs regular watering. It needs my concern, my prayers, my personal involvement, my offerings. I don't know if Zacchaeus ever watered that old sycamore. I do know what to do for my church—gladly, willingly, thankfully.

God, help me water this "tree." Amen.

> NOW FAITH IS BEING SURE OF WHAT WE HOPE FOR AND
> CERTAIN OF WHAT WE DO NOT SEE. THIS IS WHAT THE
> ANCIENTS WERE COMMENDED FOR. *Hebrews 11:1,2*

Being Sure

You're seven miles down the road after your wife said this was the right exit. There hasn't been a single sign telling you that Nashville lies ahead. You don't want to and yet you can't help asking the question, Are you sure?

Notice how the author defines faith. "Being sure of what we hope for" he says. Being "certain of what we do not see," he adds. Faith is not following a hunch or taking a blind leap into the dark. Nor is it merely hoping for the best, naively closing our eyes and wishing all will be well. Faith is having solid confidence. It brings the future into the present as if we already held in our hands what we hoped for. Faith answers the question, Are you sure? with a resounding *yes*.

I never saw the creation or the crucifixion. I wasn't present to witness the floodwaters rising above the mountain peaks or the Savior rising triumphantly from the Easter tomb. I haven't heard his actual voice pardoning my sins and promising his return. Yet I believe. For the believer, faith is a sixth sense making the invisible seen and certain.

Just so with the "ancients." Those Old Testament believers trusted God absolutely. And God commended them for their faith. He gave them an A by recording their faith in Hebrews chapter 11, the Bible's great chapter on faith. Also, just as with those ancients, a faith that is sure is God's gift, worked in me by his Holy Spirit through the powerful Word.

Lord, give me such a faith as this. Amen.

> BY FAITH ABEL OFFERED GOD A BETTER SACRIFICE THAN CAIN
> DID. BY FAITH HE WAS COMMENDED AS A RIGHTEOUS MAN,
> WHEN GOD SPOKE WELL OF HIS OFFERINGS. AND BY FAITH
> HE STILL SPEAKS, EVEN THOUGH HE IS DEAD. *Hebrews 11:4*

Still Speaking

Ever been to the National Baseball Hall of Fame in Cooperstown, New York? What a thrill to see the plaque honoring Henry Aaron, who hit more home runs during his career than Babe Ruth. Or the newer one honoring Robin Yount, the all-star shortstop of the Milwaukee Brewers.

Hebrews chapter 11 is another hall of fame. Perhaps a better label would be the "Hall of Faith." In this chapter, for my instruction and encouragement, are hung portraits of believers of the past. They were ordinary people like me. But through them God did extraordinary things. Looking at their portraits means looking even more so at the Lord whose promises were behind them and whose power enabled them.

Take Abel for example. He's described as a "righteous man." He could stand just and holy in God's presence, not because of what he did but because of what he was by faith. Abel trusted the unseen promises of God about the coming Savior, and his actions showed it. God granted his approval by recording Abel's faith on the pages of Holy Scripture. As a result, this first man who ever died still speaks to us today. "Faith's way may be rugged," Abel would remind me, "but God's grace is sufficient and his smile of approval sweet."

Time to reexamine my hold on God's promises.
Time to reconsider how much my actions reflect my faith.
Time to pray again, "Lord, give me such a faith as this." Amen.

> BY FAITH ENOCH WAS TAKEN FROM THIS LIFE, SO THAT HE DID NOT EXPERIENCE DEATH; HE COULD NOT BE FOUND, BECAUSE GOD HAD TAKEN HIM AWAY. FOR BEFORE HE WAS TAKEN, HE WAS COMMENDED AS ONE WHO PLEASED GOD. AND WITHOUT FAITH IT IS IMPOSSIBLE TO PLEASE GOD. *Hebrews 11:5,6*

Walking With God

How does one walk with God? That's what Genesis 5:24 says Enoch did. Our verse puts it, "He was . . . one who pleased God." And it tells us how—"by faith." "Without faith it is impossible to please God," it also reminds us. At once we realize we have to turn the thought around. God walked with Enoch, and because he did, Enoch could walk with him. God brought Enoch to his side by planting faith in his heart. That faith moved Enoch to walk through life in confident trust at the side of his loving Lord. It also led him to trust his God for life's greatest need, that of a Savior from sin. As always, faith, though invisible in the heart, shows itself in daily life. Enoch tried to measure his footsteps according to those of his God.

Where does such a walk lead? Since Enoch was walking with God, there was no question where the journey would end. One day on their walk together, God lengthened Enoch's stride. Before he could say good-bye to anyone, God lifted him up, both body and soul, to heaven's glory.

My destination is the same as Enoch's, though I pass through the grave first. So is the way to heaven's glory. I reach heaven's glory only by faith in Jesus. "Only Jesus can impart Comfort to a wounded heart." Only he can offer "peace that flows from sin forgiv'n." Only he can give "faith and hope to walk with God In the way that Enoch trod" (CW 385:3).

Lord, give me such a faith as this. Amen.

By faith Noah, when warned about things not yet seen, in holy fear built an ark to save his family. By his faith he condemned the world and became heir of the righteousness that comes by faith. *Hebrews 11:7*

Pounding Nails And Preaching

Talk about being convinced of "things not yet seen." Noah lived on dry land. He perhaps had never seen the sea. Most certainly he had never seen a flood rising above the highest mountain top. Yet when instructed by God, he started building an ark. "Holy fear" galvanized him into action. Unbelieving fear terrorizes and paralyzes. Godly fear stands in awe of God and goes into action at his command. So Noah, as a believer, started pounding nails.

For 120 years this "preacher of righteousness," as 2 Peter 2:5 describes him, worked on the ark. By his very actions, if not also by his words, he "condemned the world." One can only imagine what hooting and hollering he had to endure from unbelieving neighbors. Or how the morning papers and evening newscasts of his day had fun at his expense. But he pounded on, preaching to his contemporaries that an end was coming. He also pounded on trusting God and his promises. Chief among them was the promise of the Christ who was coming to rescue him by the wood of the cross. Noah was saved, not only from the waters of the flood but also from the fires of hell, through faith in God's promises.

Do I at times feel that I'm all alone in the world? That perhaps I'm wrong and all the others right? "Never mind," Noah might answer, "in my day, eight were right and all the others perished."

Lord, give me such a faith as this. Amen.

BY FAITH [ABRAHAM] MADE HIS HOME IN THE PROMISED LAND LIKE A STRANGER IN A FOREIGN COUNTRY; HE LIVED IN TENTS, AS DID ISAAC AND JACOB, WHO WERE HEIRS WITH HIM OF THE SAME PROMISE. FOR HE WAS LOOKING FORWARD TO THE CITY WITH FOUNDATIONS, WHOSE ARCHITECT AND BUILDER IS GOD. *Hebrews 11:9,10*

Just Passing Through

The central spot in the Hall of Faith belongs to Abraham. Consistently he trusted God, taking him at his word. With no map in hand, but with God's call in his heart, he headed out for an unknown land. Faith is that way. It goes forward blindfolded because it trusts God's leading.

That unknown land was to be Abraham's inheritance. Yet all he ever owned of Canaan was the burial plot purchased for his beloved wife. Like a foreigner, he moved his tent from place to place in the land that God had promised to him. Nor was it any different for his son Isaac and his grandson Jacob. They too died not having seen but having trusted God's promise.

How could Abraham do it? "By faith," the inspired author says. By faith, Abraham even looked beyond the earthly Canaan to the eternal city in heaven. His tents had pegs that were pulled and moved. This city had foundations that stand forever. This heavenly Jerusalem, the city of the living God, was his real home.

What a rebuke for me. So often I live with eyes riveted on earth's dust and fists wrapped around earth's treasures as if there were no other. And yet, what encouragement. "Press on," Abraham's portrait tells me, "it's worth it. The God you trust is absolutely reliable. He said that heaven is your home and there you shall surely stand, with us, at his right hand."

Lord, give me such a faith as this. Amen.

> BY FAITH ABRAHAM, EVEN THOUGH HE WAS PAST AGE—AND SARAH HERSELF WAS BARREN—WAS ENABLED TO BECOME A FATHER BECAUSE HE CONSIDERED HIM FAITHFUL WHO HAD MADE THE PROMISE. AND SO FROM THIS ONE MAN, AND HE AS GOOD AS DEAD, CAME DESCENDANTS AS NUMEROUS AS THE STARS IN THE SKY AND AS COUNTLESS AS THE SAND ON THE SEASHORE. *Hebrews 11:11,12*

Doing The Impossible

Modern medicine has made it possible for women in their 60s to bear children. Occasionally we hear of men in their 80s becoming fathers. But Abraham and Sarah have them beat, no thanks to modern medicine either. Abraham was past the age of begetting a child. Sarah also was barren. Yet the two conceived a child by God's miraculous working. From such a small beginning—"this one man"—and from such a miraculous beginning—"he as good as dead"—came descendants as countless as the proverbial stars in the sky and sand on the seashore.

Physically, all Israel counts its beginning from Abraham. Spiritually, all believers through his greatest descendant, Christ, call him father. So rich was the harvest that came from him. And it came by faith. Abraham "considered him faithful who had made the promise." He trusted a God who could never be unfaithful and a promise that therefore could not remain unfulfilled. God had promised that the Savior would come from his line. And what God promises, he delivers. Isaac's birth was proof and also the first step toward the fulfillment of the promise about the Savior.

When it comes to God's promises, the word *impossible* doesn't belong in my vocabulary. When a faithful God promises forgiveness for all my sins, he means it. When he assures me that he's at my side, he is. When he says he'll take me to heaven, he will. So Abraham reminds me.

Lord, give me such a faith as this. Amen.

> By faith Joseph, when his end was near, spoke
> about the exodus of the Israelites from Egypt
> and gave instructions about his bones. *Hebrews 11:22*

Going Home

Caskets speak about the brevity of life. So did the one in which Joseph's mummified body rested. But his had another message. Before his death he "made the sons of Israel swear an oath and said, 'God will surely come to your aid, and then you must carry my bones up from this place'" (Genesis 50:25). God had promised to restore his people to their homeland in Canaan. Joseph believed this promise so strongly that he bound his family by oath to carry his casket with them when the time came. For well over three hundred years his sarcophagus stood there, telling all who cared to hear, "God will take you to the homeland of Canaan."

Through all those years, his sarcophagus said something else to his people. Like other believers before him, Joseph was "longing for a better country—a heavenly one" (Hebrews 11:16). Joseph's coffin preached his confidence that a gracious God would finally take him to the homeland above. Not his striking victory over temptation in Potiphar's house, nor his skilled administration of Egypt's vast resources, but his trust in the coming Savior brought his portrait to our Hall of Faith.

"When I reach heaven above, I expect to find three wonders," said a famous Christian. "First, to meet some people I had not thought to see there. Second, to miss some people I had expected to see there. And third, the greatest wonder of all, to find myself there." All because of the same Savior from sin that a gracious God promised Joseph and you and me. Through him I will finally reach home.

Lord, give me such a faith as this. Amen.

> [MOSES] REGARDED DISGRACE FOR THE SAKE OF CHRIST AS
> OF GREATER VALUE THAN THE TREASURES OF EGYPT, BECAUSE
> HE WAS LOOKING AHEAD TO HIS REWARD. *Hebrews 11:26*

Doing Great Things For The Lord

Moses had it made. Pharaoh's daughter had plucked him out of the Nile River and adopted him. All the wisdom and wealth of Egypt were within his grasp. His picture could have been on the cover of the magazines, his exploits regularly on the 6:00 news of his day. Instead, Moses deliberately shook off his position of royal blood and chose identification with the people of God.

How could he do it? "Because he was looking ahead to his reward," Hebrews tells us. The certified public accountants of his day would have strongly disagreed with him. How could hardship and suffering as the leader of a slave people be superior to Egypt's exalted wealth and position. Folly bases its calculations on beginnings. Faith reckons with endings. Moses in faith looked all the way to the end and saw Christ's eternal riches waiting for him. With such a perspective he was ready to do great things for God.

Moses had only promises of the coming Savior. I have fulfillment. I know all about the hill called Calvary and what happened there to my Lord. I know about the empty tomb and what it means for me. Now the Lord expects me to do great things for him. No, not turning the tide of history as Moses did. Mine are more mundane—loving my spouse, raising my family, working for my church, telling my neighbor, and bringing my offerings for world missions. Such fruits of faith may not look like much, but in the Lord's eyes they are great.

Lord, give me such a faith as this. Amen.

THESE WERE ALL COMMENDED FOR THEIR FAITH, YET NONE OF THEM RECEIVED WHAT HAD BEEN PROMISED. GOD HAD PLANNED SOMETHING BETTER FOR US SO THAT ONLY TOGETHER WITH US WOULD THEY BE MADE PERFECT. *Hebrews 11:39,40*

Having It Even Better

In our tour through the Hall of Faith, the author has drawn attention to many. Their striking examples show how God, when he works faith, moves ordinary people to do extraordinary things. Yet one thing was missing for all these heroes of faith. Christ's coming to the cross and his coming on the Last Day had not occurred during their lifetimes. Only from a distance with faith's telescope did they see these events.

This delay was for me! God kept those Old Testament believers waiting so that I might join their ranks. God still delays so that "many will come from the east and the west, and will take their places at the feast with Abraham, Isaac and Jacob in the kingdom of heaven" (Matthew 8:11).

Note how the author states that God "planned something better" for me. He's not saying those Old Testament heroes of faith are second-class citizens in heaven. Christ's cross reaches both backward to them and forward to me. He's saying they operated on so much less than I do. They lived in the shadow and yet dared and died for Christ. They had so little and yet did so much.

Doesn't this thought challenge me as a New Testament reader? The full triumph of the cross is mine. The full truths of God's promises are in my hands. Now, what will I do and dare for him? Will my portrait, by God's grace, be added somewhere on the rear wall of the Hall of Faith?

Lord, again I ask that you
give me such a faith as this. Amen.

"YOU WHO HAVE NO MONEY, COME, BUY AND
EAT! COME, BUY WINE AND MILK WITHOUT
MONEY AND WITHOUT COST." *Isaiah 55:1*

No Credit Card Needed

One upscale restaurant in New York City has a $71 hamburger on its menu. Another offers a $1,000 frittata. Still another lists a $1,000 sundae. I've never been to any of these eateries, for obvious reasons. My credit card would be hard pressed to handle the bill. But regardless whether I eat out or buy groceries for meals at home, food costs.

Food for my soul also costs. The price tag on forgiveness is too much for me to handle. Even if my credit card had as much as a million dollar limit on it, I couldn't cover one sin. Admission to heaven has a tremendously high fee. Even if I could plunk down thousands of good works, heaven's cash register would still record zero. I'm more than bankrupt when it comes to buying food for my soul. I'd have to go not only starving but damned to hell.

Yet I have forgiveness of sins. I have peace with God. I have heaven as my home. All this and more is mine without charge—without charge to me, that is. The treasures of salvation cost my Lord plenty. In his love he had to send his beloved Son from heaven's glory to Calvary's gore. In his love the Son had to leave his radiant throne behind for the rough wood of the cross. In his love the Holy Spirit has to work around the clock through the Word to create and continue faith in my heart. Oh, there's a charge for my salvation—one that's out of this world. Thank God, he's paid it so that I can eat free.

Lord, feed me with salvation's rich
food till in heaven I hunger no more. Amen.

"AS THE RAIN AND THE SNOW COME DOWN FROM HEAVEN,
AND DO NOT RETURN TO IT WITHOUT WATERING THE EARTH AND
MAKING IT BUD AND FLOURISH, . . . SO IS MY WORD THAT GOES
OUT FROM MY MOUTH: IT WILL NOT RETURN TO ME EMPTY,
BUT WILL ACCOMPLISH WHAT I DESIRE." *Isaiah 55:10,11*

Raindrops Keep Falling On My Heart

Ever watch a child splashing through the puddles? A farmer standing out in the falling rain that his fields so desperately need? A city dweller marveling how an inch of rain can make brown grass green again? Rain is one of God's gifts. It replenishes earth's reservoirs. It slakes the thirst of birds and beasts. It nourishes the fields. It washes clean the landscape and streets. When God keeps the windows of heaven closed, I realize how necessary raindrops are.

My soul needs raindrops too. Isaiah reminds me that without God's Word my soul is worse off than a parched desert. Without God's Word my heart can grow only weeds and thistles. Without God's Word I'd go through life kicking up the dust of unbelief and choking on it eternally.

Thank God, I can stand in the showers of his grace. His Word has turned my heart from a desert into a field of faith. His Word irrigates my faith so that it can stay green and even grow a crop. If he were to take the news of his salvation through Jesus away, I'd hate to think what might happen. Just as with rain, only God can send his Word. Just as with rain, only God can make his Word work. Thank God, he sends the needed raindrops of his Word on my heart. One more thought—the truth that only God can send and make his Word work doesn't mean I have nothing to do. I'm to stand regularly in that nourishing rain. I'm to tell others about it.

Lord, keep the raindrops of your Word falling on my heart. Amen.

> "MEN OF GALILEE," THEY SAID, "WHY DO YOU STAND HERE
> LOOKING INTO THE SKY? THIS SAME JESUS, WHO HAS BEEN
> TAKEN FROM YOU INTO HEAVEN, WILL COME BACK IN THE
> SAME WAY YOU HAVE SEEN HIM GO INTO HEAVEN." *Acts 1:11*

Head In The Clouds

Clouds can be so beautiful. They hover like whipped cream in the heavens. They add special splendor to the sunset. They form fleecy patterns and then quickly change them. They move lazily across the sky and run like a deer before the wind. The Creator is also an artist, as his clouds clearly show.

It's fun watching the clouds. But there's more to life than that. At Jesus' ascension the disciples glued their eyes on the cloud that had covered their Savior. They missed their beloved Lord and still wanted him visibly beside them. But they weren't to stand there with their heads in the clouds. They had work to do—work that the master had left in their hands alone. And they had something to look forward to—the return of their Savior on the Last Day. While waiting for that day, they were to spread his salvation so that others might look for his return too.

Let it never be said that I'm so heavenly minded that I'm no earthly good. I'm to be looking at the clouds, waiting for my Savior to return either on my last day or the Last Day of this world. Nothing could be sweeter than his coming. But while I'm waiting, I'm to get my head out of the clouds. Waiting means working—telling my family, my friends, those around me, and even those across the world of the Savior, who wants to claim them as his own when he returns.

*Lord, keep me waiting for your return and
busy spreading the news of your salvation. Amen.*

> "WHO THEN CAN UNDERSTAND
> THE THUNDER OF HIS POWER?" *Job 26:14*

Thunder On, Lord

Rain fell as I led the devotion in Cameroon, Africa. Everyone in the open air hut ducked at the loud blast of thunder. "God's showing how strong he is," I said. All smiled and we went on.

God is all-powerful. Though his friends had advised the suffering Job to turn away from God, he could not. In words spoken before our verse, Job told his friends why he couldn't. How could he curse a God who had created the heavens and the earth? How could he ignore a God who whispered in the wind and roared in the thunder? How could he forsake a God who had complete power over death and the grave, over hell and Satan? Such a powerful God is beyond understanding. No one can fathom the thunder of his power.

Wouldn't it be something if thunder roared every time a baby received faith through Baptism? Every time the gospel word of forgiveness reached a needy heart? Every time I went back to my seat refreshed by my Savior's body and blood in the Sacrament? God's power to save is more awesome than his power as Creator and Preserver. God shows me the power of his love when his Son hangs on a cross, breathes his last breath, fills a cold grave because of my sins. And nowhere do I see more his awesome power than at his emptied tomb with its glorious preview of what will happen to my grave.

Job was right. "Who then can understand the thunder of his power?"

Lord, thank you for the power of your love.
Help me trust it for my salvation always. Amen.

> "SEE HOW THE LILIES OF THE FIELD GROW. THEY DO NOT
> LABOR OR SPIN. YET I TELL YOU THAT NOT EVEN SOLOMON IN
> ALL HIS SPLENDOR WAS DRESSED LIKE ONE OF THESE." *Matthew 6:28,29*

Better Care Than For The Lily

We were driving through Hoot Owl Valley near where my wife had grown up. It was spring and the wildflowers were in bloom. Dutchman's britches, jack-in-the-pulpits, and violets showed off their magnificent colors. No one took care of them nor could anyone duplicate their colors.

Little things can teach so much. When I look at those wildflowers, I can see the goodness of my God. He seeded them. He waters them with the rain. He brings them back to life each spring. He dresses them in grandeur that kings like Solomon would give their eyeteeth to have.

Don't those wildflowers teach me something else? Won't the heavenly Father do even greater things for me? Flowers are only inanimate objects that grace my world. God wants me to share his heaven. Flowers fade and die. God wants me to live forever. Flowers bloom for a bit. God wants me to shine like the stars forever and ever.

All this God has made possible for me. When my parents threw away the holiness in which God had created them, he gave it back. Through Baptism he puts a new heart within me—a clean heart, one that loves him. When my faith needs nourishment, God sends his Spirit to fertilize it with the treasures of Jesus. When my earthly life has needs, God takes care of them too. How can I doubt it? The wildflowers, blossoming in the ditches of life, remind me of his loving care.

Lord, point me especially to my Savior's cross
to show me how richly you take care of me. Amen.

> THERE BEFORE ME WAS A GREAT MULTITUDE THAT NO ONE
> COULD COUNT, FROM EVERY NATION, TRIBE, PEOPLE AND
> LANGUAGE, STANDING BEFORE THE THRONE AND IN FRONT
> OF THE LAMB. . . . "THEY HAVE WASHED THEIR ROBES AND
> MADE THEM WHITE IN THE BLOOD OF THE LAMB." *Revelation 7:9,14*

I Want To Be In That Number

On our picture wall hangs a copy of a tintype photo of my great-grand-father. He's wearing the blue uniform of a soldier in Grant's army of 1865. We've come a long way since the days of tintype photography. On Christmas Day we received, via e-mail, a digital photo of our son and daughter-in-law visiting with her parents in France. They were only seven hours away as we connected with them via these modern miracles.

Photography changes. But not the photo John puts before us of the number in heaven. Its members come from all four corners of the world. They speak different languages. They share different cultures. They're multicolored. But in one most important aspect they are all the same. They are all dressed in white robes. The blood of the Lamb, at whose side they stand, has washed their robes of life and made them spotless. Their every sin is gone. Their every stain has been removed the only way possible, in the fountain filled with the Savior's blood.

I said this heavenly photo doesn't change. That's true because only believers are in it. Yet, in one sense, it does change. That glorious picture is getting larger each day. The Spirit through the gospel is at work in human hearts, dressing them for heaven, adding them to Christ's family. I want to be in that number. Don't you?

Jesus, Savior, wash away all that has been
wrong today. Keep me in that number. Amen.

> THOUGH YOU HAVE NOT SEEN HIM, YOU LOVE HIM; AND EVEN THOUGH YOU DO NOT SEE HIM NOW, YOU BELIEVE IN HIM AND ARE FILLED WITH AN INEXPRESSIBLE AND GLORIOUS JOY. *1 Peter 1:8*

I Can See Him

"How can I trust someone I've never seen?" asked the doubter in my study. In reply I related the story of a son who went off to college. At the end of his first year, he told his dad, "I don't believe in God. I don't believe in anything I can't see." His father had an answer for him. "Do you have a brain?" he asked. "Yes," replied the son quickly. "Have you ever seen it?" was his father's next question.

I know my brain is real because I've seen what it does. I know the wind is real because I've seen the trees bending. I know love is real because I've felt its power with my beloved wife. And God? Only those who know what he does know how real he is. The heart that God has touched with his forgiving love in Christ knows how real he is. The soul to which a holy God has brought Christ's righteousness knows how real he is. The life that has been filled with hope through his Son's death and resurrection knows how real he is.

I couldn't argue that doubter into faith. That would be like trying to tell a blind man what an elephant looks like. Instead, I gave him a copy of the New Testament. "Read it," I urged him. "Learn what God has done for you." He never came back, so I don't know the outcome. I do, however, know that I believe in God, even though I have not seen him. He has shown himself to me by what he has done for me in Christ my Savior.

Lord, give me eyes to see and faith
to trust you as my dear Savior. Amen.

> RIGHTEOUSNESS EXALTS A NATION, BUT
> SIN IS A DISGRACE TO ANY PEOPLE. *Proverbs 14:34*

Who's Going To Help Hold Up The Light?

A father took his eight-year-old daughter to see the Statue of Liberty and told her the story behind the statue. That night as he sat down on her bed, she asked, "I'm thinking about that beautiful lady out there in the dark all by herself. Who's going to help her hold up the light?"

The torch on the Statue of Liberty was relit in 1986. But the light America really needs seems to be fading. Do the people of my land think God was exaggerating when he advised that nations receive blessings when they seek to follow his will? Do they think he was bluffing when he warned that the opposite is also true? When a nation forsakes God and forgets his way, it can expect ultimately only disgrace, decrease, destruction. America needs the light of God's Word.

Who's going to help hold up that light? God's finger points at every Christian, including me, in our land. Only God's children can truly know and want to follow his will. Redeemed by the Savior's blood, heirs of our Father's house above, we want to share our treasure. Left on earth, we view life as the time in which to spread God's Word with its blessed message of God's righteousness in Christ. The more people share in this righteousness, the more there will be outward righteousness in our land, as grateful children of God seek to walk in his ways. And the more they walk his ways, the more a gracious God will exalt the nation around them. Just think how much each of us can do for America when we do our best to hold up the light of God's Word before the people of our land.

God, help our country for your Son's sake. Amen.

THE LORD IS COMPASSIONATE
AND GRACIOUS. *Psalm 103:8*

How Merciful Is He?

On December 26, 2004, a massive earthquake and tsunami ravaged 11 countries in the Indian Ocean basin. More than 160,000 people lost their lives. Tragedies like this often raise questions about God. If he's compassionate and gracious, why does something like this happen? If he's almighty, why doesn't he prevent such a tragic loss of lives? Sometimes I may ask such questions in the smaller tragedies that hit my life too. When God takes my health, my spouse, my money, it's hard to see him as a compassionate God. When he crushes my happiness before my very eyes, it's hard not to question his goodness.

How do I know that the psalmist is right about God? By looking at Jesus! I can't think of anyone more compassionate or gracious. Look at what he has done for my ravaged soul. Sin's earthquake rocks my very existence every day. Death like some tsunami washes over my soul, threatening to carry it away to hell. There was no place for me to hide, no safe refuge in which to cower. Till a loving God launched his rescue mission. That mission brought God himself into my flesh. It laid him in a manger and elevated him to a cross. And when he was done, I was safe. My sins were paid for. Death was defeated. Hell's doors were closed; and heaven's, opened.

Tragedies come and always will. For the unbeliever, they are calls to repentance from a holy God. But for the believer, they are chastisement from his loving hand. With them he would polish my faith and point me to my ever-compassionate and gracious Savior.

*Lord, lift my eyes ever to the Savior so that
I trust your goodness in the storms of life. Amen.*

The Only Way

Driving the back roads in Montana, I stopped at a little store to ask directions. When the clerk responded, I made the mistake of asking, "Is that the best way to get there?" "Mister," he replied, "that's the only way."

Some today think there are many ways to reach heaven. For them heaven is like some mountain to be climbed from various directions—or some ocean into which many streams empty. One way is as good as the other is their claim.

That's not what Jesus said. The Savior himself claimed, "I am the way. . . . No one comes to the Father except through me" (John 14:6). That's also what the author of Hebrews states clearly. He reminds those who would abandon Jesus that there is no other source of eternal salvation. Salvation from sin comes only through the sacrifice of the God-man. Entrance to heaven comes only from his perfect payment for sin. Jesus isn't just *a* way to heaven. He's the *only* way.

I took that clerk's advice and reached my destination. So also with traveling, Jesus is the highway to heaven. When the author speaks about "all who obey him," he's referring to faith. Faith is obedience to God and is worked in me by God's grace through the gospel. My walk, not only *with* Jesus but *on* Jesus, is God's gift to me. When feet of faith are planted on his salvation, my walk is heavenward all the way.

*Lord, through your Word, keep my feet of
faith on Jesus and moving toward heaven. Amen.*

"GOD SO LOVED THE WORLD THAT HE GAVE HIS ONE AND ONLY SON, THAT WHOEVER BELIEVES IN HIM SHALL NOT PERISH BUT HAVE ETERNAL LIFE." *John 3:16*

The Whole World And Me Also

Did Jesus know what he was saying? Did he have any idea how the world since his day would mushroom in population to well over six billion today and who knows how many billions more tomorrow? He spent his 33 years on this earth in one small land named Palestine. He never flew hours around the world. He never made mission journeys, not even to the parts of the world known at his time. Yet he speaks of the world. Notice he didn't say "I am the light of Palestine" or "God so loved the Jews." Always it is the "world."

Jesus knows that all the people of the whole world need him. He came to prepare salvation for every single one of them. He did this so that many would "come from the east and the west, and take their places at the feast with Abraham, Isaac and Jacob in the kingdom of heaven" (Matthew 8:11). His love knows no limits. His forgiveness has no exclusions. He died for all and wants all to come to him.

Wonder of all wonders, he wants me also. That's what the "whoever" in his words assures me. "Whoever" is broad enough to include the whole world and yet narrow enough to mean me. I can write my own name into that "whoever." He died for Richard Lauersdorf and wants Richard Lauersdorf to believe in him so that Richard Lauersdorf "shall not perish but have eternal life."

Yes, Jesus knew what he was saying—about the world and about me. Thank God, he did.

*Dear Savior, thank you for the love that moved
you to die for the whole world and for me. Amen.*

> KEEP ME AS THE APPLE OF YOUR EYE; HIDE
> ME IN THE SHADOW OF YOUR WINGS. *Psalm 17:8*

How Precious God Has Made Me!

Eyes of the human body are certainly precious. With them I scan the pages of a book, gaze at my spouse, watch my grandchildren grow. Consider also the protection God has built in for my eyes. He surrounds them with a bone fortress, curtains them with eyelids, shields and shades them with eyelashes. I take good care of my eyes too. I want them to work when I take that driver's test. I want them to last into old age.

In our verse David compares himself not just to God's eye but to its most important part, the pupil. If God had a body, then David said he would be like the choicest part of God's eye. That's how precious God had made him. That's not what David saw, though, when he looked at himself. He saw not "the apple of God's eye" but "the object of God's just anger." He saw himself as the worthy recipient of the worst punishment God could hand out. But by God's grace, he also saw the Savior who was coming to shoulder his sin and suffer his punishment. By God's grace, David was even privileged to sing about that Savior in many of his psalms. Because of that Savior, David could turn confidently to his God and pray forcefully, "Keep me as the apple of your eye."

When a blood vessel ruptured in my eye, I was reminded of how precious my sight is. When I look up at Christ's cross, I'm reminded of how precious I am in God's sight. He's taken me, the sinner, and made me into a saint. He's taken me, his bitter enemy, and made me into his dear child. He's sent the "apple of his eye," his dear Son, Jesus, to do all this for me.

Because of Jesus I pray, "Keep me as the apple of your eye." Amen.

KEEP ME AS THE APPLE OF YOUR EYE; HIDE
ME IN THE SHADOW OF YOUR WINGS. *Psalm 17:8*

How Safe God Keeps Me!

Every spring a mother robin returned to occupy the nest she had built securely between the wall and the pipe bringing the electric service into our parsonage. There she sat with her wings completely covering her little brood. They seemed so secure in the shadow of her wings. But then one spring the neighbor's cat found the nest. She killed the mother who was trying to protect her brood and ate the little robins. So much for safety in the shadow of that mother's wings.

Not so with my God. He has more than wings over me. His nail-pierced hands shelter me. His hands speak of his love for me, a love so great that he has already rescued me from sin and hell. Now those hands will safely keep me on my journey from earth to heaven. When temptations come my way, he's my very present help in trouble. When sin comes my way, his blood cleanses me. When troubles come my way, he offers his shoulders to carry them. When death comes my way, he walks with me in the dark valley. In the shadow of his almighty, loving wings I'm safe.

I do need to seek the safety of his wings. A baby bird who tries to crawl out of its mother's nest can hardly expect to remain safe. Nor can I if I slip out from under my Savior's care. This thought makes my use of his powerful Word and of his Holy Supper extremely important.

This thought prompts my prayer, "Keep me, oh, keep me, King of kings, Beneath thine own almighty wings" (CW 592:1).

*Gracious Savior, keep me safe on
my journey to your heavenly home. Amen.*

WHEN HE REACHED A CERTAIN PLACE, HE STOPPED FOR THE NIGHT
BECAUSE THE SUN HAD SET. TAKING ONE OF THE STONES THERE,
HE PUT IT UNDER HIS HEAD AND LAY DOWN TO SLEEP. *Genesis 28:11*

My Church—A Place Of Rest

Jacob was tired, bone tired. He had traveled about 50 miles that day, every one of them on foot. His heart must have been weary also. He had left behind his loving mother, Rebekah, whom he would never see alive again. His disappointed father, Isaac, whom he had tricked into giving him the blessing. His enraged brother, Esau, who had vowed to kill him. Overhead the sky was dark, and so was his heart as Jacob lay there with his thoughts of home, his feelings of sorrow, his conscience torn this way and that with his sins. Rest was what he needed for his body and even more so for his soul. And that's what God gave him that night at Bethel.

My church may be a small building or an elaborate structure. It may even be a rented room. It may be 50 years old or almost brand new. But whatever, my church is a place of rest. Brick and stone, lumber and glass bring no rest. God's Word proclaimed in my church is what offers me rest. Like Jacob on his stone pillow, I have the burden of sin squeezing my soul. He had no corner on greed and envy, lies and trickery. I know about them too, and I fall into them regularly. Like Jacob, I don't trust the Lord to act but think I have to resort to my own schemes. Yes, I know something about sin. Those ordinary ones I wear every day like a pair of old shoes. Those special ones that jolt me like an attack of indigestion leaving my conscience with heartburn.

That's why I need to come to my church. There God through his Word offers me rest for my soul.

Lord, when I come to your house, through
your Word help me leave with the rest I need. Amen.

> HE HAD A DREAM IN WHICH HE SAW A STAIRWAY RESTING
> ON THE EARTH, WITH ITS TOP REACHING TO HEAVEN, AND THE
> ANGELS OF GOD WERE ASCENDING AND DESCENDING ON IT.
> THERE ABOVE IT STOOD THE LORD. *Genesis 28:12,13*

My Church–
A Place Of Revelation

What a revelation God granted Jacob that night! The ladder reaching to heaven, the angels using it, the Lord standing above it could mean only one thing. God still loved him and was still maintaining an intimate relationship with his erring child. Down came his holy angels, still carrying out his orders about Jacob. Up went those same angels, still carrying Jacob's prayers to God.

And the ladder—that was the main part of the revelation. Years later Jesus explained this ladder. He told Nathanael, "You shall see heaven open, and the angels of God ascending and descending on the Son of Man" (John 1:51). Christ is the ladder to heaven. With his redemptive work on Calvary's cross, Christ has opened wide the door to heaven that had been nailed shut by man's sins. With his payment for sins, Christ has made possible again a loving father-child relationship with God.

It makes no difference where my church is located or what it looks like. It's precious to me because there my God reveals himself to me. Not through special visions as to Jacob but through something just as special. Through his Word, God comes to me. In it he points me to Jesus as the only ladder to heaven. Through it he sends his Spirit to put my feet in faith upon that precious ladder. With it he reassures me that regardless what I have done or how often I have come, he is still my Father and I am still his child.

Lord, speak to me through your Word and
help me always to listen with eager ears. Amen.

[JACOB] WAS AFRAID AND SAID, "HOW AWESOME IS THIS PLACE!
THIS IS NONE OTHER THAN THE HOUSE OF GOD; THIS IS THE
GATE OF HEAVEN" . . . JACOB TOOK THE STONE HE HAD PLACED
UNDER HIS HEAD AND SET IT UP AS A PILLAR AND POURED OIL
ON IT. HE CALLED THAT PLACE BETHEL. *Genesis 28:17,18*

My Church—
A Place Of Response

I'd have been afraid too. How else can sinners react when standing in
the presence of the sinless Lord? Like Jacob, I hope I'd also have
responded with joy. Seeing the heavens opened and being assured of
God's grace brings joy. Jacob's words tumbled out. "How awesome is
this place!" he marveled. "This is none other than the house of God;
this is the gate of heaven."

The next morning Jacob's response took the form of action. The stone
that had served as his pillow he set aside for the Lord. On that very spot
he vowed to build a house for God. Appropriately he named that sacred
place Bethel—"house of God." Thankfully, he also vowed to set aside
for God's service a tenth of all God would give him.

My church is not only a place I visit to get. It's also a place where I can
give. Jacob spoke words of wonder that night. I can do the same in the
hymns and prayers each service. Jacob dedicated that spot to the Lord
and later built an altar there. I can do the same, either helping to erect
my church or maintain the one that others built for me. Jacob promised
a portion of his goods to the Lord. I can do the same through my offering envelopes. Jacob left Bethel to use his daily life in response to his
Lord's goodness. I can go home from God's house to put my life into
his service wherever and in whatever way I can.

*Lord, let my hymns, my prayers, my offerings,
my life be acceptable in your sight. Amen.*

> IN THE PAST GOD SPOKE TO OUR FOREFATHERS THROUGH THE
> PROPHETS AT MANY TIMES AND IN VARIOUS WAYS, . . . BUT IN THESE
> LAST DAYS HE HAS SPOKEN TO US BY HIS SON. *Hebrews 1:1,2*

In What Language?

Our daughter, a kindergarten teacher, called the other day with an interesting question. One of her pupils had asked, "What language does God speak?"

The God of the Bible is a God who speaks. In the Garden of Eden he spoke directly to Adam and Eve in a fellowship that will one day be fully ours again in heaven. When sin ruined that fellowship, he spoke again, lovingly and graciously, the first promise of the Savior. Beginning with Moses he spoke through his written Word, especially to repeat his promise of the Savior. When Jesus came to earth, he was God's Word made flesh. Just as words show what's in our hearts, so Jesus showed God's heart. He was the visible Word of God's wondrous love for sinners.

Notice how the main purpose of God speaking was to save! We aren't told what language he spoke. People put his words into the language of their day. Inspired by the Spirit, prophets used Hebrew and apostles used Greek to record God's saving words. Jesus used Aramaic, the language of his day, to reveal that he had come to seek and to save the lost. Today I hear this news of salvation in English. Others hear it in Spanish, Portuguese, German, French. But the message is the same—the news of his saving love for sinners in Christ Jesus.

"Tell them God speaks the language of love," I told my teacher daughter. "Tell the children that he uses whatever language he needs to let me know that he loves me dearly."

Thank you, Lord, for your life-giving words.
Help me hear them clearly. Amen.

> "No one can serve two masters. Either he will hate the one and love the other, or he will be devoted to the one and despise the other. You cannot serve both God and Money." *Matthew 6:24*

No Two-Way Devotion

Pixie, our little fox terrier, had gotten loose. Halfway down the block, she stopped. My wife called from the porch; and I, from the driveway. There she stood, turning first toward my wife then toward me. Two masters were calling, and she didn't know which to follow.

Some people have only one master. They hear the call of money very clearly and follow wholeheartedly. Like the businessman who had no interest in joining our congregation though his family were members. "I serve the almighty dollar," he told me proudly. When cancer later claimed his life, his dollars were worthless.

Some people don't know which master to follow. They want a fistful of dollars and a ticket to heaven just in case. They use this world like some giant amusement park, trying out all its rides, enjoying all its thrills. But when the rain starts falling, they want some place to hide.

Still others, like me, try to serve Jesus only. I know what loving claim he has on me. His blood paid for me. His death conquered mine. His eternal life is my inheritance in full in heaven. Where would I be without him? Yet at times the world shouts so loudly that it drowns out my Savior's voice. At times the gold of this world seems more precious to me than he does. When that happens, I pray for his forgiveness. I pray also that he will retune my ears to hear his voice only.

Lord, help it be true that you and you alone are my dearest treasure. Amen.

I WAIT FOR THE LORD, MY SOUL WAITS, AND IN HIS WORD
I PUT MY HOPE. MY SOUL WAITS FOR THE LORD MORE
THAN WATCHMEN WAIT FOR THE MORNING. *Psalm 130:5,6*

Not Just Waiting, But Expecting

On his sick bed Roy finally talked about his experiences during World War II. He related how many a night as a young Marine he struggled to stay awake in his jungle foxhole. How hard he prayed that morning would come. How glad he was when the tropical sun burst forth in the sky.

"Roy," I said, "you knew the sun would come up, didn't you?" "Yes," he replied, "but I couldn't wait till it did."

Believers also wait for the Lord. Like Roy, in the day of trouble, when the night seems so dark and so long, they pray for the Lord to come. Like Roy, their prayers are not just empty words, but confident hope. They know the Lord will come with his suitable help. They are confident of his help because he has promised it. Like Roy, they can't wait till God's help comes.

I don't know your troubles, but I do know mine. I know how often I need the reminder that I have a God who knows and cares. When I struggle under sin's weight, he knows how much I need to hear his gracious words, "Your sins are forgiven." He knows how much, in life's burdens, I need his promise that he will never leave me nor forsake me. He knows how much, in temptation's heat, I need his assurance that he will be my strength and stay. He doesn't leave me longing for daylight but shines on me with his love every minute, every hour, every day.

Lord, teach me to trust your promises more each day
and to wait confidently for the sunshine of your love. Amen.

> WHO CAN DISCERN HIS ERRORS?
> FORGIVE MY HIDDEN FAULTS. *Psalm 19:12*

Even The Ones I Don't Know

Ever try picking paint by looking at the small chip in the store? Why is it that the color always seems so different when you put the paint on the wall?

The same thing is true of sin. When I look at my daily life, I see sin. I know I'm a sinner. At the end of the day when I pray, "Forgive us our trespasses," I could list plenty of them. Where would I start? With my selfishness that didn't always put my spouse first? With my lack of trust that didn't always look to God to help me carry the day's special burdens? With my wayward thoughts that looked lasciviously at my neighbor's wife, enviously at my neighbor's house, angrily at my supervisor at work?

What does God see when he looks at my sins? I see them in miniature like that paint chip. When an all-knowing God looks at my trespasses, he sees a whole wall full. He sees the daily sins I've forgotten. He sees the ones I didn't recognize as wrong. He sees the whole load like some wrongly painted wall before him.

I need the psalmist's plea, "Forgive my hidden faults." I need a loving Lord to remind me that he has scrubbed the walls of my heart clean from all my sins, known and unknown. With Jesus' blood he has painted the walls of my heart just the color he wants—dazzling white and holy in his sight.

Lord, help me realize and rejoice in how
much forgiveness you have given me. Amen.

> WHEN I SAID, "MY FOOT IS SLIPPING," YOUR
> LOVE, O LORD, SUPPORTED ME. *Psalm 94:18*

A Steady Hand
For Unsteady Steps

At our granddaughters' ball games, we look for seats on the bottom row of the bleachers. Sometimes, though, we have to climb higher. Then comes the problem of getting back down. Because of my wife's arthritic knees I usually go first. She puts her hand on my shoulder to steady herself, and we make it safely down to the floor.

The bleachers of life are not only steep but slippery. Many a bruise comes because I think I can make it alone. Foolishly I lean on my own intellect and skill to chart a course through life's ups and downs. Foolhardily I flex my own muscles, thinking I can handle the problems of the day. Till I get tired of their crushing weight. Forgetfully, I shrug aside the seriousness of my sins. Till I look honestly at myself in the mirror of God's law. It's no fun lying with your nose on the gym floor because you can't handle the bleacher steps.

Where would I be without God's shoulder to support me? His divine shoulder is an awesome one. It's his love. That love doesn't let me lie there in my sins but lifts me up to his Son's cross. There I find pardon for my missteps and power to walk safely. That love doesn't ignore me in the other steps of life either. It's there like solid concrete under my feet when troubles crowd in and when death comes near. Leaning on his love, I can walk through today and into tomorrow.

Where do I find that loving shoulder? In his Word! In it God walks ahead of me and steadies me.

Lord, lead me into your Word so
that I lean more on you in life. Amen.

> IN HIS HAND ARE THE DEPTHS OF THE EARTH,
> AND THE MOUNTAIN PEAKS BELONG TO HIM. *Psalm 95:4*

The Whole World And Me In His Hands

My gift for subscribing to a magazine was an inflatable world globe. As I held that world in miniature, I thought about God's hands. How big they must be to hold the whole world.

He is God of the universe. He made the world and upholds it. The mountains and the meadows are his, the streams and the stars also. He rules down deep where men have sunk their mine shafts, high up where man has not yet soared. "Depths of the earth" refer to regions yet unexplored by man. "Mountain peaks" indicate the granite masses in which he has deposited his chemicals, minerals, and treasures for his creatures to discover. The whole world is in his hands.

So am I. God's omnipotence reassures me when I look at the world around me. The natural disasters that come are not by chance. God intends them to call the wicked to repentance and to assure his children of his control. The amazing discoveries mankind reveals are not surprising at all. God has only led his creatures to ferret out what he made in the beginning.

And all this for me! He holds the whole world in his hands but still has time for me. I am the object of his concern. Above all, I am the object of his love. The power with which he runs the universe is secondary to the power of his love. His love for me, a sinner, is so strong that it sent his own Son to prepare for me an eternal world where I can praise him forever.

Lord, keep your hands tightly around the world and me. Amen.

> THE LORD IS GOOD AND HIS LOVE ENDURES
> FOREVER; HIS FAITHFULNESS CONTINUES
> THROUGH ALL GENERATIONS. *Psalm 100:5*

Through All Generations The Same

Several years ago the congregation I had served for many years celebrated its 150th anniversary. Standing in the pulpit on that festive day, I thought back to past generations. They, their children, grandchildren, and great-grandchildren had sat there. I also thought ahead to the future. What about the next generations, the children, grandchildren, great grandchildren to come?

Faces change. Names change. Some come and some go. But God remains the same. He is a Lord who "is good." His thoughts toward his people are always thoughts of love. His actions toward them are always designed by his love. His salvation of them is the product of his love.

Moreover, "his love endures forever." His face can be holy and stern. He wants mankind to be holy as he is holy. He punishes those who disobey him and transgress his commandments. But the face he prefers to show is one of enduring love. He doesn't will the sinner's death but that the sinner turn from his way and live. Through the gift of his own Son, he's made heaven possible.

"His faithfulness continues through all generations." How could I trust him for pardon if he's a God who forgets? How could I trust him for heaven if he's a God who changes his mind? My heart leaps for joy when I hear again that he is a faithful God. And not just *my* heart but the hearts of the believers who have gone before and who will follow after me.

Unchanging Lord, thank you for
your daily love and faithfulness. Amen.

> WHEN HIS MASTER SAW THAT THE LORD WAS WITH HIM AND THAT
> THE LORD GAVE HIM SUCCESS IN EVERYTHING HE DID, JOSEPH
> FOUND FAVOR IN HIS EYES AND BECAME HIS ATTENDANT. *Genesis 39:3,4*

Enslaved, Yet Faithful

Poor Joseph! Once his father's favorite son, now he was a slave in a strange land. Once filled with dreams of others bowing down to him, now he had to bow down to the will of a heathen master. The life that stretched ahead of him in Potiphar's house seemed to offer less than little, with no visible hope for change. Who could have blamed him if he had groaned, "What's the use of trusting God?" and if he had grumbled through the remainder of his life?

But not Joseph! Though he had been stripped of his coat, he still had his character. The Christian virtues of piety, industry, and honesty are spelled the same whether the times are good or bad. So Joseph went to work in Potiphar's house, and the Lord visibly blessed his work. What was the secret to Joseph's faithfulness? "The LORD was with him," our verses answer. And Joseph knew this secret. He trusted a God who does not forsake or forget his children—a Lord whose promise and presence are always near. Though he couldn't see God's plan, he faithfully followed God's lead. Joseph left the outcome of it all in God's hands. The work before him, Joseph took into his own hands. In serving his master, Joseph was serving his Lord.

What matters is not what I am or what I do but who I am and how I do it. Like Joseph, by God's grace, I am God's beloved child. Like Joseph, I'm to serve my Savior faithfully wherever he places me in life. Like Joseph, I'm to follow the Lord's leading, even when I can't see his plan.

Savior, impress on me your love and
salvation so that I trust you wherever you lead. Amen.

> HIS MASTER'S WIFE TOOK NOTICE OF JOSEPH AND SAID, "COME TO
> BED WITH ME!" BUT HE REFUSED . . . "HOW THEN COULD I DO
> SUCH A WICKED THING AND SIN AGAINST GOD?" *Genesis 39:7-9*

Tempted, Yet Faithful

Life seemed to be picking up for Joseph when, like a bolt of lightning out of the blue, fierce temptation fell on him. His physical beauty caught the roving eye of his master's wife. She kept coming at him with a shameless proposition. To say no once was difficult enough. To say it day after day demanded real strength. The day came when he happened to be alone with her in the house. Catching him by the coat, she tried to force herself on him. But Joseph fled from the house, leaving his coat behind in her grasp to be used later as circumstantial evidence against him.

Joseph's answer to temptation revealed the secret of his faithfulness. Surely he didn't want to abuse his master's confidence in him. Yet for Joseph the overriding concern was "How then could I do such a wicked thing and sin against God?" Joseph said no to Potiphar's wife because he said yes to God. Joseph knew that sin against mankind is sin against God. He could not do this to the Lord who had done so much for him.

The moral atmosphere of my world is so heavily polluted. So many, including some church bodies, compromise with sexual sin as an expedient adjustment to prevailing circumstances. Joseph's no needs repeating. What a call to faithfulness his words are for me! "How then could I [a child of God bought with his Son's blood] do such a wicked thing [for that's what it is, not just sowing wild oats or following the times] and sin against God [my holy, loving God]?"

Lord, in temptation's hour, strengthen
me to say no to sin and yes to you. Amen.

WHEN HIS MASTER HEARD THE STORY HIS WIFE TOLD HIM, SAYING,
"THIS IS HOW YOUR SLAVE TREATED ME," HE BURNED WITH ANGER.
JOSEPH'S MASTER TOOK HIM AND PUT HIM IN PRISON. *Genesis 39:19,20*

Imprisoned, Yet Faithful

Can we even imagine Joseph's feelings as the prison doors slammed shut behind him? Now the favored son was labeled a felon with no hope of parole. Yet how much worse if he had been guilty as charged.

But Joseph remained faithful. Soon his positive attitude and actions brought him to the attention of the chief jailer. Eventually it brought him to the position of head trustee in that prison. Again we have to ask, "How did Joseph do it?" He had no way of knowing that the prison had not been chosen by accident. He couldn't see that the Lord had already planned how to open those doors and lead him to the vice presidency of Egypt. He did know, though, that the doors shutting him in could not shut his Lord out. He could see the Lord at his side sustaining his heart through those dark days. See the secret to Joseph's faithfulness? He looked, in the changing circumstances of life, to a faithful God and his reliable promises.

After the funeral, relatives found Grandma's Bible among her possessions. On the inside cover of that well-worn volume was written the following: "Lord, lay any burden upon me, only sustain me. Send me anywhere; only go with me. Sever any ties but that which bind me to your service and to your heart." That elderly believer had found the secret to faithfulness in life. So had Joseph. Pray God, so have I.

Lord, take my hand and lead me with
your faithful promises over life's rough ways. Amen.

I CONSIDER THAT OUR PRESENT SUFFERINGS
ARE NOT WORTH COMPARING WITH THE GLORY
THAT WILL BE REVEALED IN US. *Romans 8:18*

There's No Comparison

In my closet is an old pair of athletic shoes. They're stained green from trips behind the lawnmower. Part of the sole has loosened from the side on one of them. Next to them stands a pair of shiny black shoes. I keep them polished for preaching. I don't want dirty, scuffed up shoes to attract attention when I'm bringing the Word to God's people.

Life in this world is often like that pair of athletic shoes. Repeated problems leave their stain. Suffering rips loose the sole. If I had my choice, I'd never wear those old shoes. I'd prefer a life that is free from problems, pain, and imperfection. But I don't have a choice. A gracious God knows what is good for me. He knows how pain toughens faith's fiber. He knows how sorrow raises my eyes to the only Comforter.

Some may bear sufferings tons heavier than others. God has measured the shoulders and knows how much and how far each one can carry the load. Sometimes the sorrows seem unending, even as they increase in intensity. Should this be the case in my life, God has an answer for me. "Think of the shiny black shoes," he says. Think of how good it will be to walk with my Savior-God in his perfect heaven. There, no more sorrow will flood my eyes with tears. No more pain will cause my spirit to sag. No more temptation will assault my soul. When I'm finally there, all the sufferings of this life will seem like nothing compared to the glory I'll have at Jesus' side.

Lord, through your Word keep my eyes
on the joys waiting for me in heaven. Amen.

> JESUS DID NOT ANSWER A WORD. SO HIS DISCIPLES CAME
> TO HIM AND URGED HIM, "SEND HER AWAY, FOR SHE
> KEEPS CRYING OUT AFTER US." HE ANSWERED, "I WAS
> SENT ONLY TO THE LOST SHEEP OF ISRAEL." *Matthew 15:23,24*

Expect Testing

Jesus seemed to ignore her. The Canaanite woman had a demon-possessed daughter. No doctor could help her. So she turned to Jesus in her hour of need. "Lord," she said, with the eye of faith understanding his heavenly position. "Son of David," she continued, recognizing him as the Savior who came from King David's line. If anyone could help her, Jesus could.

But the Savior just kept on walking as if he didn't care. So she hurried after him, voicing her plea over and over again. Jesus' reply was meant more for her than for his disciples. God's salvation covers Jew and Gentile alike. But Jesus had come to work primarily among the Jews. His disciples in turn would move out among the Gentiles. With his reply the Savior wasn't refusing her. He was testing her faith. Through the testing he wanted to make her faith even stronger.

Ever felt that Jesus wasn't listening or didn't care? My song is "Jesus, still lead on," but when the road is potholed with trouble, it becomes "Jesus, are you leading?" When the road of life is less than well-lit, it's not that Jesus doesn't care. It's his way of making sure that I know he hears and cares. Tomato seedlings that never leave the safety of the greenhouse remain spindly things. Plant them out where the wind and the sun hit them, and watch them toughen and produce. So the Lord has his ways of testing my faith in order to toughen it.

Jesus, when the way is cheerless,
remind me that you still lead the way. Amen.

> HE REPLIED, "IT IS NOT RIGHT TO TAKE THE CHILDREN'S
> BREAD AND TOSS IT TO THEIR DOGS." "YES, LORD," SHE
> SAID, "BUT EVEN THE DOGS EAT THE CRUMBS THAT
> FALL FROM THEIR MASTERS' TABLE." *Matthew 15:26,27*

Keep Trusting

The Canaanite woman wouldn't take no for an answer. Seemingly rebuffed and ignored by the Lord, she kept right on coming. At Jesus' feet she fell, humbly begging, "Lord, help me." His reply about the children's bread sounds tough until we note the word he used for dogs. It meant the little dogs kept in the house as pets by the children. For the woman, that was a ray of hope. Didn't those pets get the crumbs? "Help my daughter," she pleaded in confident trust. "Give me the crumbs that fall from the table, and I'll be satisfied."

It's hard to be satisfied with crumbs. More often, I make hot demands for Jesus' help, even insisting that he cover it with a thick layer of cream. More often, I tell Jesus just exactly what to do for me instead of begging for his help. Know why? It's because I forget what I really am. An old Lenten hymn says it well: "Would he devote that sacred head for such a worm as I?" In God's sight I'm no better than a worm. I'm even worse than a worm for what good can God see in me, a lost and condemned sinner. Only when I throw myself on his mercy, as shown in his full payment for my sins, can I even think of approaching him at all. Nor do I come demanding or dictating but humbly accepting what comes from his merciful hand.

When I come asking for crumbs, I'll receive the whole loaf, as that Canaanite woman did.

Lord, teach me in humbleness and yet
confidence to expect more than crumbs from you. Amen.

JESUS ANSWERED, "WOMAN, YOU HAVE GREAT FAITH!
YOUR REQUEST IS GRANTED." AND HER DAUGHTER
WAS HEALED FROM THAT VERY HOUR. *Matthew 15:28*

Emerge Triumphant

She was well known in the congregation for her simple faith in God and serene calmness in trouble. One day a member facing severe trial visited her. "You have such great faith," the younger woman marveled. "No," replied the older one, "I have a little faith in such a great God."

The Canaanite woman's faith was great. Jesus himself said so. But the Lord in whom she trusted was even greater. He promised that her daughter was healed. When the woman reached home, that's exactly what she found. When Jesus tests faith, it's to strengthen its hold on his great promises, especially the promise of salvation.

Haven't I learned from experience that my great Savior answers faithful prayer? Sometimes he gives me a loaf made of different flour. The "whole wheat" flour of trouble is more nourishing than the cake flour I asked for. Sickness can strengthen more than health and loss more than gain. Loneliness can drive me closer to him than the company of loved ones. Need can make me seek him more than plenty. In all the changing scenes of life, he's there and gives me what I need.

How can I be so sure? Perhaps the better question is, How can I ever doubt? Look at his cross. The cross is the measuring stick of God's abundant mercy. His love drove him to the cross to take care of my spiritual needs. His love won't be stingy when it comes to my earthly needs.

Lord, teach me to cast all my cares on you,
knowing from your cross that you care for me. Amen.

THE APOSTLES SAID TO THE LORD,
"INCREASE OUR FAITH!" *Luke 17:5*

Such A Necessary Prayer

Sometimes, I have to confess, I wonder why Jesus doesn't get sick of me. I sit at his feet. I read his Word. I hear the sermons about him. My Savior hangs bleeding on his cross. My Savior cries out to me, "My blood makes your scarlet sins as white as snow." And I don't thrill as I might to his wondrous message or else don't go home with the rest I need. How I need to join the disciples in their prayer to the Lord, "Increase our faith!"

Sometimes I almost wish I wouldn't wake up to face another day. Yesterday's troubles wait beside my bed for me to hoist them up again. I don't know how much more trouble, sorrow, pain I can stand. I should know that my Savior still invites, "Come to me and I will give you rest." But I wonder. How much I need to join the disciples in their prayer, "Increase our faith!"

Sometimes I get so tired of being tempted. I become so weary of dog paddling in my sinful world. How long can I hold my head above its polluted waters? The devil never goes on vacation but bugs me every day. My sinful heart is like some dried-out grass, just waiting for a passing spark to ignite it. Yes, I know Jesus said through his apostle, "Resist the devil and he will flee from you." Yet I wonder. How much I need to join the disciples in the prayer, "[Lord,] increase our faith!"

Better still, I need to remember how Jesus increases faith. It's through his Word. His promises offer sure pardon for sin, power when tempted, and help in the day of trouble.

Lord, help me increase
my use of your Word. Amen.

THE LAST ENEMY TO BE DESTROYED
IS DEATH. *1 Corinthians 15:26*

It's Worth Waiting For

For Thanksgiving dinner my wife usually makes three kinds of pie—lemon meringue for me, pecan for our son-in-law, and pumpkin for herself. "Why can't we start dinner with pie instead of potatoes?" I like to tease her. But no, I have to wait for dessert till we're all done with the rest.

Death is a far cry from lemon meringue pie. It's hardly a dessert that I can't wait to get to. More likely, it's something I'd go to great lengths to avoid. But come it will, sometimes for the young and always for the old. In a sense, it's the last enemy that I have to face in life.

Notice, though, what Paul says Jesus will do with death. When the world ends, Jesus will wipe out forever that horrible enemy called death. Ever since my first parents fell into sin in Eden's garden, death has had its way. Mortal man has to die. For unbelievers, the moment of death means the plunging of the soul into hell's dungeons where their bodies go also on the Last Day. For believers, it means the ushering of the soul into heaven's bliss to be joined by their perfected bodies on the Last Day. But death there will be until Jesus returns. With his death and resurrection, he has already paid for sin and conquered death. On the Last Day when he returns, he will wipe death out forever. Never again will it rear its ugly head.

That sounds like dessert to me! No wonder the apostle teaches me to pray, "Come, Lord Jesus" (Revelation 22:20).

*Lord Jesus, teach me to
long for your return. Amen.*

> FOR ALL HAVE SINNED AND FALL SHORT OF THE GLORY OF
> GOD, AND ARE JUSTIFIED FREELY BY HIS GRACE THOUGH THE
> REDEMPTION THAT CAME BY CHRIST JESUS. *Romans 3:23,24*

A Perfect Score

Jim and I had gone out to the rod and gun club for some practice. I hadn't used my shotgun in some time so wondered what would happen. To my surprise, and Jim's too, I hit seven out of the first ten clay pigeons. "Not bad, Dad," my son said.

If I could keep some of his commandments, would my heavenly Father say, "Not bad"? Or would it be, "Nowhere near good enough"? My Father has said that he wants me to keep every commandment every single moment of my life. He wants me to be constantly and consistently right on target. When I'm not, when I miss, when my score is zero for ten, he's more than displeased. As a holy God, he has to punish my every sin, not with a bad scorecard but with the eternal fires of hell.

Thank God for his grace that has changed me from the target of his anger to the recipient of his forgiveness. He sent Jesus to do what I couldn't do. His Son took my place on the "firing range" of life to work out a perfect score for me. With his holy life he has kept 10 out of 10 of God's commandments. With his innocent blood, he has paid for my misses in life, erasing my sins from his scorecard as if they've never happened. Because of Jesus, my heavenly Father now looks at me and says, "Perfect, my child."

Lord, hear my humble confession and
blot out all my sins. Make and keep me perfect
in your sight through your Son's redemptive work. Amen.

> WE DID NOT FOLLOW CLEVERLY INVENTED STORIES WHEN WE TOLD
> YOU ABOUT THE POWER AND COMING OF OUR LORD JESUS CHRIST,
> BUT WE WERE EYEWITNESSES OF HIS MAJESTY. *2 Peter 1:16*

Not Just A Story

"That's what you say," replied my neighbor. Visiting in the backyard, the discussion turned to religion. When I told him what the Bible says about Jesus, that's how he responded. Like so many others, he regarded the Bible as only a storybook. Everyone knows that "once upon a time" and "they lived happily ever after" are what stories are made of and not necessarily true.

Peter faced such reaction in his day too. But, by the grace of God, he knew better. He had seen firsthand Jesus' glory on the Mount of Transfiguration. He had witnessed in person Jesus' victory over the grave when the risen Savior appeared to him that first Easter. For him the story of redemption was not just a story but wonderful fact. Of that risen Savior, Peter preached to those around him and even penned his epistles so that I could know Jesus too.

What do I tell my neighbor? I can't argue him into seeing the truths of salvation. The only One who can convince my neighbor is the Holy Spirit. The Savior has promised that he sends his Spirit to work through the Word to conquer unbelief and create faith in the human heart. So I'll try to tell my neighbor again when the opportunity presents itself.

Also I'll live in the Word myself. Before I tell others, I need to be convinced myself. As the Spirit strengthens my faith in the sweetest story ever told, I'll want to share it with everyone I can.

Lord, help me tell the true story
of Jesus and his love to others. Amen.

> GOD EXALTED HIM TO THE HIGHEST PLACE AND GAVE HIM
> THE NAME THAT IS ABOVE EVERY NAME, THAT AT THE NAME
> OF JESUS EVERY KNEE SHOULD BOW, IN HEAVEN AND
> ON EARTH AND UNDER THE EARTH. *Philippians 2:9,10*

Everyone, On Your Knees

Our granddaughter wears knee pads while playing volleyball. They protect her from floor burns and other injury. Watching her play with those kneepads made me think of what Paul once wrote about Jesus.

The apostle wasn't talking about the Jesus who came to earth in all humility to save mankind. Rather, he was looking in wonder at the victorious Savior who had completed the work of the cross. That Jesus now rules powerfully over heaven, earth, and hell. The devils in hell get floor burns kneeling before him. They've lost the battle of the ages, and they know it. The people on earth also kneel before the One who rules over them. They seldom recognize, much less accept, his dominion, but they can't escape it. They need knee pads too, but they don't have them.

The sinless angels in heaven need no knee pads. They kneel before their Lord in joyful awe. So do the believers who have already passed to glory. In perfect bliss, they kneel before the One who has loved and redeemed them. No knee pads for them either.

Nor for me. The name of Jesus is sweet in the believer's ear. Kneeling before my Savior causes me no injury. It brings joy to my heart, humble obedience to my life, and calm trust in his reign.

Lord, before your throne I humbly bow,
for you are Lord of all and my Savior. Amen.

NO ONE HAS EVER SEEN GOD, BUT GOD THE
ONE AND ONLY, WHO IS AT THE FATHER'S
SIDE, HAS MADE HIM KNOWN. *John 1:18*

Better Than A Brochure

I've always wanted to visit Australia. Perhaps it's because that continent is like a last frontier. Last summer I even went to a travel agent. He gave me brochures showing Ayers Rock, the Great Barrier Reef, and the Sydney Opera House. From those brochures I learned much about Australia. What I learned made me even more eager to get there.

In a sense, Jesus is like those travel brochures. He shows me what God is like. God is a spirit without flesh and bones. But, humanly speaking, he certainly has a heart. Jesus came to show me how much God loves sinners. Jesus is God's love walking and talking, dying and rising again to save sinners. Do I want to learn about God's love? Then I need to look at Jesus.

God is also merciful. His heart goes out to the needy, and his power reaches down with help. Again Jesus shows me the Father's heart of mercy. He healed the sick, comforted the sorrowing, befriended the lonely. Do I want to learn about God's compassion? Then I need to look at Jesus.

In fact, Jesus is far better than a travel brochure. Its pictures and words can give me only some ideas about Australia. Jesus gives me a far clearer picture of the God of my salvation. When I see Jesus on the pages of the Word, I see God. What I learn about God from Jesus makes me eager to see him face-to-face in heaven.

*Jesus, let me see your loving face on the pages
of the Word so that I may see the Father. Amen.*

> JESUS REPLIED, "LOVE THE LORD YOUR GOD
> WITH ALL YOUR HEART AND WITH ALL YOUR
> SOUL AND WITH ALL YOUR MIND." *Matthew 22:37*

No Leftovers For Him

I couldn't believe it. Someone brought a half-eaten hot dish to the church potluck. How cheap can a person be? All of us eat leftovers at home. That's part of life. But we don't bring them to serve others. That's why my wife tells me to keep my fingers off the dessert she's made for Bible class.

God doesn't want leftovers either. Notice how emphatic he is. Three times he says "all." He wants *all* my heart, *all* my soul, *all* my mind. That means all of me—period. That's a lot of love, but that's what my God asks of me.

He has a right to ask such love from me. Hasn't he shown total love for me? When he planned my salvation, he didn't go halfway. When his Son came to earth, he didn't stop short of the cross. When his Spirit works faith in my heart, it's not for a day or two. Thank God, his love is complete, giving me his all.

My love for him so often falls short. As hard as I try, I can't keep the fork of my selfishness out of what I offer him. Instead of giving him the main room in my heart, I shove him into the closet. I bring him leftovers when it's all of me he wants. Thank God, he forgives me. His Son's cross assures me of his pardon when my love falls short. His Son's cross also offers me power to work at bringing him all my love.

Lord, through your Word draw me closer
to your cross so that I may love you more. Amen.

> PETER CAME TO JESUS AND ASKED, "LORD, HOW MANY TIMES
> SHALL I FORGIVE MY BROTHER WHEN HE SINS AGAINST ME?
> UP TO SEVEN TIMES?" JESUS ANSWERED, "I TELL YOU, NOT
> SEVEN TIMES, BUT SEVENTY-SEVEN TIMES." *Matthew 18:21,22*

Thank God He Doesn't Keep Track

My wife helped me clean up our workshop in the garage. As we swept up the sawdust from the planer, router, and saw, I couldn't help wondering how many particles there were. Was it a thousand or even closer to a million? No way could we count them. There were just too many.

Sometimes we feel like counting when someone sins against us. A spouse may keep track of her partner's wrongs. A relative may tally up another family member's transgressions on the calculator of his mind. Forgiving once or twice or maybe even seven times takes a lot of doing. It's so much easier to remember and retaliate.

What if God treated me the same way? What if when he saw me coming, he'd groan, "No, not you again." What if when I bring the same old sins to him day after day, he'd hold up his hand and say, "That's it. You've reached your limit." Or what if he'd never forgive me for even a single one of my sins against him?

God's forgiveness has no limits. How could it? On the cross, Jesus paid for all the sins of the whole world. That means mine are covered too. That blessed truth tells me something about forgiving others. I'm to be God-like in my forgiving those who sin against me.

Lord, thank you for forgiving my many sins.
Help me forgive others as you forgave me. Amen.

MANY PEOPLE SPREAD THEIR CLOAKS ON
THE ROAD, WHILE OTHERS SPREAD BRANCHES
THEY HAD CUT IN THE FIELDS. *Mark 11:8*

Red-Carpet Treatment

Some years ago Queen Elizabeth of Great Britain visited the Canadian city in which we were living. When her launch reached the dock of the waterfront park, the city officials rolled out a red carpet for her. That was their way of welcoming this important person.

On Palm Sunday some of Jerusalem's citizens rolled out the so-called red carpet for Jesus. Some carpeted the street with their cloaks. Others cushioned it with branches cut in the fields. We can only speculate how many of them recognized Jesus as the promised Savior. We do know that by Friday many of Jerusalem's inhabitants were calling for his red blood to run on Calvary's cross.

Red-carpet treatment—that's what Jesus deserves from me every day. This King of love, who shed his blood on Calvary's cross, wants my undying adoration. This King of love, who rose from the grave to show his blood had paid for all my sins, has a right to unending royal treatment from me. This King of love, who will one day elevate me to heaven to rule with him in glory, expects me to treat him like my loving ruler constantly.

I'd better not criticize the citizens of Jerusalem for so quickly rolling up the red carpet they had given Jesus. I do the same all too frequently. Much better for me to ask my King to forgive me and to help me keep the red carpet rolled out for him.

Alleluia! Jesus, thank you for coming
in the name of the Lord to save me. Amen.

> YOU SHINE LIKE STARS IN THE UNIVERSE AS
> YOU HOLD OUT THE WORD OF LIFE. *Philippians 2:15,16*

Shining Through

At first glance those windows didn't look like much. We were standing before the famous Notre Dame Cathedral in Paris. The stained-glass windows looked like dirty pieces of glass held together by faded strips of lead. Once we were inside, however, their beauty appeared. Lit by the sun shining through, the windows were alive with magnificent color.

Ever think of believers as stained-glass windows? I'm less than beautiful. The glass in my life is dirtied by the ravages of life. The lead holding the pieces together is even dirtier. But when the Son shines through, I gleam like the brightest star. In the midst of this sin-polluted and sin-darkened world, I'm to be a ray of light. People around me are to notice that I march to a different beat and serve a different master. They are to wonder about my walking with my feet on this earth but my eyes on heaven. And when they ask why, I am to tell them.

It's because of Jesus. He's the Word of life that changes everything. Because of his payment for my sins, I no longer have to live in fear's darkness. Because of his resurrection from the grave, I no longer have to wear a worried frown about my future. Because of his love, I can walk through life with a smile, knowing he takes good care of me.

As a believer I shine with beautiful light. Really, though, it's Christ the Son shining through me.

Shine, Jesus, shine on my
heart and through my life. Amen.

Remember Your Baptism

The congregation I serve purchased a portable defibrillator last month. When someone's heart suddenly stops beating, this machine tries to shock it back to life. Sometimes it brings the "dead" individual back to life. Sometimes it doesn't.

Something far greater occurred at my baptism. My baptism did more than restart a heart that had stopped beating. It actually brought life to a heart hopelessly dead in sin and unbelief. By birth I was a spiritual corpse, having no faith in Jesus and no power to produce such faith. In my baptism the Holy Spirit worked his miracle of creating a new heart within me. Through this means of grace, he made me a sharer in the salvation Christ's death earned for me. By the washing of water with the Word, the Spirit transformed me into an adopted member of God's family.

So what's the date of my baptism? It should be more important to me than my physical birth date. What a day to celebrate each year—the day God in his grace gave me the life that counts! Also, what an incentive to live each day as God's adopted child! When Paul wrote of living a new life, he was referring also to my daily walk as God's child. People who are alive show it. Believers, made alive by the Spirit in Holy Baptism, show it too. Each day my baptism powers me to live more like my Father's holy child.

Lord, thank you for the miracle of Holy Baptism.
Help me use its power to walk with my Savior. Amen.

> THE NEXT DAY JOHN SAW JESUS COMING TOWARD HIM AND SAID, "LOOK, THE LAMB OF GOD, WHO TAKES AWAY THE SIN OF THE WORLD!" *John 1:29*

Weed Killer For Sin

Last year our youngest daughter and her husband bought their first little "nest" from an aged couple. Helping the kids with the neglected yard, we tackled the creeping charley that had taken over the lawn. This weed had grown so thick with such twisted roots that you couldn't pull it out. Even a liberal dose of weed killer didn't take care of it. This summer we'll try Weed-B-Gone and see what it does to that obnoxious weed.

Sin is like creeping charley. It creeps into my life like that first little clump. If I don't root it out, it just keeps spreading. One sin leads to another and another and another. Nothing spreads faster than sin left untended. The final outcome is no grass left, only weeds in the heart, as former believers have learned by experience.

How can I get rid of sin's creeping charley? John reminds me in our verse. Regardless of how strong sin's roots are in my heart or how many sins have spread across my life, God's Lamb takes care of them. On the cross he has already paid for all my sins with his precious blood. That blood is no *maybe* weed killer for my sin. It's the *sure* weed killer. It has already knocked my sins dead. It also serves as the power I need to battle sin as it seeks to reseed itself in my heart.

John said "Look" at this precious Lamb of God. That reminds me not to leave this heavenly weed killer in the container but to use it regularly.

Lord, keep my eyes on Jesus. Amen.

> "I HAVE CALLED YOU FRIENDS, FOR EVERYTHING
> THAT I LEARNED FROM MY FATHER I HAVE
> MADE KNOWN TO YOU." *John 15:15*

Friends Of Jesus

Scripture calls me as a believer by many names. I'm a sheep in the Shepherd's flock, an heir of his heaven, a servant of the Lord. Each name has much meaning for me. But can any be better than the name friend?

Let me be clear right up front as to how this friendship came to be. I had nothing to do with it. With my sinful heart and sinful life, I deserved to be called God's enemy and Satan's slave. Friendship with Jesus was the furthest thing from my mind and from my reach. Till Jesus in his unexplainable love stepped in. How do I explain a love that came seeking someone who wanted nothing to do with him? A love that gave the ultimate on the cross for someone who in no way deserved it? A love that looks at me, a sinner, and chooses me to be his friend? I can't, but I certainly do thank him for it.

As my friend, Jesus has so much to say to me. As I listen to him in Scripture, I hear words of loving forgiveness. "Nothing you have done can ruin our friendship," he assures me as he forgives me. I hear words of loving care. "Nothing you face can rip you loose from our friendship," the Savior comforts me, even as he puts his arm around me. I hear also words of loving assurance. "Not even death can dissolve our friendship," the Savior cheers me when it's time to walk through the valley of the shadow. What a friend I have in Jesus, thanks to his love.

Lord, help me treasure
our friendship every day. Amen.

DO NOT BE ANXIOUS ABOUT ANYTHING, BUT IN EVERYTHING,
BY PRAYER AND PETITION, WITH THANKSGIVING,
PRESENT YOUR REQUESTS TO GOD. *Philippians 4:6*

A Carefree, Not Careless, Life

"God will take care of me," replied the member I was visiting. She had some physical problems but didn't want to hear about going to the doctor. "God surely does take care of you," was my response. "But he uses doctors to do it."

When Paul urges me not to be anxious about anything, he's speaking about sinful worry. He's reminding me that God wants me to care. He wants me to do what I can with life's problems. But when I have done my best, God wants me to leave the rest to him. So I fill my prescriptions. I practice good stewardship. I plan for the future. I put up smoke alarms. And then I place today and tomorrow in God's almighty hands.

I also pray. I know that my loving Father takes care of me, but he wants me to show that I know. My prayers don't alert him to my needs. He sees them long before I do. My prayers are my way of showing that I trust him to supply those needs. My petitions show my confidence that nothing is too big for him to handle. "Lord, I can't, but you can," I whisper as I crawl upon his lap. Even before he supplies my needs, I thank him. Asking and thanking go hand in hand. As a believer I can thank him even as I ask him, because I know he will answer. Behind each of my prayers is the sign of his Son's cross. When he gave his Son as payment for my sins, it was before I ever thought of asking him. That supreme answer to my needs assures me of all his other answers too.

Lord, hear my prayers and wipe away my
worries with the promise of your loving care. Amen.

"I THE LORD DO NOT CHANGE." *Malachi 3:6*

Our Changeless Lord

How quickly the weather can change in a Wisconsin summer. In the morning the sky is clear and the sun shines brightly. By lunchtime the clouds have moved in and a rainstorm is on the way. I don't know if I'd want to be a weather forecaster on TV.

I change too. Every Monday I step on the bathroom scale. Too often, the number has gone up. Every night I go to bed one day older, not knowing how many are left. In some ways I don't change. Every day, though I fight hard, I still fall into sin. The devil has his way with me, and I have to hang my head in repentance. Every day, I need to hear that sweet message of a Savior who wipes away each of my sins. Every day, though the problems facing me may change, I need that familiar promise of a God who is my Rock and my Fortress.

What if the Lord were to change? What if he were to say, "I've changed my mind," when I come asking him for forgiveness? What if he were to say, "You're on your own. Handle your own problems. I'm no longer going to help you"? What if he were to shake his head as I reach for his hand at my death, "I no longer care to walk through the valley of the shadow. Good luck to you"?

But the Lord doesn't change. He says so in our verse. He's always the same, always ready to forgive, always ready to bless and keep. On his unchanging love I can rely all my changing days.

Changeless Lord, help me put my trust
in you and your never-changing promises. Amen.

> "THE FOOLISH ONES TOOK THEIR LAMPS BUT DID
> NOT TAKE ANY OIL WITH THEM. THE WISE, HOWEVER,
> TOOK OIL IN JARS ALONG WITH THEIR LAMPS." *Matthew 25:3,4*

Keep The Oil Handy

"Checks returned for insufficient funds (NSF) will incur a fee of $25" read the bank's policy. That made me think of Jesus' parable about people waiting for his return on the Last Day. He compared them to people standing in night's darkness with burning lamps in their hands. In Jesus' day those may have been poles with oil-drenched rags on top. After about 15 minutes the rags needed more oil and the charred ends needed trimming. The people who brought extra oil for their lamps were the wise ones. Their torches kept on burning.

I don't know when my last day on this world or the last day of this world will come. My Lord has wisely kept that knowledge from me. Could it be that he wants me to live each day as if it were the last? Could it be that he wants me to direct my attention to the more important question of how to be ready when he does come? He doesn't want me to be like a check rejected because of insufficient funds. Hell's fires will be much worse than a $25 penalty if my faith fund is found empty when he returns.

I need regular deposits for my faith, and I know where to get them. In his Word, God offers me rich salvation through the work of his Son, Jesus. Through his Word, God works to strengthen faith in my heart. Through his Word, a gracious Lord works to keep my faith burning and my wick trimmed. Insufficient funds? Not when I draw richly on his Word.

Lord, keep me watching for my Savior's
coming with my faith kept burning by your Word. Amen.

"INDEED, THE VERY HAIRS OF YOUR HEAD
ARE ALL NUMBERED. DON'T BE AFRAID." *Luke 12:7*

Watching Over Every Detail

Yesterday when my wife cut my hair, she remarked that it was getting thinner. I could have told her that. I see three or four hairs in my comb every morning. I suppose that means I no longer have the average 140,000 hairs on my head.

God knows how many hairs I once had and how many I have left. He knows when I lose just one of them. Rather than showing me that God majors in minor things, this fact assures me that he watches over every detail. That's how much he cares about me.

The more he reassures me of this blessed truth, the more I can follow his advice not to be afraid.

When my sins give me alarm, as well they might do, I can look to my gracious Lord. He knows my daily sins. He knows also how sorry I am that I've fallen into them and how much I desire his forgiveness. "Don't be afraid," he tells me. "They've been paid for with my Son's blood." He knows my daily problems, big and little. He knows how old ones get up with me each morning and how new ones come along almost with every day. "Don't be afraid," he tells me. "Cast your cares on me, for I care for you." No facet of my life escapes his notice. No problem is out of his sight.

The hairs in my comb each morning remind me that I have a loving Father watching over every detail in my life. What reason do I have to be afraid?

Lord, forgive me for doubting your loving care.
Help me put my trust in you. Amen.

IN HIS GREAT MERCY [GOD] HAS GIVEN US NEW BIRTH INTO A
LIVING HOPE THROUGH THE RESURRECTION OF JESUS CHRIST FROM
THE DEAD, AND INTO AN INHERITANCE THAT CAN NEVER PERISH,
SPOIL OR FADE—KEPT IN HEAVEN FOR YOU. *1 Peter 1:3,4*

My Savings Bond

Going through the file the other day, I came upon a government savings bond in our daughter's name. One of the ladies' groups at church had given it when she was born. It matures in ten years and keeps on earning as long as you hold it. When she needs it, our daughter can cash it in and receive whatever it's worth.

There's a savings bond in God's file with my name on it. It was placed there when Jesus died and rose again. My name was put on that savings bond when the Holy Spirit brought me to faith in the Savior. It promises me more than a pay out of so and so many dollars. It assures me of an inheritance that nothing can ever wipe out. Peter called it "a living hope" and showed what that hope cost—"the resurrection of Jesus Christ from the dead."

This inheritance is completely God's gift to me. Just as the ladies gave our daughter her savings bond, so God has gifted me with something much more precious. I'm going to live forever in heaven with him. This inheritance is sure because my Savior has paid for it. His blood has covered the cost for my sins. His resurrection is the guarantee that my sins are gone, that my death is conquered, and that his heaven is opened for me. The day is coming when I'll cash in that heavenly savings bond. And it'll supply all I need.

Lord, thank you for preparing heaven for
me and me for heaven through Christ Jesus. Amen.

IN CHRIST WE WHO ARE MANY
FORM ONE BODY, AND EACH MEMBER
BELONGS TO ALL THE OTHERS. *Romans 12:5*

Each An Important Part

My wife and I have gone into woodworking as a hobby. Recently I ordered through the mail a bench top drill press for our small shop. When I put the pieces together, two small parts were missing. One was the chuck, the set of jaws that holds the drill bit. The other was the chuck key that tightens the bit. Both are small parts, but without them the drill press doesn't work.

It made me think of Paul's words about believers. God puts believers together in a location for a purpose. They gather together to hear his life-giving Word. They also work to serve one another and spread that Word. Each one has the same needs for the Savior. And each one has some talent, given by the Lord, to help proclaim the news of the Savior. One may have the gift of preaching. Another the talent of serving on a board or committee. Still another the gift of giving. There are many more gifts, like teaching the children in our homes and Sunday school, encouraging fellow members in their sorrow, witnessing to our neighbors, helping the needy.

What's my God-given talent? It may not be the same as the one my fellow member has. It may not show up obviously in service as some talents do. But it will be missed if I don't use it. Like that drill press, God's people can move forward in and with the Word when all the parts are functioning. Let some talents lie unused and all will feel the impact. So what's my God-given talent? Better still, what am I doing with it to help spread the news of my beautiful Savior?

Lord, show me what talent you have
given me and move me to use it for you. Amen.

"I HAVE TOLD YOU THIS SO THAT MY
JOY MAY BE IN YOU AND THAT YOUR
JOY MAY BE COMPLETE." *John 15:11*

His Majesty In Residence

We were standing before Buckingham Palace in London, waiting for the famous Changing the Guard at the queen's residence. Next to us stood a retired member of the guard. "I don't see the royal standard," he remarked. "What's that?" I asked him. "It's the flag that shows Her Majesty is in residence" was his reply.

My joy as a Christian is like that flag. It shows that the King of kings is at home in my heart and life. When in love my faith tries to walk the way of God's commandments, my Savior says he rejoices. He finds joy in my feeble efforts because they show him his love has worked in my heart.

At the same time my efforts at living a Christian life bring me joy. Some scoff that walking the way of God's commands robs me of joy. But I know better. I know there's great joy to be found in pleasing the heavenly Father, who has done so much for me.

Do I want to keep the "Jesus is in residence" flag flying in my life? There's only one way. It's to be filled with his amazing love for me. Jesus is the King of love because he filled my cross and emptied my tomb. His love brought him from heaven's glory to earth's squalor and even to hell's punishment so that I could be his own and live under him in his kingdom. When his love fills my heart, it shows in my life. The royal standard of joy flies above me every day.

Lord, show me from your Word how great your love for me is. Use that love then to fill my heart with joy and my life with service. Amen.

> WHAT A WRETCHED MAN I AM! WHO WILL RESCUE
> ME FROM THIS BODY OF DEATH? THANKS BE TO GOD—
> THROUGH JESUS CHRIST OUR LORD! *Romans 7:24,25*

Paint Me Just As I Am

In the 1600s, Oliver Cromwell led a revolution against the king of England. The war ended in victory and led to Cromwell becoming Lord Protector of England. When it was time for his portrait to be painted, the anxious artist asked what sort Cromwell wanted. Should it be flattering? Should it be realistic? "Paint me as I am," Cromwell replied, "warts and all."

What would my portrait look like if one were painted? Paul gives me more than a hint in our verse. That portrait would show a "wretched man," one who, even though he tries, is still stuck daily in his sins. My sins are more than warts blotching my skin. They are mortal scars dooming me to death in hell. Who would want a portrait like that? Yet I need such a realistic picture if I'm to appreciate the portrait God in his love paints of me.

What's that portrait like? It shows me as sinless in God's sight. It shows me with a pure and holy life before him. It shows me standing next to my Father in his family. Is such a portrait some artist's flattery, some omitting or painting over of my warts of sin? Or is it realistic? Paul gives me the answer for this question too. He says, "Thanks be to God—through Jesus Christ our Lord!" When God paints with the brush of his love in the Savior, my portrait is perfect. When the Savior covers me with his forgiveness and his perfect life, the warts of sin are all gone and I am beautiful in God's sight. Yes, "thanks be to God—through Jesus Christ our Lord!"

Lord, thank you for making me beautiful
in your sight through my Savior. Amen.

"THIS IS WHAT THE KINGDOM OF GOD IS LIKE. A MAN SCATTERS SEED ON THE GROUND. NIGHT AND DAY, WHETHER HE SLEEPS OR GETS UP, THE SEED SPROUTS AND GROWS, THOUGH HE DOES NOT KNOW HOW." *Mark 4:26,27*

Sow The Good Seed Of God's Word

Consider the tiny seeds in our hands when it's sowing time. They seem dead. There's no movement there, no heartbeat, no outward evidence of any life. But place those seeds in the ground, and before long something happens. They germinate, poke through earth's crust, and reach for the sun. Life comes from those little seeds, though I can't fully explain how. I do know that I have to sow the right kind of seed. If I put pebbles into the ground, I won't get sweet corn. If I want carrots but sow beet seeds, I know what'll happen.

The same is true when I go gardening with God. The church's garden plot is the souls of men. Only one kind of seed works in this plot, God's Word. Of that seed, Peter wrote, "You have been born again, not of perishable seed, but of imperishable, through the living and enduring word of God" (1 Peter 1:23). Of that seed, James also wrote, "He chose to give us birth through the word of truth" (James 1:18). Only God's Word has life in it and can bring life to the souls of mankind.

Some churches have forgotten how important the right kind of seed is. Or could it be that they no longer think the seed of God's Word is effective. By God's grace we still preach salvation, not sociology; redemption, not reform; Christ, not civilization. To do anything less is to invite a garden full of weeds.

Lord, thank you for sowing the right seed
in my heart. Help me sow it in others. Amen.

> "ALL BY ITSELF THE SOIL PRODUCES GRAIN—
> FIRST THE STALK, THEN THE HEAD, THEN
> THE FULL KERNEL IN THE HEAD." *Mark 4:28*

God's Power Makes It Grow

Every gardener can understand this part of Jesus' parable. Once the seed is in the ground, there's nothing more I can do. I can watch the garden but can't make the seed sprout. I can scratch around in the soil covering the seeds but can't make them grow. The best I can do is patiently wait for the seed to do its thing.

Even more so with the miraculous seed of God's Word. I sow, but the Holy Spirit has to cause the sprouting. Just how he does this, I can't fully explain. Nor do I have all the answers I would like. Why the Word germinates in one heart and not in another is a question whose answer I'll receive first in eternity. Why the Word grows and then dies in one heart and not in another is still another question eternity will answer. Why growth is more rapid in some and not in others is a third question. It's enough for now to know that only God's power makes the seed grow.

An elder pastor once told me in my early years in the ministry, "You young fellows want to go right back across the field with the combine after you've just come out with the seeder. Be patient," he went on. "Sow the seed, and trust God's power to make it work. Just sow, sow, and then sow some more." And he added, "Don't forget to give thanks that God has caused his Word to germinate in your heart and grow in your life." Good advice.

*Thank you, God, for working faith in my heart.
Keep me patiently trusting your power to bless the
seed that I sow on the hearts of others. Amen.*

> "AS SOON AS THE GRAIN IS RIPE, HE PUTS THE SICKLE
> TO IT, BECAUSE THE HARVEST HAS COME." *Mark 4:29*

Harvesttime Will Come

In our second parish, I had time for a good-sized garden. One of our favorite moments was picking the first green beans off the plants. The children would go with me into the garden and eat those sweet, crunchy beans almost faster than I could pick them. With delight they said we were out in the garden to "pickle beans" because they couldn't get the words out right.

Harvesttime has to be the best time for any farmer or gardener. In our city society, we miss the joy a farmer has when the grain runs golden in the combine wagon or the corn yellow in the storage bin. Those who garden have a taste of harvest's joy as they pick those green beans.

Imagine the joy in heaven when the Word germinates in a human heart and grows fruit in a believer's life. Not only do the angels rejoice over every sinner brought to Christ, so does my loving God. He, whose power brings life through the Word to a sin-dead heart, finds great joy in such a harvest. That's why his love sent his Son to Calvary's cross and his Spirit to work through the gospel of salvation. He finds joy also as faith grows in a human heart and fruit becomes more abundant. When he sees "love, joy, peace, patience, kindness, goodness, faithfulness, gentleness and self control" blossoming in my life, great is the joy of my heavenly gardener (Galatians 5:22). And when I stand someday with all my fellow believers in the heavenly harvest before his glorious throne, both his joy and mine will be complete.

Lord, cause your Word to spring up and bear
abundant fruit in me and in many others. Amen.

NEVER BE LACKING IN ZEAL, BUT KEEP YOUR
SPIRITUAL FERVOR, SERVING THE LORD. *Romans 12:11*

Letting It Show

When our daughter made the grade school cheerleading team, we were in for it. Every spare moment at home, she was practicing the cheers and the chants. I couldn't help but marvel at her enthusiasm. Then came the games. She and her team members stirred up the crowd with their spirited efforts. Just watching them made me tired.

As a believer I'm to be a cheerleader for the Lord and his cause. The apostle reminds me of what that involves in our verse. He urges me "never be lacking in zeal." In the original he was more emphatic. "As regards zeal—not slow," he wrote. I'm never to run out of steam in my zeal for getting the good news out about my Savior. "But keep your spiritual fervor," Paul continues. Again, in the Greek he wrote, "As regards the spirit, fervent." That word *fervent* means to "boil or seethe." Like the boiling water in which I cook pasta, I'm to bubble over with enthusiasm in my life for the Lord. "Serving the Lord," he concludes. The word really means "slaving for the Lord." Like a slave, I belong, body and soul, to my Savior. But unlike a slave, I serve him out of gratitude, not fear.

Sounds like my Savior expects enthusiasm from me. He desires action and diligence, something like I saw in those grade school cheerleaders. He even provides the power for such a response. How can I refuse to cheer for him who went to the cross and gave his all for me?

*Lord, lead me in showing
forth your praises all my life. Amen.*

> "THE ETERNAL GOD IS YOUR REFUGE, AND UNDERNEATH ARE THE EVERLASTING ARMS." *Deuteronomy 33:27*

His Arms Hold Me

Does God have arms? Isn't he a spirit without flesh and bones? Of course, but sometimes the Bible speaks in terms that help me understand. It uses word pictures so I can know God better—like saying that God has "arms." That word rings a bell. When I was sick as a child, how comforting to have my mother hold me in her arms! When I faced some problem, how reassuring to have my dad's strong arms to help me! When I returned from some mission trip overseas, how good to have my wife's arms around me again!

Sometimes those human arms may not be there for me. I may be miles from loved ones. I may hesitate to tell them my troubles. I may even fear their arms can't help me or hold me up in my needs.

How different with God's arms. Moses reminds me God's arms are "everlasting." God's arms are so strong that they can hold me in any storm. They are so loving that I can trust them to be there for me. They are everlastingly underneath me, holding me forever and ever. When I need them, I can count on them. When I don't see them, they're still there.

Am I sure? Looking at his Son's arms stretched out on Calvary's cross ought to reassure me. Because of Jesus, God wraps his forgiving arms around me. In his love he'll also hold me safely in all the other dangers in life.

Lord, keep me safe in
your arms forever. Amen.

GOD IS FAITHFUL; HE WILL NOT LET YOU BE TEMPTED BEYOND WHAT YOU CAN BEAR. BUT WHEN YOU ARE TEMPTED, HE WILL ALSO PROVIDE A WAY OUT SO THAT YOU CAN STAND UP UNDER IT. *1 Corinthians 10:13*

My Escape Ramp

"Truck Escape Ramp—One Mile" read the sign. We were traveling in the beautiful mountains of Colorado. Coming down one steep grade, we saw this sign. One mile down the road was the ramp itself, a steep upgrade with soft sand. Any trucker whose brakes were giving him trouble could steer onto that ramp and escape disaster.

In my travels through life, God also provides escape ramps for me. When I'm picking up speed down temptation's slope, God doesn't want me to end up a wreck at the bottom. When life's brakes are heating up on trouble's downhill run, God doesn't want me to become another highway statistic. He wants me to turn onto his off ramp and return cooled down to the highway.

What are the escape ramps God provides for my travels? His promises, of course. In the day of trouble, he reminds me, "The God of all grace, who called you to his eternal glory in Christ, after you have suffered a little while, will himself restore you and make you strong, firm and steadfast" (1 Peter 5:10). In the day of temptation, he urges me, "Put on the full armor of God so that you can take your stand against the devil's schemes" (Ephesians 6:11). In the day when sin has overwhelmed me, he invites me, "Though your sins are like scarlet, they shall be as white as snow" (Isaiah 1:18). Like some trucker in trouble, I'd be foolish not to use God's escape ramps.

Lord, you know my needs.
Help me remember your promises. Amen.

> LIVE A LIFE OF LOVE, JUST AS CHRIST LOVED US
> AND GAVE HIMSELF UP FOR US AS A FRAGRANT
> OFFERING AND SACRIFICE TO GOD. *Ephesians 5:2*

So Sweet Smelling

We live in a little ranch style house, built with an open concept. The kitchen, family room, and dining room blend into one another without walls. It makes our house seem spacious. It also brings problems—as when my wife fries fish or onions. The smell penetrates into all the rooms. So we light a candle. My wife's favorite scent is vanilla. Once lit, its fragrance spreads nicely.

I don't often think about Christ's sacrifice on Calvary's cross being like a sweet fragrance. More likely I view it like the acrid smell of burnt onions or garlic. His suffering was so painful; his death so gruesome. But to my loving God, the smell from Calvary is far better than any vanilla candle. It speaks of Jesus' willingness to carry out his Father's plan of salvation. It speaks of payment for all the sins of the whole world. It speaks of God's holiness being satisfied by his love. From Jesus' cross radiates the wonderful fragrance of God's saving love.

When we sit in our family room after the candle has been burning for a while, we take on some of its fragrance. The vanilla smell clings to our clothing. Something like that happens when I stand before my Savior's cross. His sweet smelling love goes with me into my daily life. True, my love is but a faint reflection of his love. Yet it's there. Because Jesus loves me, I can live in love toward those around me—but only as I absorb the sweet smell of his love.

Lord, the Savior's work of salvation
smells sweet, not only to you but to me too.
Help me carry its sweetness out into the world. Amen.

I AM STILL CONFIDENT OF THIS; I WILL SEE THE
GOODNESS OF THE LORD IN THE LAND OF THE LIVING.
WAIT FOR THE LORD; BE STRONG AND TAKE HEART
AND WAIT FOR THE LORD. *Psalm 27:13,14*

Advice For Weary Warriors

Sometimes Christians can get tired of fighting the good fight. Life grinds them down, taking the sharp edge from their faith. How long and how hard can one keep pushing in the war of life? "What would you tell a member who's ready to give up?" I would ask a seminary student sent to our congregation for field training. In answer, I would point him to our verses.

David's first answer is a long-range one. He talks about the "land of the living," or more precisely "the land of life." He speaks about being able to "see" in that land. The word *see* means to "gaze upon something with delight." And the delightful object in his sight? "The goodness of the LORD," he says. Get the picture? In those days when my heart no longer feels like beating and I'm more than ready to throw in the towel, David points me to heaven. That's the land of life—wondrous life that never ends. There only God's goodness exists. All the pain and problems of this life are totally gone. "Take the long-range view," David urges me.

David's second answer is for the here and now. "Wait for the Lord," he writes, not once but twice. So strongly does he feel about this advice. When my loving God puts his shoulders under the load with me, I can walk on. When my powerful Lord fights next to me, I can keep swinging. When my God seems to delay his help or hold back his strength, I need to wait for him. He will come and help, just as he came in the fullness of time and put his Son on Calvary's cross for me.

*Lord, I am weak and weary. Fill me with
your strength and surround me with your love. Amen.*

WHEN I CONSIDER YOUR HEAVENS, THE WORK OF YOUR FINGERS,
THE MOON AND THE STARS WHICH YOU HAVE SET IN PLACE,
WHAT IS MAN THAT YOU ARE MINDFUL OF HIM? *Psalm 8:3*

So Small And Yet So Dear

One winter night the sky was so clear that we could see more stars than usual shining in the heavens. Astronomers report that about three thousand stars are visible to the naked eye. If we use modern telescopes, the number rises to 30 billion. And this count is only what man has discovered so far.

How many stars did the Creator make? I'll never know. Yet he knows each one of them. Those stars are the work of his fingers. All the heavenly bodies were like so much finger work for God. He created them so easily and just as easily takes care of them. How do I rate when compared to those magnificent stars? Some might reply, "Small and insignificant." To many, man seems like a small drop in the ocean or a single grain of sand on the beach compared to the vast universe. Humanly speaking, that assessment is accurate.

Now listen to the Lord. He reminds me that I am the most important part of his creation. He intended me to walk at his side in perfect fellowship forever. When sin wrenched me from his side, he didn't just shake his head and say, "Too bad. So sad." Instead, he came down to earth to reclaim me. He wrapped himself in my skin, took up the burden of my sin, took it to the cross, took it away forever. His love for me made it possible for me to be his dear child and heir of his heaven. While I wait for heaven, he takes care of me day by day, even more so than he does those stars. I'm so small when compared to the stars but so dear because of God's love.

Lord, thank you for your love that raises
me above the stars and readies me for heaven. Amen.

For God, who said, "Let light shine out of darkness," made his light shine in our hearts to give us the light of the knowledge of the glory of God in the face of Christ. *2 Corinthians 4:6*

Lord, Shine In My Heart

Last night my wife sort of scolded me. When we get up from our recliners to head to bed, I'm usually ahead of her. She uses her eye medicine from the fridge and then follows. On my way to the bedroom last night I forgot and turned off the family room light on her. "Do you know how dark it is and how hard to make my way around the furniture?" she chided.

Sin's darkness is far denser. Unbelief's fog is far more impenetrable. I'd still be stumbling down the sin-darkened slope to hell if it weren't for God's grace. With the power of his gospel, he lights up my dark heart. He dispels unbelief's darkness and does away with sin's fog. Now glorious light floods my heart. I know Jesus as the Light of the world. I see his cross as the beacon lighting the road to heaven. I follow his Word as the bright light for my path in this world. God's marvelous light of salvation shines all the way ahead of me to heaven.

Do I pause often enough to thank God for bringing his light in Christ to me? Many a morning I wake up to the light God created in this world and forget to thank him for it. Let that not be true of the light he has created in my heart. My wife rightly scolded me when I turned off the family room light on her. Let God never have to ask why I forget to thank him for the light he turned on for me.

Lord, how marvelously you lit up the world at creation.
Thank you even more for marvelously lighting up my heart
with the light of salvation. Keep me walking in your light. Amen.

> THEY GAVE THEMSELVES FIRST TO THE
> LORD AND THEN TO US IN KEEPING
> WITH GOD'S WILL. *2 Corinthians 8:5*

My Heart Or My Money?

Last Sunday in church I heard a familiar question. A young family sat down in the bench behind us. A moment later the mother whispered to her little boy, "Do you have your church money?"

Money for church is important. Who wants to sit in an unheated or unclean building? What would we do without a pastor in the pulpit or teachers in our classrooms? How would missionaries ever be sent to foreign lands?

Church money was important in Paul's day too. He took up a collection for the needy Christians in Jerusalem. From believers in Macedonia had come an offering more liberal than the apostle had thought possible for them. But Paul knew why they had sent such an offering to him. It was because they had first given themselves to the Lord. They gave, even out of their need, to the Lord who had given his all to meet their needs.

Why do I give money for church? The answer's simple. Look at what God has given me. Not only life in a beautiful world but eternal life in a far more beautiful heaven are gifts from his hand. Christ's birth, Christ's bloodshed, Christ's burial, Christ's breaking the bonds of his and my grave, Christ's building the free road to heaven—all this God has given me without any merit or worthiness on my part. How can I help loving him who first and so well loved me? Money for church? Yes. But first my heart, my soul, my life, my all for the One who gave himself for me.

Lord, take my heart and then my money. Amen.

"MY SHEEP LISTEN TO MY VOICE; I KNOW
THEM, AND THEY FOLLOW ME." *John 10:27*

How Good
To Know My Shepherd!

"What do people do who don't have Jesus?" asked a grief-stricken husband
who had just lost his mate. A similar question came from a Christian
before surgery and from a penitent sinner sitting in my study. Let's turn
that question around. Let's ask what it means for me to know Jesus.

Before I can talk about my knowing Jesus, I have to thank him for
knowing me. "I know them," Jesus said of his sheep. He's telling me that
I'm not just one among many who make up his flock. He knows me, my
name, my needs, my sins. He knows all about the times each day I drift
away from him, disregard his words, despise his love. He knows how
headstrong I can be in my sins. How wavering in the battle of Christian
life. How foolish if left to my self. He also sees every disappointment
that burdens me. He feels every pain that afflicts me. He's aware of every
trouble that weakens me. All this he knows, and with all this, he will help
me. That's what his words "I know [my sheep]" assure me.

But the question today is, Do I know the Shepherd? Thank God's grace,
I can answer, "Yes." He's made me Jesus' sheep by gifting me with faith.
Now, when sin dirties my daily life, I know the Shepherd whose blood
cleanses me. When trouble causes bitter tears, I know the Shepherd who
whispers in faith's ear, "Never fear, I am near." When life's losses knock
me for a loop, I have a Shepherd who cradles me close to his caring
heart. How good it feels to nestle down in my loving Shepherd's arms
and to say with God-given faith, "He knows me and I know him!"

Please, Shepherd of your tender sheep,
hold me tightly in your loving arms. Amen.

"My sheep listen to my voice; I know them, and they follow me." *John 10:27*

How Good To Listen To My Shepherd!

Those in the know tell us that although sheep are among the most stupid of animals, they do have one redeeming feature. They know their shepherd's voice. No imposter can lure them away. They follow only their own shepherd.

In my 21st-century world, all kinds of voices clamor for my attention. Pleasure sings with suggestive voice, "Everybody's doing it. Have some fun. It can't hurt you. Times have changed, you know." "Follow me," beckons another false shepherd, the one named possessions. In my modern world, right and wrong have been blurred, if not buried under, by the mad rush to get as much as you can, in any way that you can, from anyone that you can. Even in the area of religion, false shepherds call invitingly. "Follow me," they promise, "and I'll give you prosperity in your life, answers to your prayers, a short-changed sort of heaven that never flies above this earth."

But the question today is, Do I listen to the Shepherd? Thank God's grace, I can answer, "Yes." Quietly, without splash or splendor, he called me at the baptismal font, made me his lamb, and lifted me up in his arms. Quietly, yet sweetly and systematically, he speaks to me through his Word as I have opportunity to hear it, read it, ponder it. In his Holy Supper, he speaks to me again, softly, urgently, of sins forgiven and faith strengthened. Oh, how he speaks to me! And I who am his sheep, what do I do? He has told me, "My sheep listen to my voice." How good it is to hear his voice and to listen to his love as revealed in his words!

Lord, open my heart to hear as my
Shepherd speaks to me through his Word. Amen.

"MY SHEEP LISTEN TO MY VOICE; I KNOW
THEM, AND THEY FOLLOW ME." *John 10:27*

How Good
To Follow My Shepherd!

The shepherd calls. The sheep raise their heads and perk up their ears. Then they drop those heads back down to their grazing. No, that's not how it works. Instead, the sheep fall in behind their shepherd and follow wherever he leads.

Those who love the Good Shepherd understand the need for such following. Knowing the Shepherd and listening to his voice are inward things, actions centered invisibly in the heart. Following the Shepherd is the outward result that shows in the Monday through Sunday affairs of daily life. His sheep don't just sing, "Savior, lead." They also add, "We follow you." His sheep know that what they think, what they say, what they do is the final test as to whether they truly have the Shepherd.

But the question today is, Do I follow the Shepherd? Thank God's grace, I can answer, "Yes." To that answer I quickly add my prayer, "Good Shepherd, help me. Help me accept your Word whether I can understand it or not. Help me follow it whether it agrees with my wishes and the world's fancy or not. Help me to make your life my pattern and to cut as close to that pattern as possible. Help me to go only where you would go, to think only as you would think, and to do only as you would do. Even when you lead through thorny ways of trouble or across deserts of sorrow, help me follow with as little hesitation and complaint as possible. Through all the changing scenes of life, let me confidently follow as one who has the Shepherd.

Savior, fill me with trust in your leading
and with power to follow your directions. Amen.

> "I GIVE THEM ETERNAL LIFE, AND THEY
> SHALL NEVER PERISH; NO ONE CAN SNATCH
> THEM OUT OF MY HAND." *John 10:28*

How Good
To Be Safe In My Shepherd!

At the Memorial Day celebration, a tug-of-war was a favorite feature. Strong men lined up for the contest on each end of the rope. With all their might and muscle, they tugged. Slowly the flag in the middle moved in one direction, then back in the other. Finally the stronger team prevailed and the shout of victory went up.

There's a lot of tugging going on in my life. The muscles of the devil, the world, and my flesh aren't to be sneezed at. With all their might, they pull away, trying to inch me over the finish line into hell.

But on the other end of the rope is my Shepherd. Safely cradled in his arm, I can watch as the tug-of-war over my soul goes on. I know who will win. My Shepherd will keep me safe. He says of his sheep, "I give them eternal life." Further he promises, "They shall never perish." Even more, he asserts, "No one can snatch them out of my hand." He can make such promises because he's the author of the eternal life he grants. His blood bought it. His resurrection guaranteed it. His grace gave me the faith to believe it. In his arms he keeps me safe till he carries me home to his heaven. How good it is to sing, "Who so happy as I am, Even now the shepherd's lamb? And when my short life is ended, By his angel hosts attended, He shall fold me to his breast, There within his arms to rest" (CW 432:3).

Lord, hold me close so I never have to ask,
"What do people do without the Shepherd?" Amen.

> HE ANOINTED US, SET HIS SEAL OF OWNERSHIP ON US,
> AND PUT HIS SPIRIT IN OUR HEARTS AS A DEPOSIT,
> GUARANTEEING WHAT IS TO COME. *2 Corinthians 1:21,22*

A Foolproof Guarantee

Have you ever been "burned" by a guarantee? I bought a used car with a 60-day warranty. Sure enough, the brakes went out after 40 days. But the dealer wouldn't cover the cost because of some fine print in the warranty. That guarantee wasn't worth the paper it was printed on.

Notice the guarantee Paul says we have from God? "He anointed us," Paul writes. In the Old Testament God's prophets, priests, and kings were anointed as they began their work. The anointing showed that God had separated them for his service. In his grace, God has set me aside to be his beloved child and heir of his heaven. "He set his seal of ownership on us," Paul continues. That seal tells me that I am his and tells others to keep their hands off. He "put his Spirit into our hearts as a deposit," Paul further states. Like a down payment, his Spirit goes with me, assuring me that I belong to God and that he will claim me for heaven.

I am reminded of my baptism. Through that miracle, God's Spirit created faith in me. Like an anointing, that sacrament set me aside as someone special in God's eyes. At my baptism God put on me his seal—his Son's cross with its blessed assurance that Christ the crucified has redeemed me. At that moment, the Spirit also took up his dwelling in my heart, sweeping my heart clean of sin and filling it with faith. With these actions of his grace, God promises that he will continue the good work he has begun in me until he takes me home to heaven. What a foolproof guarantee—one on which I can pin my trust!

Lord, lead me to trust you and your
foolproof promises as I look forward to heaven. Amen.

> ONCE MADE PERFECT, [JESUS] BECAME
> THE SOURCE OF ETERNAL SALVATION
> FOR ALL WHO OBEY HIM. *Hebrews 5:9*

The Best Source Of All

We were watching the milking contest at the state fair. Behind us a youngster piped up excitedly, "Look, momma, milk comes from cows." What an eye opener! The little one had learned that the milk on his cereal and in his ice cream came not from waxed containers but from cows.

From cows comes milk. From Jesus, and Jesus only, comes eternal salvation. That's what the words "Once made perfect" point out. That expression literally means "having reached his goal." Earlier the author had told what that goal was for Jesus. It included the cross with its pain-filled payment for my sins. Also the tomb first filled with my Savior's lifeless body and then emptied because he was no longer dead. And the throne to which he ascended with his mission of salvation completed. No more needs to be done. The Savior has done it. Now he offers it to me.

"For all who obey him," the author goes on. Let Scripture itself explain his words. In 1 John 3:22,23, I'm told, "We obey his commands and do what pleases him. And this is *his command: to believe in the name of his Son, Jesus Christ.*" Faith is the obedience God in his grace works in me through his Word and the sacraments. My faith in Jesus as the only Savior is God's gift to me. It's the hand he has given me to take hold of Jesus and his eternal salvation. Both cows and Jesus are sources of something good. But Jesus is the best source of all. From him comes my eternal salvation.

Lord, thank you for sending your Son to save
me and for giving me faith to believe in him. Amen.

> HE WHO HAS THE SON HAS LIFE; HE
> WHO DOES NOT HAVE THE SON OF
> GOD DOES NOT HAVE LIFE. *1 John 5:12*

Which Direction?

The sign indicated we were standing at the Continental Divide. From this spot in the Rocky Mountains the waters separate, some flowing east into the Mississippi, the others flowing west into the Pacific Ocean. They must flow either east or west.

John in our verse speaks also of a great divide. One side leads to hell. On that horrible road are all who do not have the Son of God. Unbelievers walk and talk in this world but do not really have the life that counts. They are only animated corpses, ahead of whom waits the never-ending death of hell. People don't like to hear of hell. But that place of outer darkness and fiery torment is the sure destination for those who are dead in unbelief and sin.

Much rather would I hear about those on the other side. Those who have faith in Christ Jesus have the life that counts. Through faith they live in the joy of salvation already on this earth. When they leave this earth, they enter the never-ending joy of life in heaven at their Savior's side.

Only two directions—either to life or to death, either to heaven or to hell—one for a believer, the other for an unbeliever. And not just a believer in something or anything but a believer in Christ as the one and only Savior. Thank God for the blessed gift of faith. Thank God that I'm going in the right direction.

Please, Lord, keep me in faith in
Jesus so that heaven is my home. Amen.

> I RESOLVED TO KNOW NOTHING WHILE
> I WAS WITH YOU EXCEPT JESUS CHRIST
> AND HIM CRUCIFIED. *1 Corinthians 2:2*

At The Top Of The List

Somewhere I read the results of a survey asking people to list the most important events in history. They gave first place to the discovery of America by Christopher Columbus. Second place went to Gutenberg's invention of the printing press. Way down in 14th place, tied with the flight of the Wright brothers and the discovery of the X ray, was the crucifixion of Jesus Christ.

I very much disagree! So did the apostle Paul. Nothing was more important for him than Christ's crucifixion. Was he correct? Stop and consider that all the other events brought changes only for life in this world. They were important, and I still benefit from them. But Christ's death on the cross far surpasses them in benefit. His payment for sin frees me from sin's guilt. I can lie down in peace each night, knowing I am right with God. His crucifixion also frees me for God's service. I can rise up each morning to follow my Lord in daily life. And Christ's death guarantees that when my evening and mornings end, I'll be at home with my Savior in his heaven.

I won't need any airplanes in heaven because heaven will be my final destination. No X rays will be necessary because no sickness will be there. Though I enjoy reading books now, in heaven praising the Lord will be my joy. Nor in heaven will I need the continent Columbus stumbled upon. But I do need the Savior's death and resurrection as the only way to get there. Doesn't that make Christ's crucifixion the most important event in the world?

*Lord, let me never stop marveling at the
beautiful truth that Jesus was crucified for me. Amen.*

> PUT ON THE FULL ARMOR OF GOD
> SO THAT YOU CAN TAKE YOUR STAND
> AGAINST THE DEVIL'S SCHEMES. *Ephesians 6:11*

Well Equipped For Battle

No soldier wants to go into battle with little or no equipment. Our country spends thousands of dollars outfitting each soldier for battle. Among the items issued are body armor, a strong helmet, night-vision goggles, and up-to-date weapons.

As a Christian I'm engaged in an ongoing war. Satan never stops attacking me. His schemes can be so clever that I don't always recognize that I'm under attack. He can make sin look so inviting that I can hardly resist. And he knows exactly what my weak points are. How am I going to stand up against such a clever opponent?

I need the body armor of God's Word if I'm to win the victory. When God's strong promises surround me, the devil's bullets may bruise but can't penetrate. I need the helmet of salvation if I'm to stay standing when the devil aims his weapon at me. How can Satan accuse me of sin when Jesus has paid for them all? I need the night goggles of God's will if I'm to scope out the enemy. How can Satan trick me when I know God's commandments? I need the weapon of God's Word if I'm to beat off the devil. Nothing sends the devil scurrying faster than those simple words "It is written." Above all, I need the Savior when I fail in battle so that my wounds won't be fatal. Also, I can't forget my need for ongoing training. The best equipment does little good if I don't know how to use it. I need to be in God's Word if I'm to win in this war.

Lord, draw me into your Word for sin's
pardon and for power in the battle against sin. Amen.

> "STORE UP FOR YOURSELVES TREASURES IN HEAVEN,
> WHERE MOTH AND RUST DO NOT DESTROY, AND
> WHERE THIEVES DO NOT BREAK IN AND STEAL." *Matthew 6:20*

How Much Can I Get? Or How Much Can I Keep?

"Wanted," a humorous ad in a farm magazine read, "marriageable lady with tractor. Please send picture of tractor." I may chuckle at that bit of humor. But am I not often like that? I get my values mixed up. I'm more concerned about how much I can get instead of how much can I keep. This Labor Day week it might be beneficial for me to reexamine my priorities in life.

Of course, I need earth's treasures. Without money in the checking account, how would I buy groceries, make the mortgage payment, and pay the utility bills? So it's off to work I go, using the talents God has given me to acquire what I need for daily life. Sometimes I forget why I labor. I act as if the world's things are the only thing. I let possessions possess me rather than just using them as I pass through this life. Then when moth and rust in modern dress make their attack, I lose sleep. I worry about interest rates, inflation's rise, job security. I spend my energy trying to hang on to what I have or in getting more. How much I can get becomes the driving force in life.

So it's time to reevaluate—time to remember that no Fort Knox can contain the gold found at the foot of the cross. No billions can buy the divine peace found in my forgiveness. The whole world packed into all the Brinks and Wells Fargo armored trucks ever built isn't rich enough even to stand near the treasures I have in Jesus. That treasure is so great it took the blood of God's own Son to purchase it for me. That's the treasure a gracious God wants me to keep.

Lord, help me examine my priorities in life.
Make me rich with the treasure of salvation. Amen.

> JUST AS YOU RECEIVED CHRIST JESUS AS LORD, CONTINUE
> TO LIVE IN HIM, ROOTED AND BUILT UP IN HIM, STRENGTHENED
> IN THE FAITH AS YOU WERE TAUGHT. *Colossians 2:6,7*

Keep Your Roots Deep

Two young boys lived side by side in a little town. Their parents' gardens were also side by side and a source of competition. One morning Fred noticed that Cal's father's plants were growing faster than his father's. So Fred pulled his father's plants up a bit. The next morning he pulled them up still more. The third morning those plants were hanging their heads. Fred had pulled their roots loose from the nourishing soil.

The moral of the story is easy. When the Spirit brought me to faith, I was like the plant that started growing in Fred's garden. If I'm to grow stronger in Christian faith and life, I need to stay rooted in Christ and his Word. God's Word, with its central message of Jesus' payment for my sins, is the only soil in which faith can germinate and grow. Rooted in such soil I'll know the truths of salvation. I'll be powered by the Spirit. I'll yield more and more fruit of Christian living.

If my roots are disturbed, I'll also be like that plant in the garden. My faith will hang its head. Eventually it'll be dead like some dried up plant uprooted in the garden. The devil knows this and does his best to tug on my roots. I also know this and will do my best to keep my roots down deep in Christ's Word. Makes my church attendance more than just a habit, doesn't it? Weekend worship is putting-down-the-roots time. Makes my home devotions more than just a chore, doesn't it? Daily use of God's nourishing Word is also putting-down-the-roots time. Without the good soil of God's Word, there's no root of faith and no fruit of Christian living.

*Lord, keep my faith deeply rooted in your
Word so that it may grow and produce. Amen.*

> "THE LORD IS MY STRENGTH AND MY SONG;
> HE HAS BECOME MY SALVATION. HE IS MY
> GOD, AND I WILL PRAISE HIM." *Exodus 15:2*

He Is My Savior

"Give it to me; it's mine," shouted our granddaughter. Her older sister was playing with her Christmas gift, the electronic game we had given her. And she wanted it back. *Mine* is a word that often creeps into my vocabulary. Sometimes it's a raw reminder of my selfishness. Other times it indicates my proper concern for what is dear to me.

Standing on the shores of the Red Sea, Moses spoke of "my God." Israel's leader had just seen the Egyptian troops swallowed up by rushing waters. He had just witnessed the Lord's mighty deliverance of his chosen people. Wouldn't you think Moses would have said, "our God"? Yet it's "my God," and properly so. To the best of my knowledge, this is the first time Scripture records those words "my God." And it does so in connection with "salvation" or deliverance.

God has done more for me than rescue me from enemies that chase me. He has saved me from my sins. The waves of hell's punishment were ready to wash over me, but his Son took my place. Now ahead of me waits the peaceful shore of heaven. That's *my* song. The Lord is *my* God. He is *my* strength and *my* salvation.

First it's with that pronoun "*my* salvation." Then I can tell others about *our* salvation. First it's God's gift to *me*. Then I'll want to make it *our* gift, as I share it with those around me.

*Lord, thank you for saving me. In the joy of
my salvation, help me share you with others. Amen.*

"YOU ARE TO GIVE HIM THE NAME
JESUS, BECAUSE HE WILL SAVE HIS
PEOPLE FROM THEIR SINS." *Matthew 1:21*

His Name Fits

After all the baptisms I've officiated at, I've given up wondering how people pick names for their children. Do they pick the name of a relative like a grandparent? Do they choose a name because they like the way it sounds? Is it because they hope the name will fit their child? With our long last name, my wife and I looked for short first names like Beth, Mark, James, and Anne. That way their names would at least fit on a driver's license or a credit card receipt.

God picked the name for his Son. It was the same as Joshua in the Old Testament. And it had special meaning—"God saves." Best of all, the name God chose fit exactly. The miracle child conceived by the Holy Spirit and born of the virgin Mary is the Savior of sinners. The Old Testament hero Joshua had led God's people to the promised land of Canaan. God's Son, the greater Joshua, came to lead God's people to the promised land of heaven. Jesus came to be a hero in the greatest battle of all, the battle against sin and Satan. When he had finished, Satan lay in the dust of defeat and heaven was open in victory.

For me the name of Jesus is above all other names. By God's grace I know "there is no other name under heaven given to men by which we must be saved" (Acts 4:12). For me the name of Jesus is the power for my prayers. When I stand before the heavenly Father, he will give me whatever I ask in Jesus' name (John 15:16). Thank God, I can call him *my* Jesus.

Lord, may it ever be Jesus—
name of wondrous love—my Savior and my King. Amen.

> JESUS LOVED MARTHA AND HER SISTER AND LAZARUS.
> YET WHEN HE HEARD THAT LAZARUS WAS SICK,
> HE STAYED WHERE HE WAS TWO MORE DAYS. *John 11:5,6*

Handled With Care
By His Great Love

"HANDLE WITH CARE" was stenciled on both sides of the box. But somewhere along the line someone couldn't read or didn't care. Looking at the dented container and damaged contents, I had to wonder, "You call that handled with care?" The two sisters at Bethany had the same question. Why didn't Jesus come when they told them about their sick brother? Why did he wait till Lazarus was in the grave? Didn't Jesus love them? Weeping at their brother's graveside, they must have asked, "You call that handled with care?"

Haven't I asked that same question? In life's tears and losses, when this has gone stale and that has gone sour, it's so easy for me to complain. Behind my complaint lies a deeper question, Does Jesus love me? If he loves me the way he says he does and the way I thought he did, why didn't he handle me with care? At such times, I need to recall what finally happened at Bethany. At the grave of his dear friend, Jesus showed his love plainly and powerfully. "Lazarus, come out!" his love shouted. No longer could Mary and Martha question Jesus' love. Their brother, alive again, was a visible reminder that the Savior always handles his own with loving care.

When I question the Savior's loving care of me, I can go to no better place than to another grave. When I see my Savior being laid lifeless in a borrowed tomb, I know how much he cares. When I see him rise from that tomb, I know what his love has prepared for me. Handled with care? "Always," comes back the answer. His great love won't allow him to do anything else.

Lord, forgive me for when I wonder. Let
your cross and grave assure me of your care. Amen.

> SO THE SISTERS SENT WORD TO JESUS, "LORD, THE ONE
> YOU LOVE IS SICK." WHEN HE HEARD THIS, JESUS SAID,
> "THIS SICKNESS WILL NOT END IN DEATH." *John 11:3,4*

Handled With Care
With His Great Power

The sisters' prayer was a model one. They didn't tell Jesus what to do. They simply told him their problem. They didn't lay claim to an answer. Instead, they relied on his love. Then they waited for his help. And waited. Jesus' answer, "This sickness will not end in death," seemed to promise help. But those sisters must have wondered as they carried their brother to his grave.

Don't I wonder too when it happens to me? So often, unlike those sisters, my prayers are far from model ones. So often I use prayer to dictate man-made solutions to Jesus instead of asking for God-made solutions for me. At times I use prayer like aspirin, like taking two prayers and expecting my headache to disappear quickly and completely. When the Savior doesn't seem to answer, I'm tempted to shrug my shoulders and complain, "You call this handled with care?"

At such times I need to remember what finally happened at Bethany. What a Helper of the helpless those sisters found Jesus to be as they hugged their brother made alive by Jesus' great power. What a visible reminder Lazarus was of how the Savior always handles his own with care.

I don't need more promises about God's loving care. Scripture offers many of them. I need God's Spirit working through Word and sacrament to strengthen my grip on those promises. Then I'll be able to tell myself and others, "Handled with care. Always! God's great power will see to that."

Lord, give me the faith to trust your
answers and follow your leading. Amen.

WHEN HE HEARD THIS, JESUS SAID, "THIS SICKNESS WILL
NOT END IN DEATH. NO, IT IS FOR GOD'S GLORY SO THAT
GOD'S SON MAY BE GLORIFIED THROUGH IT." *John 11:4*

Handled With Care For His Great Glory

A woman, plagued by many problems, asked her pastor, "*When* am I going to get out of these troubles?" He wisely replied, "Maybe you should ask, *What* am I going to get out of them?"

One thing I know will always come out of God's handling of my life. That's his glory. He may put a cross on my shoulders because I've started to stray from him. He may use a burden to wake me up again and draw me closer to him. He may use my troubles and how I react to them as a powerful sermon to others. He may use affliction as a mechanic uses a blowtorch and hammer to pound the dents out of my faith. But always what he does is for his glory and my good.

Mary and Martha learned this valuable lesson at the grave of their brother. More glory came to Jesus at Lazarus' graveside than would have come at his bedside. Healing a sick Lazarus would have brought Jesus glory, but nowhere near as much as raising a dead Lazarus. Jesus is much more than the Great Physician. He is the Resurrection and the Life. He not only helps with life's problems, he heals sin's disease and defeats death completely.

Someday in heaven looking back, I'll have to say, "I could have done without many pleasures, but I could not have spared one sorrow that God allowed into my life." Or to put it another way, I'll have to say, "Handled with care always for his great glory."

*Lord, in life's troubles show me your
sure help and the glory it brings you. Amen.*

"BEHOLD, I WILL CREATE NEW HEAVENS AND A
NEW EARTH. THE FORMER THINGS WILL NOT BE
REMEMBERED, NOR WILL THEY COME TO MIND." *Isaiah 65:17*

A Jerusalem Where All Is New

Sometimes I find myself, as the airlines put it, "Socked in by the fog." The problems of everyday living hang over me like a thick cloud, leaving me barely a glimpse of heaven's brightness. Whether I'm 18, 28, or 80, I need to slow down, part the fog, and look forward to heaven.

That's what Isaiah does in our verse. Admittedly I can't understand all he writes about heaven. Though he uses earthly colors to paint the heavenly scene, yet some colors are too brilliant for me. One such example is when he quotes the Lord about creating a new heavens and a new earth. Bible scholars have long disputed whether this will be a new creation after the present world has been annihilated or a restoration after the world has been reduced to its original elements. We can't tell from Holy Scripture, not because God has left it unclear but because our limited ability cannot understand the deep mysteries of God. My view of the heavenly Jerusalem is like that of a grandma with macular degeneration looking at her grandchild. I can make out the form but can see and know only what I need to see and know. In the heavenly Jerusalem, I will have a perfect existence in a perfect heaven with a perfect God. And I know how to get there—through Jesus my Savior.

When Leonardo da Vinci finished his famous painting of the Last Supper, he found people focusing too much on the cup in Jesus' hand. Taking his brush in hand, he boldly wiped out the goblet. "Look at the Savior's face," he insisted. Instead of getting my attention caught up in details that I can't understand, I need to look at the Savior's face. Only through him can I reach that Jerusalem where all is new.

Lord, keep my focus on Jesus, the only way to heaven. Amen.

"I WILL REJOICE OVER JERUSALEM AND TAKE DELIGHT
IN MY PEOPLE; THE SOUND OF WEEPING AND OF
CRYING WILL BE HEARD IN IT NO MORE." *Isaiah 65:19*

A Jerusalem
Where All Is Joy

Joy highlights this verse. First it's the Lord's joy in his new Jerusalem. When he speaks of Jerusalem, he means his holy Christian church, the eternal gathering of all believers in Jesus as their Savior. What joy to see eternally at his side those whom he has cleansed with his own Son's blood and covered with Christ's robe of righteousness! They are perfectly holy and a source of eternal joy to the Lord, who has made them such.

For believers also heaven will be only joy. Banished forever will be the sound of crying. The evils of sin that cause sobbing will be completely erased. Just imagine—no more sin or temptation to sin. No more Satan trying to worm his way into my heart through the holes in my faith. Just imagine—no more pain in my body, no more weariness in my soul, no more conflicts because of the past or concerns about the future. Just imagine—no more death like a shadow one step behind me, and no more hospitals or cemeteries. Yes, just imagine—the apple of joy without any worms at all in it.

On one of my trips to the mission field in Puerto Rico, a young family with a little boy sat across the aisle from me. As the plane banked and we got our first cloudy view of the island, the boy piped up, "Momma, where are the palm trees? Where are the coconuts? I can't see them." Puerto Rico meant coconuts to that little boy, and he wanted to see them first of all. Heaven means joy, perfect joy, to the believer. When I get there, the first one I'll want to see is my Jesus. He's the One through whom the Father has made me his joy. He's the One who will be the center of my joy in heaven.

Lord, keep me in true faith till
in heaven I see my Savior's face. Amen.

"THE WOLF AND THE LAMB WILL FEED TOGETHER, AND
THE LION WILL EAT STRAW LIKE THE OX, BUT DUST WILL
BE THE SERPENT'S FOOD. THEY WILL NEITHER HARM NOR
DESTROY ON ALL MY HOLY MOUNTAIN." *Isaiah 65:25*

A Jerusalem Where All Is Peace

What's the Lord trying to tell me with this verse? Will there come a time when God's church will know only peace on earth? A time when the impossible will happen? Like a wolf eating with the tender sheep instead of tearing it to pieces? Like a lion eating hay like some tame animal instead of pouncing on others? Or like a serpent putting his venomous fangs into the earth's dust instead of into living flesh?

Or is the Lord describing his heaven where all will be peace? His words, "they will neither harm nor destroy on all my holy mountain," give me the answer. He's talking about the holy mountain of his heaven. He's using picture language I can understand to give me some idea of the perfect peace waiting for me in his heaven.

Let others reduce this heavenly peace to some millennium on earth where there'll be no more wars and no more strife. That's reducing the millions of Christ's peace waiting for me in heaven to leaden nickels and dimes. Let others lower their eyes from heaven's golden crown of glory to a tin crown of earthly reign and riches. Let others be satisfied with such filmy, flimsy cotton candy that only leaves you sticky. I prefer the perfect peace that's spelled H-E-A-V-E-N and that is reached only through the One whose name is spelled S-A-V-I-O-R.

Lord, lift the fog in life and let
my eyes of faith see your heaven. Amen.

> WE ALSO REJOICE IN OUR SUFFERINGS, BECAUSE WE KNOW
> THAT SUFFERING PRODUCES PERSEVERANCE; PERSEVERANCE,
> CHARACTER; AND CHARACTER, HOPE. *Romans 5:3,4*

A Lesson In Patience

I learned patience the hard way. Laid low by a bad disk in my back, strung up by traction in that hospital bed, I could do nothing. "Never again," I told my wife, "will I say to someone in a hospital bed, 'Just be patient.'" Patience can be a hard commodity to come by.

When my friend, a fellow pastor, visited me, he read me our verse. "Sounds strange," he said, "but suffering can actually bring a believer joy." Then he went on with Paul's words, "Suffering produces perseverance." Suffering teaches God's child to wait patiently for the Father's deliverance. How true. On that hospital bed, I could only look up, at my God. "Perseverance produces character," my friend read on. Again, how true! Like the battle-tested soldier who has made it through tough times, patient waiting for the Lord's help conditions me for the day of trouble. "And character produces hope," he finished. The day of suffering has a way of making us rely more deeply on the Lord. Sinking times are praying times. Troubled times are reach-for-his-precious-promises times. A Christian's hope is not some nebulous hope-it's-true reaction to God's promises. It's confidence cemented in the rock-solid promises of a loving God.

God taught me patience through that hospital bed. He taught me more. He raised my eyes again to his Son's cross. With his Son's suffering and death in payment for my sins, he has given me a hope that will never disappoint.

Lord, help me appreciate suffering as
blessed training tools from your loving hand. Amen.

BLESSED IS HE . . . WHOSE SINS
ARE COVERED. *Psalm 32:1*

Getting Rid Of Sin's Waste

In the paper this morning was an article about the Yucca Mountain nuclear waste dump project in Nevada. An adverse court decision has put a roadblock in the way of this proposal. As a result, the president's budget has cut back its funding for it. But something needs to be done. You can't put nuclear waste in the city landfill. You can't burn it or throw it into the ocean. The best we can do is to bury it deep in some deserted dump so that its radiation won't hurt people.

The article made me think about sin's waste. With sin it's not a matter of preventing the contamination of people. Everyone is born "radioactive" with sin. Because of my inherited sinful nature, the Geiger counter of God's law races madly when held against my daily thoughts, words, and deeds. Ahead of me looms only a sure and painful wasting away in the punishments of hell.

How do I get rid of sin's waste? I don't. There's nothing I can do to decontaminate my soul. Nor do I have to. What does the psalmist tell me? He says that my sins are covered. God has buried them deep with the death and resurrection of his Son, Jesus. When Jesus went to Calvary's cross, he bore the "nuclear waste" of the world's sins. When he rose from the grave, he left my sins covered forever, not with dirt but with his forgiveness. In his love God has buried my sins so deep that they can never hurt me again. My world still has to search for ways to handle nuclear waste. Thank God I don't have to worry about how to get rid of the contamination of my sins.

Lord, show me that fountain filled with blood drawn from Immanuel's veins, where I have cleansing from sin's every guilty stain. Amen.

> LET THE WORD OF CHRIST DWELL
> IN YOU RICHLY. *Colossians 3:16*

Can't Run On Empty

One of the families of our mission congregation in Canada lived 30 miles out of town. One Sunday afternoon we drove out to visit them. Part way there the car sputtered to a stop. I had forgotten to fill the tank with gasoline. Leaving my pregnant wife in the car, I started walking to the gas station. "You can't run on empty" was the painful lesson I learned that day.

How come I sometimes think faith can keep running without refueling? Or that it can run on the fumes of last week's fill up? Like my car, my faith needs regular stops at the "gas pump." Regularly it needs the hose of God's Word pumping the necessary strength for faith and life.

Does the rich forgiveness God has prepared for me on Calvary's cross dim in value? Then it's time, through the Word, to kneel before Jesus' cross. Does the desire to walk like his disciple diminish in daily life? Then it's time, through the Word, to fill up with his pardon and in responsive gratitude get back on his road. Does the prospect of heaven seem like some distant dream? Then it's time, through the Word, to be reminded that this world is only my motel on the road to my real home.

The American Automobile Association reminds members to check their tanks. For good reason! Many of the calls it receives involve empty gas tanks. Our verse also stresses the importance of keeping faith's gas tank full. In fact, it urges me to top it off regularly with the Word.

Lord, remind me how much I
need your Word for faith and life. Amen.

> DO NOT BE DECEIVED: GOD CANNOT BE MOCKED.
> A MAN REAPS WHAT HE SOWS. *Galatians 6:7*

When God Settles His Accounts

While growing up on the farm, we had a neighbor who had nothing to do with church. On Sundays, when we would pause for worship, he went right on working. One day he said facetiously to my dad, "I plow on Sunday. I plant on Sunday. I cultivate on Sunday. And in October I harvest as much, if not more, than you do." My dad didn't say much. But on the way home he told me, "Remember, God doesn't always settle his accounts in October."

That's what Paul emphasizes in our verse. Why do so many think they can pull the wool over the eyes of the all-knowing Lord? They waste their days in worldly pursuits. They fill their pockets with worldly treasures. They live as if there were no eternity coming. They almost delude themselves into thinking they'll never have to step before a righteous God and give account for their lives. Unlike the farmer who knows that you can only harvest what you sow, they think otherwise. In the judgment, their empty lives will plainly reveal their empty hearts of unbelief.

When Paul reminds me that I'll reap what I sow, he's not saying I can earn heaven. He's rather stating the clear scriptural principle that faith in the heart shows in daily life. Heaven is God's free gift to me. His Son prepared this gift on Calvary's cross when he paid for my sins. My life of faith is my gift to God. It's my showing him, with the Spirit's power, how much his free gift means to me. In the judgment, my "sowing" will be the visible evidence of a heart filled with faith.

Lord, fill my heart with trust in the Savior
and my life with grateful response to him. Amen.

THOSE WHO HOPE IN THE LORD WILL RENEW THEIR STRENGTH. THEY WILL SOAR ON WINGS LIKE EAGLES; THEY WILL RUN AND NOT GROW WEARY, THEY WILL WALK AND NOT BE FAINT. *Isaiah 40:31*

Fly Like An Eagle

Hiking in Alaska's Kenai Peninsula, we spotted an eagle's nest high up in a tree. Soon that magnificent bird came swooping down and settled on its nest. Watching it, I could understand why our country's founding fathers adopted the eagle as our national emblem.

I'm hardly like an eagle by myself. What strength do I have to get rid of my sins? To handle life's daily, wearisome problems? To withstand the stormy blasts of sudden trouble? I'd never make it out of the nest, much less survive in such storms. I'd be left like some baby robin, dropped out of the nest right after hatching, with no hope for survival.

Do I want to fly like an eagle? There's one way. It's to hope in the Lord. When by his grace I know Jesus as my Redeemer, sin can no longer damn me. Satan can no longer accuse me. Hell can no longer claim me. With the strength of God's free salvation, I can fly above sin's down currents. Also when I hope in the Lord, I can fly through the storm of death. When by God's grace I know that Jesus has died for me, my death becomes not the wage for sin but the entrance to life eternal. When I hope in the Lord, I can fly also over the highest peaks of life's problems. Like some eagle with the strength of the Lord, I can make my way safely through life. Our nation's founding fathers picked the eagle because of its strength. For me that eagle speaks of the greatest strength of all, my God and my Savior.

Lord, through your Word fill me with your strength that I may fly like an eagle. Amen.

> MY EYES ARE EVER ON THE LORD,
> FOR ONLY HE WILL RELEASE MY
> FEET FROM THE SNARE. *Psalm 25:15*

Turned Toward The Sun

Near the farm where my in-laws lived was a field of sunflowers. Those tall plants with their large flowers were a sight to behold. They not only looked like the sun, but followed the sun. In the morning they'd face toward the east. By evening they'd be pointed toward the west. All day long they turned toward the sun on which they depended for life.

Sounds like what David said about the believer. "My eyes are ever on the LORD," he wrote. Like a sunflower turning toward the sun, a believer turns toward the Lord at all times. Where else can I find nourishment for my faith? Only God's Holy Spirit, as he works through Word and sacraments, can light up my dark heart in faith. I need the constant sunshine of God's life-giving Word if faith is to continue. Where else can I find release from all my sins? I need Jesus as the Sun of Righteousness, shining on me with his love and goodness, if my heart is to know peace. Where else can I find rescue from life's problems or, as David called them, life's "snare"? I need the Lord as my strength and my light in life's darkest night.

Later this fall those sunflowers will be harvested. They'll be squeezed into oil and processed as food for man and beast. Someday I too will be harvested. The Lord will take me home to stand in the glorious sunshine of his saving love forevermore. Then my eyes will be ever toward him.

Lord, send your Spirit to keep me turned
ever toward the sunshine of your love. Amen.

> "MY SON, DO NOT MAKE LIGHT OF THE LORD'S DISCIPLINE,
> AND DO NOT LOSE HEART WHEN HE REBUKES YOU, BECAUSE
> THE LORD DISCIPLINES THOSE HE LOVES." *Hebrews 12:5,6*

Life's Hard Roads

Are you more careful driving on a straight, well-paved road or on a bumpy, curving one? On a bumpy road, the sharp curves and deep potholes have a way of keeping us awake. We keep our eyes on the road and our foot near the brake. On smooth, straight freeways, we can become sleepy and less vigilant.

Can I understand why God doesn't always put a smooth road ahead of me in life? Sometimes he takes me down the bumpy road to keep me awake. When he does, I need the advice of the author of Hebrews. "Do not make light of the Lord's discipline," he urges me. God may be saying something important that I as his child can hear better when kept awake by the bumps than half asleep on the smooth freeway. Nor am I to lose heart when he rebukes me. God never forsakes his own. When he tests, he also toughens. However heavy the discipline, his grace will cover. However deep the ruts of trouble, his hand is on the wheel.

The right reaction when life runs down hard roads is confidence in God's love. He disciplines me because he loves me. If he didn't care about me, he'd leave me alone and I might end up as a statistic in the ditch. Because he loves me, he puts me on alert to sin's seriousness and directs me straight ahead on heaven's highway. Can I expect anything less from a God whose love has made me his own through his Son's sacrifice?

Lord, pilot me on life's
highway with your sure love. Amen.

THE GOSPEL HE PROMISED BEFOREHAND
THROUGH HIS PROPHETS IN THE HOLY
SCRIPTURES REGARDING HIS SON. *Romans 1:2,3*

God's Good News

Don't you get tired of reading the newspapers or listening to the news reports on TV? So often it seems like they report only the bad news. The headlines speak about the latest car bombings in far-off lands or the latest murders on city streets. Seldom do stories about human kindness and concern make it to the front page or to TV's breaking news.

What if hell were to publish a newspaper? What do you think it would report? I wonder whether there'd be an updated statistic about how many souls were locked up eternally that day. Or how many souls Satan claimed with his roadside bombings. Or how many casualties his temptations caused. Who'd want to read hell's newspaper? It would be filled only with bad news.

How about if God were to publish a newspaper? What would it contain? Paul tells us. He says good news, for that's what *gospel* means. Paul even gives us a summary of that good news. It's "regarding his Son," he explains. And Paul also reminds us that God has published this good news about his Son, the Savior. That was the heart and center of the Old Testament Scriptures. God's prophets spoke of many things, but none was more important than the coming Savior. Then God gave us his New Testament. In it he highlighted the good news of how his Son did come, paid for all sins, and made it possible for needy sinners like me to live forever in heaven. Now that's good news I can never hear too much of!

*Lord, keep the attention of my eyes and
ears on the good news of my salvation. Amen.*

> I HAVE FOUGHT THE GOOD FIGHT. I HAVE FINISHED THE
> RACE. I HAVE KEPT THE FAITH. NOW THERE IS IN STORE
> FOR ME THE CROWN OF RIGHTEOUSNESS. *2 Timothy 4:7,8*

Champions, One And All

When I was in grade school, I ate a cereal described as "the breakfast of champions" almost every morning. On the front of the box would be a picture of the latest champion in some sports field. I hoped that cereal would make me into a champion baseball player.

Well, I never made it. But like Paul, the author of our verse, I'm a champion in the truest sense of the word. Near the end of life, he could speak of victory. Regardless of what enemies of his own faith and of God's church he had to battle, he kept going. Regardless of how many potholes and bumps tried to throw him off heaven's highway, he kept on running. Ahead of him now beckoned the crown of righteousness, that perfect existence at his Savior's side in heaven.

Paul was not bragging about how good an athlete he was. He could speak of heaven as his home only because the Lord had strengthened him for the race and sustained him on the course. Faith and its continuation are always God's gracious gift. So is the object of faith whom we know as Jesus our all sufficient Savior. Paul could claim the crown of victory only because his loving God had nourished him well.

My breakfast cereal didn't do much for me. But God's Word does. Through it God keeps me strong for heaven's race. Through a regular diet of it, I can be a champion just like Paul.

Lord, keep me on a regular
diet of your nourishing Word. Amen.

> NOW MAY OUR GOD AND FATHER HIMSELF
> AND OUR LORD JESUS CLEAR THE WAY FOR
> US TO COME TO YOU. *1 Thessalonians 3:11*

Large Petitions For My King

As God's children we pray. Frequently we crawl up on the knee of our heavenly Father. Fearlessly we pour out our hearts to that Father, trusting him to hear and answer for Jesus' sake. The temptations, the tears, the triumphs of life offer more than enough material for our daily petitions. Yet we need the reminder to pray and for what to pray!

In our verse Paul had a large petition for his King. To that God, the heavenly Father, who alone could do what was right for his children, and to his Son, that Lord Jesus Christ, who alone can make us God's children, Paul turned with a prayer. He wanted that gracious God to direct his way back to the Thessalonian believers. Paul wasn't asking for directions along the road or a companion for the way. He prayed for a safe journey back to his fellow Christians.

Paul's example shows me that prayer is a daily affair for a believer. He reminds me that no petition is too insignificant and none too impossible for a Father who has made me his very own through his Son's blood. Life's shuddering emergencies are times for prayer. So are those daily decisions and routine relationships, those "nuts and bolts" of my daily life. Could it be that I wrestle with my daily life because in the morning, I forgot to pray, "Please, Lord, send your help today"? Then, in the evening, tired out with life's problems, do I also forget to say, "Thank you, Lord, for your help today"? Any petition I bring in Jesus' name is a large petition for my King.

Lord, lift my heart heavenward in prayer
throughout the day for things large and small. Amen.

> MAY THE LORD MAKE YOUR LOVE INCREASE AND
> OVERFLOW FOR EACH OTHER AND FOR EVERYONE ELSE,
> JUST AS OURS DOES FOR YOU. *1 Thessalonians 3:12*

Larger Petitions For My King

Yesterday we saw how Paul prayed for a safe journey back to the believers in Thessalonica. Today we hear him ask the Lord to make their "love increase and overflow for each other and for everyone else." With this larger petition Paul wanted the Lord to cause their love, like some rising river, to overflow its banks and flood all those around them.

Paul wasn't asking for just any kind of love, but one that reflected God's love for them in Christ Jesus. God had showered his love unselfishly on them, not because of, but in spite of, what they were. God's love came to give to them, not to get from them. His only Son dying on the cross to pay for unworthy sinners is proof of this. Through the gospel of his saving love, Paul asked the Lord to increase their faith, so that resulting love for others might glow and grow in their lives.

If my love for others is drying out like an uncovered cake in a pan or shrinking down like a leaking tire, perhaps it's because I haven't looked often enough at God's love for me in Christ. A love that endures all things from fellow human beings can be found only in him who on Calvary's cross endured all sins for me. A love that is not self-seeking can be found only in him who on the cross sought the good of me, a sinner. A love that is not proud can be found only in the One who humbled himself even to death on the cross. Only because God has so loved me, can I love those around me. To him I bring my larger petitions for love.

Lord, fill me with your amazing love so
that I can reflect it toward those around me. Amen.

> MAY HE STRENGTHEN YOUR HEARTS SO THAT YOU WILL BE BLAMELESS AND HOLY IN THE PRESENCE OF OUR GOD AND FATHER WHEN OUR LORD JESUS COMES WITH ALL HIS HOLY ONES. *1 Thessalonians 3:13*

Largest Petitions For My King

So often Paul prayed in concern for the souls of people. When he did, so often he had the greatest goal of all in mind. He wanted them to be found blameless when the Lord Jesus would return on the Last Day. The apostle's greatest prayer for fellow believers was that they would stand with the sacred throng around the throne of the Lamb on that glorious day. What greater request could he have made, and to whom could he have made it, than to the Lord who in his grace through the gospel keeps us in the faith?

Do I forget the matter of Christ's return when I bring my petitions to my King? Am I so busy asking for the nickels and dimes for my earthly needs that I tend to forget about the millions Christ offers for my soul? Of course, I pray about family needs, health concerns, financial matters. Such items are part of daily life. Help with them comes from the merciful hand of my King. Even more so, am I to pray about strength for faith, forgiveness for sin, help with temptation, steady endurance as each day brings me one step closer to the Last Day.

For myself and my family, for my neighbor down the block and around the globe, I can offer no greater prayer than "When he shall come with trumpet sound, Oh, may [we] then in him be found, Clothed in his righteousness alone, Faultless to stand before his throne" (CW 382:4).

Lord, remind me that your grace and power are such that I can never ask too much. Amen.

> BE JOYFUL ALWAYS; PRAY CONTINUALLY; GIVE
> THANKS IN ALL CIRCUMSTANCES, FOR THIS IS GOD'S
> WILL FOR YOU IN CHRIST JESUS. *1 Thessalonians 5:16-18*

Clear Commands
For Christians

During the Vietnam War, our congregation lost two young men. After the funeral services, as I stood by the hearse, the military honor guard marched down the church steps. The leader's commands were sharp and clear. The soldiers followed with well-trained precision.

That was for a funeral. How about life? "Be joyful always," Paul commands. These aren't the shallow words of some simple optimist who doesn't know that life involves a great deal of pain. They are rather the words of one who had found "inexpressible and glorious joy" in Christ (1 Peter 1:8). In Christ I have joy that no sorrow can shut off. Shallow happiness is based on what happens today. Joy comes from knowing what awaits me in heaven because of Jesus.

Paul's next commands follow quite naturally. As a joyful believer, I "pray continually." Constantly, I lift my wants and wishes to my loving Father in heaven. Confidently, I walk tuned in to him who's ready to listen at any time, in any place, to any thing. "Give thanks in all circumstances," Paul also said. Sure of God's saving love for me in Christ, I can also expect that he will make both the "chocolate cake" and the "sour pickles" in life serve for my good.

Unlike that military honor guard, my response to my Lord's commands isn't always precisionlike. More often I sorrow instead of rejoicing, forget to look up to God in prayer, and grouse instead of giving thanks. Then it's time again to look at what God has done for me in the Savior and, filled with his love, to march on.

God, help me to do so. Amen.

> IF ANYBODY DOES SIN, WE HAVE ONE WHO SPEAKS TO THE
> FATHER IN OUR DEFENSE—JESUS CHRIST, THE RIGHTEOUS ONE.
> HE IS THE ATONING SACRIFICE FOR OUR SINS. *1 John 2:1,2*

What If I Sin?

Sin troubles people who think seriously about their relationship with God. As a believer I know what sin can do to that blessed Father-child relationship. I hear Scripture warning me not to sin. Daily I fight against and yet fall into sin. What can I do when I sin? Is there no hope for me?

In answer, John points me beyond the Bethlehem manger, past the Calvary cross, up to the throne room in heaven. There stands One who restores fellowship with God when I sin. His name is Jesus Christ, the Righteous One. Powerfully and personally he steps before my Father. As my lawyer he pleads for me, and my loving Father listens willingly. Behind his pleading stands the cross where he sacrificed himself as the perfect payment for the world's sins and for mine. "Case dismissed," the heavenly Father says as Jesus points to the nail prints in his hands and feet. "Not guilty" is the verdict, not because I don't sin but because Jesus has paid for all my sins.

Without Jesus Christ, the Righteous One, the question, What if I sin? would be a horrible one. It would haunt me all the way to hell. Without him each sin would be a mountain-high barrier between my God and me—one that I could neither blast through nor burrow under. I pray that I never reach the point where my daily sins don't trouble me. When I sin, I pray that my gracious Lord keeps leading me to the Savior's manger bed and Calvary cross. Even more, I ask that he lift my eyes to the throne room in heaven where the Savior keeps pleading for me.

Lord, take me deeper into your Word with
its comforting message of forgiveness in Christ. Amen.

> DO NOT BE SURPRISED, MY BROTHERS,
> IF THE WORLD HATES YOU. *1 John 3:13*

What Do You Expect?

"If you were on trial for being a Christian, would there be enough evidence to convict you?" That was the question on a poster in a religious bookstore. In our verse, John points to one evidence of Christian faith. He reminds me that as a believer I should expect hatred from the world.

Ever since the fall into sin in the Garden of Eden, the human heart by nature has no love for God or fellow human beings. Instead, hatred broods there, planted by and patterned after the original "wicked one," the devil. This hatred manifests itself in life, in world wars, in family feuds, in large upheavals, and simple impoliteness. For the world, hatred is a way of life.

From such a world, I as a child of God can expect to receive hatred. When our Lord came to earth, that's what he received. Because his words and life exposed people's sinfulness, they picked up stones to throw at him and finally nails to pierce him. As Christ's follower can I expect better? Jesus reminds me, "If the world hates you, keep in mind that it hated me first" (John 15:18).

What happens when I step away from a crowd speaking filth or shut my ears to gossip making the rounds? When I label abortion and premarital sex as sin? When I refuse to play fast and loose with God's Word? I'll meet opposition from the world. Such opposition, though it hurts deeply, is a sign that I'm alive in Christ. God give me strength to be in the world but not of the world, regardless what it thinks of me.

Savior, through your Word,
power me to walk closer to you. Amen.

> GOD IS LOVE. WHOEVER LIVES IN LOVE
> LIVES IN GOD, AND GOD IN HIM. *1 John 4:16*

Love Says It All

"God is love," John states in his epistle again and again. More than a description of God, this phrase is an all-inclusive name for him. Luther once wrote, "If we should desire to paint a picture . . . to represent God, it would have to be a picture of pure love, to bring out the fact that the divine nature is, as it were, a furnace aglow with love that fills heaven and earth."

I can learn more about this God of love from his actions. "Do you love me?" children might ask their parents. In response they receive a big hug and kiss from them. "Do you love me?" I ask God. In response he points me to Calvary's cross. There on the cross is God's love in action. There's proof that he loved me first, when I was unlovable in my sins and deserving of damnation. There his love stretched out nail-pierced arms in the warmest and widest hug my world will ever receive. Then he also reached with those loving arms down to me. He sent his Spirit through the gospel to bring me to faith so that I can know and rejoice in his amazing, saving love.

See what his love has made of me. I can now stand right next to God without fear. He's my Father and I'm his child. And he stands right next to me. John says that God dwells in me. What a picture of the close, intimate union his love has brought me. Here on earth I'm joined with my Father, though sin often gets in the way. In heaven I'll have a perfect union with him without sin's interruption—all because of God's love. Praise God that he is love!

Thank you, Lord, that I can sing, "God loves me dearly, grants me salvation. God loves me dearly, loves even me." Amen.

> "No one can come to me unless the Father who sent me draws him, and I will raise him up at the last day." *John 6:44*

Drawn By His Powerful Love

Yesterday, in the children's sermonette, our pastor used an interesting illustration. He tied a piece of rope to an iron fireplace grate. Then he asked the children to talk to the grate. "Tell it to come here," he said. Some of the children did, but nothing happened. Then he had the children take hold of the rope and pull. You can guess what happened.

The pastor's illustration made me appreciate what a gift my faith is. Like some iron chunk, I couldn't come to God. I could only sit there heavy in unbelief and grimy with sin. Actually, my condition was even worse. When I heard the good news of salvation, I didn't want it. I could only punch it aside with my fist of unbelief. There I remained, far more distant from God than that iron grate was from the children at the foot of the chancel.

Till God put the rope of his grace on me. At my baptism he tied invisible twine around my heart and pulled it close to him in faith. No longer was I far distant from him but right in his family. Through his Word he pulls me closer to his love. In his Holy Supper he pulls some more. What a gift of his grace my faith is! What a powerful rope his gospel is to pull me close!

On the way home from church, I saw a pickup truck pulling an old beater car with a nylon rope. "That's me," I thought, "thanks to God's grace."

Lord, thank you for the gift of faith. Through your gospel keep pulling me closer to you. Amen.

> YOU ALSO, LIKE LIVING STONES, ARE BEING BUILT INTO A
> SPIRITUAL HOUSE TO BE A HOLY PRIESTHOOD, OFFERING SPIRITUAL
> SACRIFICES ACCEPTABLE TO GOD THROUGH JESUS CHRIST. *1 Peter 2:5*

Strange Building Materials

During the 2004 Olympic Games in Athens, much was said about Greece. For example, one broadcaster talked about the famous Parthenon. This ancient building doesn't have a straight line or perfect 90-degree angle in it. But instead of being ugly, it's beautiful. Though an explosion ruined much of it, yet tourists come by the thousands to it each year.

Looking at the Parthenon on TV, I couldn't help thinking about God's church. Peter says that God builds his church out of "living stones." Stones aren't perfect. They are crooked and jagged. Some have cracks and some have holes. So it is with the people God turns into the stones for his church. He takes crooked sinners like me and lays us in a perfect line with other stones in his spiritual house. Beginning with Adam and Eve; continuing with Abraham and Isaac, Peter, James, and John; my parents and my spouse; God, the master builder, is at work bringing sinners to faith and cementing them into his eternal church. And because of his grace in Christ, we ugly stones become a beautiful building.

Just as Greeks like to have people view the Parthenon, God wants people to look at his church. He wants to use me to help others marvel at his grace and goodness. "Spiritual sacrifices" is how Peter described it. I'm to shine with his love and reach with his saving Word that others might not just marvel but become part of his church.

Lord, thank you for shaping me
into a living stone for your church. Amen.

"I AM THE LIVING BREAD THAT CAME DOWN
FROM HEAVEN. IF ANYONE EATS OF THIS BREAD,
HE WILL LIVE FOREVER." *John 6:51*

Better Than Peanut Butter And Jelly Sandwiches

My wife likes peanut butter and jelly sandwiches. Sometimes she eats one for breakfast, other times as a snack before bedtime. Such a sandwich has a way of satisfying her hunger.

Strange that Jesus should describe himself as bread. We don't toast him. We don't cover him with peanut butter and jelly. But he does taste good. And he does have a way of satisfying my soul's hunger.

Only Jesus can take away the hunger pains caused by sin. Sin starves my soul, reducing it to skin and bones fit only for hell's bone pile. How much I, a sinner, need the nourishment of Jesus' forgiveness. Not one day goes by when I don't need him as bread for my soul. Only if my daily life were free from sin could I do without this heavenly bread.

When Jesus speaks of eating this bread, he means believing in him. God's Spirit turns me in faith toward Jesus, like my wife heading for the bread drawer. Earthly bread does me no good if I don't eat it. Jesus, the Bread of Life, nourishes when I "eat" him in faith. Thank God for the gift of faith that reaches for him. Earthly bread satisfies for a while. Jesus satisfies forever. Those who believe in him "will live forever." He's the only bread that sustains till heaven's shores. Only his forgiveness satisfies the heavenly judge and makes me fit for eternity.

*Jesus, bread of heaven, feed me through
your Word till I reach heaven's shores. Amen.*

> THOSE WHO SUFFER ACCORDING TO GOD'S WILL
> SHOULD COMMIT THEMSELVES TO THEIR
> FAITHFUL CREATOR. *1 Peter 4:19*

Tailor-Made For Me

Life had been tough for the aged Christian. He had lost his wife suddenly. Heart surgery had followed. Then came cancer and the necessary treatments. When I visited him, he wondered, "Does God know how heavy my life has been?"

In response, I told him the story of the Christian who complained about the cross he had to carry. So the Lord took him to the cross storehouse in heaven and told him to take his pick. He tried on one but kept tripping because it was too long. Another was too compact and quickly wore out his back. Another was too wide and kept slipping off his shoulders. Finally he found one near the door that fit exactly. Out the door he went with the same cross he had carried in.

I did more than tell him this old story. I also read to him our verse. When some heavy cross drives my nose to within an inch of life's pavement, I need to lean on a faithful God. He's my Creator. He, who made me in the womb of my mother, remade me at the baptismal font into his beloved child. He won't let a cross that's too heavy break my back. Or one that's too splintery tear up my shoulders. He's a faithful God, who takes good care of his own. Committing or entrusting myself to his gracious care at times seems like quite a stretch. But then I raise my eyes to his Son's cross and see what he has already done for my salvation. My loving God tailors even the crosses I carry.

Lord, when I weary under life's burdens,
strengthen me with the promise of your love. Amen.

> "LET YOUR LIGHT SHINE BEFORE MEN, THAT
> THEY MAY SEE YOUR GOOD DEEDS AND PRAISE
> YOUR FATHER IN HEAVEN." *Matthew 5:16*

The Right Kind Of Filament

When Thomas Edison worked on the first light bulb, he had trouble finding the right material for the filament. He tried fibers made out of paper and then wood, but they didn't burn long enough. He tried more than six thousand filaments composed of vegetable fibers, but they didn't work either. Finally he came up with a bamboo filament that would burn longer. Today a very thin wire, usually made of tungsten, is used because it can take a lot of heat and last a long time.

But a filament doesn't glow without a source of electricity. Pick up a lightbulb and look at it. It doesn't do a thing until screwed into a lamp that is plugged into the power. Sounds like a Christian, doesn't it? I'm supposed to shine before men. But, on my own, I'm a lifeless "filament." Only when I'm plugged into Christ can I shine. He's the light of the world. He's the only One who lights up a sin-darkened world with forgiveness. When the Spirit through Word and sacrament plugs me into him, I shine like a bulb in a turned-on lamp.

The Lord doesn't light me up in faith just for myself. He wants to use me to help others know Jesus as their light and salvation also. What do they see when they look at me? Can others learn from me something about what it means to be a Christian? What it means to have the joy of salvation? What it means to have a purpose in life? What it means to face life's reversals and life's end? Bulbs that are plugged in shine. Am I a 15- or a 40-watt bulb? How brightly is my filament shining?

Lord, help me shine more brightly
with the light of your salvation. Amen.

"Where, O death, is your victory? Where, O death, is your sting?" But thanks be to God! He gives us the victory through our Lord Jesus Christ. *1 Corinthians 15:55,57*

Victory In

"Garbage in—garbage out" is an old saying that relates, among other things, to computer use. If what I feed into the computer is wrong—if it's garbage—the computer can only give me garbage back. On the other hand, if I program and feed the computer properly, there's so much it can do for me.

In our verse, Paul's writing about "victory in." What might that victory be? It's Christ's conquest of sin and death. Thinking people dispute the fact that death is the greatest enemy of all. They may not recognize sin as the cause behind that enemy. But they do shudder at the sight of the endless line inching toward the grave, knowing they must join it. They do tremble at the realization that there's no exit ramp before sin's road leads them to the judgment seat of God.

God himself came down from heaven to win the battle I couldn't fight. On Calvary the battle raged. When it was over, Christ was the glorious victor. His empty tomb proclaims that sin's debt had been canceled, death had been overcome, and hell conquered. This is the victory Paul wants plugged into my heart. He wants me to know that death is no longer a jailor to lock me in some grave and, even worse, in hell. It's the gatekeeper to usher me into eternity. He wants me to live victoriously in the joy of Christ's resurrection.

For me it's "victory in" because of Christ's saving work and God's grace.

*"Thanks be to God! He gives us the
victory through our Lord Jesus Christ." Amen.*

> THEREFORE, MY DEAR BROTHERS, STAND FIRM. LET NOTHING
> MOVE YOU. ALWAYS GIVE YOURSELVES FULLY TO THE WORK
> OF THE LORD, BECAUSE YOU KNOW THAT YOUR LABOR
> IN THE LORD IS NOT IN VAIN. *1 Corinthians 15:58*

Victory Out

How profound for those plugged into Christ's glorious victory over sin and death! As a believer I'm to stand firm and let nothing move me. Like some two-ton rock, I'm to stand solidly on Christ the resurrection and the life. How? By staying close to his Word through which the Spirit plugs his victory into my heart.

Then I can always give myself fully to the work of the Lord. Christians, filled with the victory over sin and death, get busy. For them each day is an opportunity to serve their Lord wherever he has put them. When I wonder whether such work is worthwhile, I look again at the risen Savior's promise. "Your labor in the Lord is not in vain," he assures me. How can it be? I'm doing his work when I tell others of his great victory. Success will come as he grants it.

One day in his studio Leonardo da Vinci worked at a painting with his own matchless genius. Suddenly handing the brush to one of his students, he commanded, "Paint on." The student protested that he was both unworthy and unable to paint on that which his great master had begun. But da Vinci silenced him with the question, "Will not what I have done inspire you to do your best?" "Paint on," the risen victor commands me, "wherever I put you, at whatever work I place before you. Let my victory inspire you." Let it be "victory in—victory out."

Risen Savior, fill me with the joy of your victory and help me share it with others. Amen.

> [THE LORD] PASSED IN FRONT OF MOSES, PROCLAIMING,
> "THE LORD, THE LORD, THE COMPASSIONATE AND
> GRACIOUS GOD, SLOW TO ANGER, ABOUNDING IN LOVE
> AND FAITHFULNESS, MAINTAINING LOVE TO THOUSANDS,
> AND FORGIVING WICKEDNESS, REBELLION AND SIN." *Exodus 34:6,7*

How Would You Describe Him?

On Mount Sinai the Lord gave Moses as good a description of himself as we're ever to going to read. Note that it's a description of the Lord, the unchangeable God of grace. He has another side too—that of eternal and just judge. But here it's the God of salvation being described.

He's a "compassionate" God, using a word that means "tenderly pitiful." Whenever I see a father taking care of a crippled child, I can appreciate this picture. Though sin has crippled my heart, he won't sweep me aside with an impatient hand.

He's also "gracious." That word reminds me that he loves me because he wants to, not because I deserve his love.

He's "slow to anger." Yes, he becomes angry when his mercy and grace are rejected or ignored. But he'd much rather bless. Have there been times I thought I had worn out his grace with my repeated or "special" sins? Then these are words I need to hear.

"Abounding in love and faithfulness," the description continues. Like some full glass still held under the tap, he overflows with his saving love for sinners.

His last words leave no doubt about sin forgiven. He forgives "wickedness, rebellion and sin." Whatever sin I have is not just covered, but removed. When God looks at me, it's as if my sin never happened. So completely the blood of his Son cleanses me from sin.

Lord, thank you for revealing
yourself to me as my Savior-God. Amen.

> THE WORD BECAME FLESH AND
> MADE HIS DWELLING AMONG US. *John 1:14*

When God Tented Among Us

Vacation time in the early years meant packing our tent into the station wagon. With four kids, we couldn't afford motels or restaurant meals. So it was a Coleman stove, sleeping bags, and a six-person tent. Good times were had by all as we visited the national parks.

Our verse says that God "made his dwelling among us." Literally the words mean that he set up his tent, or tabernacle, among us. In Old Testament times, God had Israel make a tent, called the tabernacle, as an outward sign that he was dwelling in their midst. That tent was visible proof that he was their God and they were his people. When Jesus was born, the Lord came to dwell in person among us. Though he is "very God of very God," yet he tented among us as the eternal Word. In Jesus, who came to our planet and into our flesh, God gave us a living picture of his heart. He used Jesus as his walking, talking Word to communicate with us.

Jesus came to earth not to vacation with me but to save me. As God's Word, he came to show me that God's heart is filled with wondrous love for me, a sinner. When I see the God-man on the cross, I see how far divine love was willing to go for me. I see a God whose heart takes no delight in the death of the wicked but, instead, bleeds and dies to save sinners like me.

On vacation with our six-person tent, we had good times. Because Jesus came to tent on this earth, I have better times waiting for me in heaven.

Lord of love, thank you for sending Jesus
to save me and to live with you in heaven. Amen.

> ONE WHO WAS THERE HAD BEEN AN INVALID FOR
> THIRTY-EIGHT YEARS. WHEN JESUS SAW HIM LYING THERE, . . .
> HE ASKED HIM, "DO YOU WANT TO GET WELL?" *John 5:5,6*

From The Divine Physician, A Word Of Compassion

It was called Bethesda, or "house of mercy." Composed of porches built around a pool that promised healing, it was filled with the sounds and smells of sickness. Among the patients was a paralytic confined to his pallet for 38 years. Many people in those days didn't even live that long. For him it must have seemed like forever.

Can't you feel Jesus' compassion as he bends over that man's weary, wasted form? From the Savior's lips come no empty platitudes like "I feel so sorry for you." Instead, he asks, "Do you want to get well?" Jesus was asking about more than healing for the man's body. Later verses reveal the Savior's concern for the sin that gripped the man's heart and paralyzed his soul. *Compassion* is one of Scripture's big words. *Compassion* means "love, sympathy, concern, and a desire to help." It encompasses both the heart that feels and the hand that reaches out to help.

My church is a modern Bethesda. In this house of mercy, I find what my soul desperately needs. In the preaching of the Word, I hear my heavenly "specialist" inviting, "Do you want to get well?" From that Word, I receive the healing prescription, "God, my heavenly Father, has been merciful to me and has given his only Son to be the atoning sacrifice for my sins." From such a compassionate Savior, I can look for help with life's other concerns. He who heals my soul will handle my bodily needs also. What a hospital! What a physician!

Lord, help me come to you with
every need of body and soul. Amen.

> THEN JESUS SAID TO HIM, "GET UP! PICK UP YOUR
> MAT AND WALK." AT ONCE THE MAN WAS CURED;
> HE PICKED UP HIS MAT AND WALKED. *John 5:8,9*

From The Divine Physician, A Word Of Compulsion

The Great Physician said, "Pick up your mat and walk." And the man did! No crutches or canes, no weeks of therapy, just instant walking. What a feeling that must have been for him when he carried off the mattress on which he had lain for so many years. What a greater feeling when he walked away with the greater healing for his soul. Later Jesus pointed to this healing when he told the man, "Stop sinning or something worse will happen to you" (6:14).

Why do I go to the worship services held in the Bethesda known as my church? Isn't it to hear my Great Physician say about those sins of the past that still chew on my conscience and those sins of the present that repeat themselves, "There is a fountain filled with blood—Immanuel was slain—And sinners who are washed therein Lose ev'ry guilty stain" (CW 112:1)? Isn't it to go home with the confidence, "Jesus sinners does receive. Even I have been forgiven. And when I this earth must leave, I shall find an open heaven. Dying, still to him I cleave—Jesus sinners does receive" (CW 304:7)?

Isn't it also to thank him for the lesser healing? Behind a surgeon's knife, a doctor's skill, a prescription bottle stands my divine healer with his compelling power. When he doesn't send healing, he builds up my muscles of faith to carry the cross. His powerful Word reminds me of this blessed truth in my Bethesda week after week.

Savior, thank you for healing my sin-sick
soul. Deal with my body as you know best. Amen.

> LATER JESUS FOUND HIM AT THE TEMPLE AND SAID
> TO HIM, "SEE, YOU ARE WELL AGAIN. STOP SINNING
> OR SOMETHING WORSE MAY HAPPEN TO YOU." *John 5:14*

From The Divine Physician, A Word Of Concern

Healed people are happy to leave the hospital. They want to get back to family and friends. Would to God that some of them were just as eager to get back to church to praise and thank their God. Perhaps that failure shows that, though the body is well, the soul is still ill.

Not so with the healed man in our verses. Sometime later Jesus found him in the temple, no doubt praising God. There in the temple came the heavenly physician's third word to this man. "See, you are made well again," Jesus told him. "Stop sinning or something worse may happen to you." Even worse than relapses into sickness are relapses into sin. "Go, live as my healed child," Jesus was telling him. In concern the Savior spoke to him about the life of repentance and faith. "Throw off. . . the sin that so easily entangles," Jesus was urging him (Hebrews 12:1).

I want to live the healthy lifestyle of God's grateful child. I want my religion to be more than come and grab on Sunday mornings and then go my own way the rest of the week. That's why I turn to his Word every chance I get. Modern medicine deals more and more not just with cure but with prevention. That's what my heavenly physician does. When he, in loving concern, urges, "Stop sinning," he offers me the power I need at the same time. Through his Word, he shares with me his strength against Satan, the world, and my own flesh. With his power I can win more and more in the ongoing battle of life.

Savior, to you I turn with praise for help
received and with prayer for renewed strength. Amen.

> "SEE, I HAVE ENGRAVED YOU ON THE
> PALMS OF MY HANDS; YOUR WALLS
> ARE EVER BEFORE ME." *Isaiah 49:16*

God's Tattoos

We were waiting for a stoplight to change. All at once a car swooped alongside us, scraped our front fender, and sped quickly off. Quickly I wrote its license number on the palm of my hand or else I would never have remembered that important number.

God says that he has something written on the palms of his hands. Of course, he doesn't have a hand. Nor does he have any trouble remembering anything. Rather he's using a picture to reassure me. Like some tattoo, he's written my name on his palm. Nothing can wash my name away. No dirt or soap or passing of time will obliterate me from his mind. Just as I look at my palms often each day, so God has my name in his sight.

Why does he remember me? I'm hardly worthy of his concern. As a sinner I deserve the back of his holy hand slapping me away. But in love that I'll never understand this side of heaven, he's stretched out his hands on Calvary's cross to cover all my sins. In love, he's stretched those hands down in Holy Baptism to cradle me as his very own. In love, he'll stretch those hands down to carry me home when my time comes. Those same loving hands take care of my "walls." He watches over my comings and goings each day. He sees my successes and my sorrows. He knows my tears and my fears. When I think because of trouble's heat that he has forgotten me, he reminds me that he has my name tattooed on the palms of his hands.

Thank you, Lord, for the love that keeps
me in your care. Help me never forget you. Amen.

> IN CHRIST WE WHO ARE MANY FORM ONE BODY, AND EACH
> MEMBER BELONGS TO ALL THE OTHERS. WE HAVE DIFFERENT
> GIFTS, ACCORDING TO THE GRACE GIVEN US. *Romans 12:5,6*

Members Of God's Orchestra

There weren't many notes for the piccolo player in the piece the orchestra was rehearsing. So he sat there daydreaming and missed his part. The conductor, banging his baton on the stand, pointed directly to him, and scolded, "We need your part. The music is incomplete without you."

Ever think of believers as being members in God's symphony orchestra? He gives each of us individual talents. Some can preach and teach, as called by God's people. Some can lead and direct in the affairs of his people. Others can encourage and share on the basis of God's Word. Like sections in an orchestra, each has his or her spot and would be missed if caught daydreaming.

God knows which talents are best for each one of us. What if the trumpet section of the orchestra would quit and join the string section? What if the violins wanted to be kettledrums instead? Or the clarinets would refuse to play unless they could be trombones? The result wouldn't be sweet music, but a cacophony of sound. But when each chair plays its notes, sweet is the sound.

The question isn't, What chair do I fill in God's orchestra? but, How am I filling it? The sweet music God's wants his people to produce is the song of salvation. He wants each of us, wherever he has placed us, with whatever talent he has given us, to sound forth with, "To God be the glory; great things he has done! He so loved the world that he gave us his Son" (CW 399:1).

Lord, help me use the talents you have given
me to sing of your salvation and your praise. Amen.

"ALL MEN ARE LIKE GRASS, AND ALL THEIR GLORY IS LIKE THE FLOWERS OF THE FIELD; THE GRASS WITHERS AND THE FLOWERS FALL, BUT THE WORD OF THE LORD STANDS FOREVER." *1 Peter 1:24,25*

One Thing Never Changes

My dear mother passed away at the age of 97. Just think of the changes she saw in this world. She could remember washing clothes in water heated on a kerosene burner. Refrigeration was an ice box filled with frozen chunks cut from the river. When the radio came on the scene, that was really something. Enjoying the modern conveniences, she more than once commented about the changes she had lived through.

But one thing never changes. From her mother, she had learned God's Word in German. As a Christian mother, she taught me about Jesus. To me she taught it in English. But the message was the same one about a God who so loved that he gave his one and only Son. As a Christian mother, she brought me to worship services, first in her arms, next on her lap, and then at her side. Though she lived through three different hymnals, the theme was always the same. For her and now for me, it is God's grace in Christ Jesus. As a Christian mother, her life preached the gospel of her Savior. "Let your light shine" means the same thing regardless what century it is.

Time changes many things. But one remains constant. That's God's Word. It stands forever. What my mother taught me, my wife and I have tried to teach to our children. What the pastors preached in her day is what I was called to preach in my day. The Word with its saving message of Jesus remains the same throughout all generations. Thank God for that!

Lord, help me treasure your unchanging
Word and find my salvation there. Amen.

WHATEVER IS TRUE, WHATEVER IS NOBLE, WHATEVER IS RIGHT, WHATEVER IS PURE, WHATEVER IS LOVELY, WHATEVER IS ADMIRABLE . . . THINK ABOUT SUCH THINGS. *Philippians 4:8*

Milking The Mind's Poison

The other day on the Discovery channel we watched a show about snakes. It showed a man in the Far East, milking a cobra. Grabbing the deadly snake at the back of the neck, he squeezed till its mouth opened. Then he pressed the glands and the white liquid oozed out. He also told how three hours later he could milk that same cobra again and get still more venom to sell for antivenin purposes.

Yesterday, stung by a sour remark from someone, I felt like that cobra. My mind was filled with poison. Though I held my cool, I still thought my share. And the thoughts weren't pretty. Nor was this the first time my mind had gone astray. The devil has his way of filling my mind with all kinds of thoughts that are far from being pure, noble, lovely, and admirable. Left to build up in my heart, those thoughts become words. The words become deeds. And people are stung all along the way. I need someone who can grab me and, with knowing hands, milk sin's poison from me. Thank God for Jesus. When my mind produces poison, Jesus points me to his cross. There he paid in full for all my wayward thoughts. When I want those thoughts replaced with ones that are good and pure and lovely, again Jesus points me to his cross. There he crushed the head of Satan, the old serpent. Satan has to retreat when I stand in God's Word beneath my Savior's cross.

Lord, cleanse my heart from sin's poison
and fill it with pure and lovely thoughts. Amen.

> "IF RIGHTEOUSNESS COULD BE
> GAINED THROUGH THE LAW, CHRIST
> DIED FOR NOTHING!" *Galatians 2:21*

No Need For Both

My wife had a relative who came to her family reunion wearing both a belt and suspenders. When I teased him, he replied that he was just being sure that his pants would stay up. Some people try the same thing when it comes to their salvation. They want to rely both on what Christ has done and on what they are doing in their lives.

People like that existed in Paul's day too. They claimed to follow Christ as their Savior. Yet, at the same time, they insisted that all the old laws about circumcision, clean food, and Sabbath days needed to be kept. Paul had strong words for them. "If you think that you have to do something to save yourself," he warned, "then what Jesus did for you means nothing."

The devil can't erase Christ's payment for sin. That's a done deal. It stands recorded in Holy Scripture. "It is finished," the Savior shouted from his Good Friday cross as he stamped "paid in full" on the debt of every sinner. Nothing more is needed. So the devil tries to get people to question this full payment for sin. "Don't I have to do something to get to heaven?" he gets them to ask. "Don't I have to give my offerings, work for my church, run my score up higher if God is going to accept me?" he gets them to think. "Finished" means "paid in full." To question this blessed truth is to doubt my Savior's word. Even worse, it takes away the confidence his word brings me. It makes me reach for my suspenders.

Lord, fill me with the joy of your full
salvation and help me reflect that joy in my life. Amen.

> LET US THROW OFF EVERYTHING THAT HINDERS AND THE
> SIN THAT SO EASILY ENTANGLES, AND LET US RUN WITH
> PERSEVERANCE THE RACE MARKED OUT FOR US. *Hebrews 12:1*

It Doesn't Get Any Easier

In our previous congregation we had a member who ran the Boston Marathon each year. One day I asked about the race. "It's physically draining," he said, "especially the last few inclines. You just don't know if you're going to make it."

The author of Hebrews spoke much the same way about the race of faith. He calls it a "race," a Greek word that means exertion and struggle. He's talking about a constant contest, in the Greek writing, "Let us keep on running." And he's talking about an extremely difficult contest, one that requires perseverance. That word means holding out under stress, not stopping or slowing down for any reason. The race of faith is not some hundred-meter dash, but a lifelong marathon. In this marathon, like the Greek runner, I need to eliminate everything that might slow me down. Particularly, I throw off "the sin that so easily entangles." Like some flopping warm-up robe, sin of any kind can wrap itself around my legs and trip me on the track to heaven.

The last inclines seem so steep. Some days I don't know if I'm going to make it. Sometimes people think older Christians have an easier time of it in this race. But that's not true. The devil seems to double his attacks the closer I get to the finish line. I wouldn't be in this race if Jesus hadn't died for me. I can't continue in this race if Jesus doesn't strengthen me. But with his power as he channels it through the gospel, I can cross heaven's finish line.

Lord, thank you for putting me on heaven's
path. Help me run the course in faith. Amen.

> "IT IS EASIER FOR A CAMEL TO GO THROUGH THE
> EYE OF A NEEDLE THAN FOR A RICH MAN TO
> ENTER THE KINGDOM OF GOD." *Mark 10:25*

Camels And The Kingdom Of God

I almost chuckled out loud. On the way home from church, our grand-daughter asked in all seriousness, "Grandpa, a camel can't go through a needle's eye, can it?" She had seen camels at the Milwaukee zoo. She had also seen how small the eye on grandma's sewing needle is.

Jesus wasn't saying that a rich person couldn't make it into heaven. He was referring instead to those who make riches their God. There are plenty of them out there who take the letter "l" out of *gold* and end up with *god*. There are also rich people who trust God instead of gold. Like Abraham, David, Nicodemus they don't serve their riches but put their riches into service for the Savior. There are also other barriers to the kingdom of God besides riches. Anything on which people set their hearts becomes their god, making them too wide and high for heaven's door.

No, camels can't pass through the eye of a needle. They're too huge for such a small opening. Neither can a person who trusts in something other than Jesus enter heaven's narrow door. But, yes, those who are rich in Jesus make it through. Later Jesus told his disciples that God makes the impossible possible. He takes sinners and through faith fills them with the riches of his pardon and peace. Covered by God's grace with Jesus' blood and righteousness, they pass through heaven's doors. I'm glad that God hasn't blessed me with earthly riches. That temptation he has kept from me. But I'm even more glad that he's made me rich in Christ and ready for heaven.

Lord, I can never thank you enough for
bringing me to faith and readying me for heaven. Amen.

SINCE, THEN, YOU HAVE BEEN RAISED
WITH CHRIST, SET YOUR HEARTS
ON THINGS ABOVE. *Colossians 3:1*

Vulture Or Hummingbird?

Somewhere I read that two kinds of birds fly over the California deserts. One is the vulture. It soars aloft looking for some carcass on the desert sand. Down it swoops to feast on the carrion. The other is the hummingbird. It spots a tiny blossom on a spiny cactus and spears it with its sharp bill. The vulture sees only the carcass. The hummingbird seeks the sweet cactus flower.

Can you guess which is the believer and which the unbeliever? Unbelievers don't think of themselves as vultures. Yet they feed on the world's dead things. Sometimes this carrion looks so good, smells so sweet, and tastes so great. The unbeliever's humanitarian efforts and concern for the world's betterment attract applause. Sometimes it's disgusting what unbelievers sink their teeth into. Pornography, illicit sex, disregard for marriage vows are a few examples. These examples, though, are dead carcasses in the eyes of God, who looks into the heart.

What about the believer, the one whose sinful flesh died with Christ and whose new life of faith rose with Christ? The believer wants to center his life on things above. Hearts cleansed from sin by the Savior seek to walk the clean road of Christian living. Hands filled with Christ's heavenly riches use, not abuse, the things of this world. Feet traveling on heaven's path don't trample over others on the way. The world laughs at and takes advantage of hummingbirds like us. But I'd rather have the sweet blossom of the cactus than carrion any day.

Lord, keep my eyes lifted up to heaven's shores
even as I walk as your child here on earth. Amen.

> DO NOT BOAST ABOUT TOMORROW,
> FOR YOU DO NOT KNOW WHAT A DAY
> MAY BRING FORTH. *Proverbs 27:1*

Only One Sure Thing

Our friends lost their son last month in the Middle East. Bad weather took his plane down in the mountains. The crash killed all 104 people on board. Their son had left his commission in the Navy and gone to work for a civilian contractor. Now he was gone, leaving a wife and family behind.

Solomon's words of wisdom come to mind. None of us can "boast about tomorrow." That fact doesn't mean that I shouldn't prepare for tomorrow. What it means is that I can't lay claim to tomorrow. Only God's grace can give me another day. Jesus once said, "It is not for you to know the times or dates the Father has set by his own authority" (Acts 1:7). He was speaking to his disciples about the Last Day, but his words apply equally to my last day.

Solomon's words of wisdom remind me of something else. Though I can't lay claim to another day, I can use today to get ready for tomorrow. My Savior wisely commands, "Seek first his kingdom and his righteousness, and all these things will be given to you as well" (Matthew 6:33). Today is the time of grace he gives me to prepare for my eternal future. When I use each day to grow closer to my Savior, I've used it wisely. When I leave tomorrow in his loving hands, I'm on safe ground. Regardless of my age, the psalmist's prayer fits, "Teach us to number our days aright, that we may gain a heart of wisdom" (90:12).

Lord, thank you for today. Help me
leave tomorrow in your loving hands. Amen.

NOTHING IN ALL CREATION IS HIDDEN FROM GOD'S SIGHT.
EVERYTHING IS UNCOVERED AND BARE BEFORE THE EYES
OF HIM TO WHOM WE MUST GIVE ACCOUNT. *Hebrews 4:13*

No Shield For Sin

Although our van has no trunk in which to conceal valuable items, it has a nice feature. Its windows are treated in such a way that no one can look through from the outside.

Sometimes I think that I can treat the windows of my life so that God can't see my errors. Because I can hide my envious, lustful thoughts from others, I think I can do the same with God. Because I can fool others by sweeping sin's dirt under the carpet, I think God won't notice either.

"Wrong!" the verse tells me. "Nothing in all creation is hidden from God's sight," it warns. God has X-ray vision that pierces through everything. "Everything is uncovered and bare" before his eyes, it says so that I can't miss the warning. My secret sin, my stowaway temptation, that little speck of decay, everything lies wide open before him.

Best of all, the verse reminds me that he who sees all is the One to whom I must give an account. If I were an unbeliever, this thought ought to bring me up short. It's the stern warning that I can't fool this righteous judge, but I must one day face him. As a believer, though, this verse is gospel. It warms me with the thought that God knows all my weaknesses and stands ready to provide in Christ all I need. When I stand before him on my last day, he won't see my sins. Not because they're hidden behind some colored glass but because they're covered by Jesus' blood.

Lord, thank you for Jesus' blood that covers
my sins so that I can stand holy in your sight. Amen.

BOTH THE ONE WHO MAKES MEN HOLY AND THOSE WHO
ARE MADE HOLY ARE OF THE SAME FAMILY. SO JESUS IS
NOT ASHAMED TO CALL THEM BROTHERS. *Hebrews 2:11*

My Big Brother

I never had a brother. Many times I've wished that I had. It seems like it would be more fun playing ball and going fishing with brothers than with sisters. Perhaps some of you have brothers. If so, then you know what I mean.

I'm glad that I have Jesus as my big brother. He has done things for me that no human brother ever could. He makes me "holy," the verse says. That's why he came to earth. He became flesh and blood just like me. Yet unlike me, he had no sin. His heart was perfectly holy and so was his life. But also, unlike me, he could do something about my sin. As God's own Son his blood was precious enough to make payment for all my sins. He took my place on the cross, suffered the punishment of hell I had deserved, and now hands this perfect payment for sin to me. It's mine! No, I didn't prepare it. My big brother did. But it counts for me.

By God's grace, I can call Jesus my brother. Because of God's love, Jesus calls me his brother. Can anything be sweeter than to hear Jesus tell my heavenly Father, "Here, he's my brother—a son in your family just as I am"? Just think what is mine here on earth and forever in heaven because Jesus in his love became my brother.

I never had a brother. But I certainly don't ever want to be without Jesus as my big brother.

Lord Jesus, thank you for becoming my
brother to save me and make me your brother. Amen.

> WE HAVE THIS TREASURE IN JARS OF CLAY TO
> SHOW THAT THIS ALL-SURPASSING POWER IS
> FROM GOD AND NOT FROM US. *2 Corinthians 4:7*

Not The Container
But The Contents

I still use my old metal tackle box. Its hinges are rusted and its top dented. I've replaced the handle with rope. But I take it with me when I go fishing. Inside are all my fishing treasures—the lures that I've acquired, the Hopalong Cassidy jack knife that I bought as a kid, the extra line and sinkers that I need. My wife wonders why I don't buy a new one. But I tell her it's the contents that count.

Ever wonder why God put the treasures of his salvation into our hands? Surely he could have found a much more suitable container for such precious contents. I know how often I didn't tell my neighbors about their only Savior. Or if I tried, how often I seemed to botch the job. I know how often I passed by the opportunity to teach my children about Jesus. I know how often as a pastor I could have done better. So why in the world did God put the priceless message of his salvation into my rusty, dented hands?

Could it be that he wanted to remind me where the power behind his message lies? Not in the one telling it but in the One of whom it tells. Not in the one preaching but in the One who is the central message of all preaching. It's God's message. It's his message about his Son, the only Savior from sin. And it's God's power that makes the message work in the hearts of people. I'm only a rusty, dented container, but the contents God entrusted to me are more than precious.

Lord, help me be a better witness
of your message of salvation. Amen.

> YOU ARE NO LONGER A SLAVE, BUT A SON;
> AND SINCE YOU ARE A SON, GOD HAS
> MADE YOU ALSO AN HEIR. *Galatians 4:7*

What Is His Is Mine

My wife and I in our retirement have gone into woodworking. The more we get into it, the more tools we need. The other day on the phone, I told my son about buying a planer so that we could make rough boards smooth. "Do you think you'll get your money out of that planer?" my son asked. "Probably not," I replied, "but you will." Someday that machine will be his.

When my heavenly Father brought me to faith, he already shared his treasures with me. At my baptism he made me his own son. That means I already have his forgiveness to make my sin-rough life smooth. That means I already have peace with him, a peace that comes from knowing him as a loving Father in whose family I stand. Through his Word he continues to share his possessions with me. Not just some woodworking equipment that will wear out, but the eternal treasures of his grace are mine.

In heaven, someday my inheritance will be complete. When the Father invites, "Come, . . . take your inheritance, the kingdom prepared for you since the creation of the world," he'll share with me the life in heaven prepared by the blood of his Son (Matthew 25:34). At that moment I'll exchange life *for* him on earth for life *with* him in heaven. I enjoy this blessed life with my Father already here on earth. But that's nothing compared to what he has waiting for me in heaven at his side.

Father, thank you for making me your child.
Help me appreciate what you give me. Amen.

> WHEN I WAS A CHILD, I TALKED LIKE A CHILD, I THOUGHT
> LIKE A CHILD, I REASONED LIKE A CHILD. WHEN I BECAME
> A MAN, I PUT CHILDISH WAYS BEHIND ME. *1 Corinthians 13:11*

Seeing With Grown-Up Eyes

One day our two boys were playing with little toy cars called Hot Wheels. The next day, or so it seemed, they were behind the wheels of their own cars. What a difference from racing those toy cars to running a real one on the highway. So quickly life races on and our perspectives change.

It's the same with my life as a Christian. So often in this life my knowledge of God's Word is partial and my understanding incomplete. I believe what he has told me even though I don't understand. Like our boys, I long to be grown up. I wait for the time when I can know my gracious God more perfectly and understand his ways more completely.

For example, the incarnation of his Son. How could God, who is timeless, enter this world of time as a man? How could he, who is sinless, take on my load of sins? And the love behind it all? What kind of love is this? Or the mystery of the Trinity. How could the true God be one God and yet three, equal, eternal persons? How could this marvelous triune God be so interested in my salvation? Or the inspiration of Scripture. How could a book written by human beings be his errorless, always true Word? Here in this life I'm like a child still playing with toys when it comes to understanding such divine mysteries.

When members would ask me questions that I couldn't answer, I'd respond, "That's one to ask God when we get to heaven." Then I'd pause and say, "In heaven we won't need to ask. We'll know all the answers."

Lord, I can hardly wait! Amen.

> THE FOOLISHNESS OF GOD IS WISER THAN MAN'S
> WISDOM, AND THE WEAKNESS OF GOD IS STRONGER
> THAN MAN'S STRENGTH. *1 Corinthians 1:25*

When Foolishness Is Wisdom

I was on a flight to Mexico to visit our missionaries. Sitting next to me was a lawyer going to Acapulco for rest and recreation. As we conversed, I tried to tell him about Jesus my Savior. His reply was frosty: "I don't want to hear about your Christ. All I need is to be good, do good, and God will be good to me."

What I believed as the wisdom of God was foolishness to him. Nor is he the only one. By nature people think they can reach whatever eternity there might be by their own actions. So they scratch around in this world, tally up their works, and hope that they're good enough. "Wisdom," they call this. But it's only foolishness. How can people know when the sum of their works is high enough to buy entrance into eternity?

Nor is the cross of Jesus the answer for such worldly wise. To them the cross is a symbol of weakness. Even if the unbeliever sees Jesus on that cross, the Savior hardly seems strong enough to pay for a world's sins. Who wants to rely on someone who was crucified for entrance into heaven?

I do! I know that in God's kingdom things are topsy-turvy. What unbelievers consider foolish, God proves is wisdom. What they consider weakness, God proves is strength. Unbelievers see the cross of Jesus as foolishness and weakness. For me, God has made it the greatest truth I can ever know.

Lord, keep me wise unto salvation
through faith in Christ Jesus. Amen.

I WANT TO KNOW CHRIST. *Philippians 3:10*

Knowing Christ—Impossible

Once upon a time for Paul, it was, "I despise Christ and want to destroy his followers." Why? Because Christ was a threat to Paul's way to heaven. Paul planned to earn heaven with his own works. A Savior who offered heaven as a free gift was beyond his comprehension. Nor could Paul do anything to change his reaction. Later he told the Corinthians, "The man without the Spirit does not accept the things that come from the Spirit of God, for they are foolishness to him" (1 Corinthians 2:14). He wrote to the Ephesians, "You were dead in your transgressions and sins" (2:1). Saul was dead in unbelief and had no more power than a corpse to change his condition.

Wasn't it the same with Martin Luther? Luther thought he had to earn heaven. He was taught a Christ who was his judge, not his Savior. Even in the monastery where he slaved away, he had to cry, "My sins, oh, my sins." Luther knew *of* Christ but didn't really know him. Nor was there any way for him to change that. Not "Jesus loves me, this I know" but "Jesus will judge me, and this I fear" drove him to struggle with his sins and strive with his works.

I know Christ. I can hardly remember a time when I didn't. But do I remember how come I know him? Left to myself, I'd still be loading my own deeds into a cardboard box that wouldn't hold up in the journey across the eternal sea. But as with Paul and Luther, God has been gracious to me. He has brought me out of unbelief's death to faith's life. It is by his miracle alone that I can sing, "Jesus loves me, this I know, for the Bible tells me so."

Thank you, Lord, for the miracle of faith. Amen.

I CONSIDER [THE THINGS I'VE LOST] RUBBISH, THAT I MAY GAIN
CHRIST AND BE FOUND IN HIM, NOT HAVING A RIGHTEOUSNESS
OF MY OWN THAT COMES FROM THE LAW, BUT THAT WHICH IS
THROUGH FAITH IN CHRIST—THE RIGHTEOUSNESS THAT
COMES FROM GOD AND IS BY FAITH. *Philippians 3:8,9*

Knowing Christ—Incredible

"Rubbish," Paul called his former works. All his striving for heaven
seemed now like something fit only to be shoved out of sight. "I want
to be found in Christ," he shouts, "having a righteousness that is
through faith in Christ." Ever since that day on the Damascus road
when the risen Christ had come to him, cracked open his dead heart,
and changed his rebellious spirit, Paul had one treasure. His goal was to
have Christ and to get to know his Savior better.

Wasn't it the same with Martin Luther? As Luther prepared his lectures
on Paul's letter to the Romans, God said, "Let there be light." And
Luther saw his Savior. God's grace showed Luther that the righteousness that counts is the one Christ earned by his spotless life and his
innocent death for sin. "Then the whole Scripture was opened to me
and also heaven itself," Luther wrote with joy. "Immediately I felt as if
born anew, as if I had found the open gate to paradise," he exulted. He
knew Christ was the most incredible treasure in the world for him.

Do I stop often enough to consider how incredible my knowing Christ
is? I know that in Christ my sins are forgiven. In Christ I have a peace
that I surely can't live or die without. In Christ I have victory spelled
L-I-F-E when the grave opens before me. This and so much more I have
when by God's incredible grace I know Christ.

Lord, thank you for making Jesus—
his blood and righteousness—my dearest treasure. Amen.

> I AM OBLIGATED BOTH TO GREEKS AND NON-GREEKS, BOTH TO THE WISE AND THE FOOLISH. THAT IS WHY I AM SO EAGER TO PREACH THE GOSPEL ALSO TO YOU WHO ARE AT ROME. *Romans 1:14,15*

Knowing Christ–Unstoppable

If there were one word to use in describing Paul after his conversion, it would be *unstoppable*. From that Damascus road he went out to the known roads of his world to tell others about Christ. The countries he visited, the mission congregations he founded, the souls he led to the Savior are a matter of divine record. All of this was for Christ and for those souls. "I am obligated," Paul said, "to preach the gospel." For him no hill was too high, no sea too wide, no suffering too severe to slow him down. He just had to tell others.

Wasn't it the same with Martin Luther? Till he breathed his last, his zeal to tell others was unstoppable. He preached, wrote, taught, fought, went himself, and sent others, with one concern in mind. He wanted people to know Christ as he did. "The very best of all works," he wrote, "is that the heathen have been led from idolatry to the knowledge of God."

It's not enough for me to say, "I know him." Not enough to say, "My spouse knows him." Not even enough to say, "My children and grandchildren know him." How about my neighbors, not just those who share my culture but also those who are different? How about those nameless, faceless people in cities that are distant and countries far away? By God's incredible grace the impossible has happened to me. I know Christ in the truest sense of the word. Now let my efforts to tell others be unstoppable too.

Lord, let Paul's words fit me too:
"I am so eager to preach the gospel." Amen.

> THEREFORE, STRENGTHEN YOUR FEEBLE
> ARMS AND WEAK KNEES. *Hebrews 12:12*

Always In Training

We knew we'd be doing a lot of walking on our trip to Prague. Many of the streets of this beautiful European city are steep. So my wife and I conditioned ourselves by some serious walking in the weeks before the trip. Still we had to pause at times and catch our breath.

The road of faith is no cakewalk. The incline to heaven is steep. Faith's knees need conditioning if they are going to make it. Also, the enemies along the road are no pushovers. The muscles in faith's arms need toning if they are going to beat off the foe. Unlike our exercising before the trip to Prague, faith's conditioning is a lifelong process. I never reach the point where I can stop and rest. I can never bend my knees, flex my arms, and say, "That's strong enough."

How to exercise my faith is the important question. Working out in some gym or power walking some miles won't do a thing for my faith. I need to work out in God's Word. I need to power walk regularly in his Word. That's why the author of Hebrews, before talking about bulking up faith's muscles, urges me to fix my eyes on Jesus, the author and perfecter of my faith (12:2). Jesus is my Savior, my sure source of pardon for sin and steady source of power for my battle against sin. He's my hope, the one who walks with me on heaven's road and carries me when my legs give out. He sends his Spirit to work in my heart through his gracious Word so that not only are faith's feet on heaven's road but they keep walking there. God's Word is the gym in which I need to work out regularly if I'm serious about conditioning for heaven's walk.

Please, Jesus, send your Spirit to increase
my faith as I work out in your Word. Amen.

> "LET NOT THE WISE MAN BOAST OF HIS WISDOM. . . . BUT LET HIM WHO BOASTS BOAST ABOUT THIS: THAT HE UNDERSTANDS AND KNOWS ME, THAT I AM THE LORD." *Jeremiah 9:23,24*

The Right Wisdom

"How stupid do you think I am?" scoffed the young man. His parents had asked me to visit with him. He was at the university, working on his doctorate. He also hadn't darkened the church doors for several years. And his parents were concerned about his soul. As I tried to converse with him about his need for Christ, that vehement question was his answer.

We need wisdom and learning in our world. They can bring us so much in life. Our great grandparents would view with astonishment the high-definition televisions and wireless phones, the jet engines and space capsules, the surgery techniques and organ transplants that man's wisdom has brought our way. We need to pursue wisdom, but we dare not make it a god on which we pin our hopes or to which we give the glory. When we do, we're putting the limited mind of the creature up on the throne of the eternal Creator. Such a use of wisdom means no more than to be miserable intelligently.

How often don't I run into people who consider themselves "smart" enough to solve their own problems and set their own destinies? "Why do I need God?" such "wise" ones ask. "I can take care of myself." At times, I too may think the same thing. Then I need Jeremiah's reminder. He reminds me that I may know about many things. I may even know many things. But unless I know THE thing, the cross by which I'm saved and the wisdom of God behind it, I'm the greatest fool on earth.

Lord, thank you for making me wise unto salvation through faith in Christ Jesus. Amen.

> "LET NOT . . . THE STRONG MAN BOAST OF HIS STRENGTH. . . .
> BUT LET HIM WHO BOASTS BOAST ABOUT THIS: THAT HE
> UNDERSTANDS AND KNOWS ME." *Jeremiah 9:23,24*

The Right Strength

"Might makes right" is how the world puts it. Everybody admires and desires worldly strength. Might carries people for a while. But then comes the fall, and hard it is indeed.

A brief glance at history reveals that power rises only to fall. The histories of ancient Greece and Rome, more recently of Communist Russia, show that at the point a nation flexes its muscles it's already on the decline. In our own nuclear power age, it should be all the more obvious that there's no sense in boasting in strength. The nuclear power we have created has become the Frankenstein that threatens our existence. Earthly power may win today, but what about tomorrow? It may conquer in many battles, but what about the war with death?

Do we need Jeremiah's warning? When we're young, we think we can handle anything. No job is too big or challenge too tough. Even as we grow older, the desire for power and drive for position propel many a person. How quickly we can forget that the gravestones of some at the cemetery may rise higher than others, but underneath all lie at the same level.

Do I want to boast about strength? Then let it be in the One whose strength is made perfect in my weakness. Let my trust be firm in the power of a loving God, who has already destroyed death by his Son's cross and given me entrance into eternity through my Savior's emptied tomb.

Lord, I am weak, but you are strong.
Hold me always with your powerful hand. Amen.

"LET NOT . . . THE RICH MAN BOAST OF HIS RICHES,
BUT LET HIM WHO BOASTS BOAST ABOUT THIS: THAT
HE UNDERSTANDS AND KNOWS ME." *Jeremiah 9:23,24*

The Right Riches

Have you ever met a poor man who trusted in riches? I have. Some days I'm even that person. When I fear that my retirement plans won't keep pace with the economy, I'm exhibiting the symptoms of spiritual affluenza. When I'm dissatisfied with my house, my job, my position in life, I'm hugging the things of this world more tightly than I ought. Not just the rich trust in their wealth. So do those who are dissatisfied with what God has given them and long for more.

One week this past summer, a band of clever thieves hit our community. They would enter a store in a group. One or two of them would separate from the group. The rest would cause a disturbance in another part of the store. While the clerks were distracted, the accomplices filled their pockets with merchandise. Then all would leave. Hours later, perhaps days later, the victimized merchant would discover his loss and call the police. Too late! How the devil delights in using this tactic. He tries to divert my attention to the money and goods of this world while his evil angels attempt to steal away my salvation.

Do I want to be rich? Really rich, that is? Then it's time to head for Jesus' cross. There the Savior dispenses freely the riches of his salvation. What can compare to having forgiveness for my sins? What can come close to having the robe of his righteousness wrapped around me? What can be more precious than the crown of life waiting for me in heaven?

Jesus, may I treasure your blood
and righteousness now and eternally. Amen.

> YOU SHOW THAT YOU ARE A LETTER FROM CHRIST,
> THE RESULT OF OUR MINISTRY, WRITTEN NOT WITH INK
> BUT WITH THE SPIRIT OF THE LIVING GOD, NOT ON TABLETS
> OF STONE BUT TABLETS OF HUMAN HEARTS." *2 Corinthians 3:3*

Living Letters
Of Recommendation

Many times high school graduates, whom I had confirmed, would use my name as a reference. Or they would ask me for a letter of recommendation as they applied for a position or for entrance into college. Usually I was happy to oblige.

Did you ever think of a believer being a letter of recommendation? That's how Paul described the Christians at Corinth. A "letter from Christ," he called them. We write recommendations with ink on paper. The Holy Spirit had written this letter on their hearts and in their lives when he brought them to faith in the Savior. Paul had done the preaching, but the Spirit had done the writing. Now Paul could point to those Corinthian Christians as his credentials. They showed his ministry was genuine and even more so was the Savior he preached.

"I learned the gospel from my mother. Sometimes she even used words," a layman with whom I worked on a synodical board told me. His mother was a Christ letter. She taught him by word and deed. "What you do speaks so loudly, I can't hear what you say" is how another person put it. What do those around me read from my daily life? What kind of recommendation am I for the One who gave his all for me? Will those who look at and listen to me want to read more about their only Savior? I pray so. God make me so—a living letter of recommendation for Jesus.

Lord, you used others to show me the
Savior. Now use me to show him to others. Amen.

> THEREFORE, I URGE YOU, BROTHERS, IN VIEW OF
> GOD'S MERCY, TO OFFER YOUR BODIES AS LIVING
> SACRIFICES, HOLY AND PLEASING TO GOD. *Romans 12:1*

Me, A Sacrifice? What?

What kind of sacrifice does God desire from me? Paul's answer almost takes my breath away. "Offer your bodies," he says, "as living sacrifices . . . to God." Of course, when he says *body*, he means me and all that I am. Everything I am and have is to be offered willingly to God. God wants me—period!

Me? A sacrifice? Is that how it goes in daily life? Do I tell him, "Take my moments and my days" but then let a little rainfall, a late Saturday evening, a vacation away, get in the way of an hour's time to worship him? Do I sing, "Take my will and make it thine" but then let some pet sin that has worked its way into the fabric of my daily life rule my days? Do I vow, "Take my hands, my feet, my voice, my lips" but then sidestep with, "Lord, you know how busy I am"? And, I haven't even said a word about "my silver" and "my gold."

Me? A sacrifice? You must be mistaken, Lord. That's not quite what I see when I look at my life in closer detail. Maybe a bit here and a bob there—a short burst here and a slow crawl there. But me, totally, all the time, Lord, is that really what you want? Oh, Lord, please forgive me.

Time to look again at Calvary. That was no halfway sacrifice stretched out on that awe-full hill. That was God's Son completely given by a God of total and complete love.

*God, help my grateful response to run
in a similar vein. God, help me pray, "Take
myself and I will be, ever, only, all for thee." Amen.*

> THEREFORE, I URGE YOU, BROTHERS, IN VIEW OF
> GOD'S MERCY, TO OFFER YOUR BODIES AS LIVING
> SACRIFICES, HOLY AND PLEASING TO GOD. *Romans 12:1*

Me, A Sacrifice? Why?

That's the main question, isn't it? If I'm convinced about the "why," then the "what" will follow. Why should I show concern for my family, my church, my country, my world, when others laugh at what it seems to cost? Why should I save myself for my marriage partner when around me others flit from partner to partner and seemingly with so much pleasure? Why should I serve my church and spend all that time when many seem to do so little? Why should I be concerned about what God wants when it's much easier and pleasing, at least so it seems, to do what I want? In short, why should I offer myself as a living sacrifice to God?

Do I need to ask? Don't I know? Yes, but how I need the constant reminder! Nobody can force me into offering myself more fully to God. There's only one way service comes—only one force that can make me want to be a living sacrifice for my God. Paul says it with one little expression in our verse. "In view of God's mercy," he says and, with that phrase, takes me right to the foot of the cross.

For me, God's Son felt the rough wood of the Bethlehem crib and the even rougher wood of the Calvary cross. For me, he was wrapped in swaddling clothes and weighed down with sin's sordid load. For me, he sweat drops of blood in Gethsemane's dust and sighed life's last breath in Golgotha's darkness. For me, he paid sin's debt in full, pushed open heaven's door, prepared an eternity filled with joy. For me! All this for me! Now what will be my response "in view of God's mercy"?

God, help it be, "Me! A sacrifice!" Amen.

> WHEN TEMPTED, NO ONE SHOULD SAY, "GOD
> IS TEMPTING ME." FOR GOD CANNOT BE TEMPTED
> BY EVIL, NOR DOES HE TEMPT ANYONE. *James 1:13*

Put The Blame Where It Belongs

So, you're being tempted! Sin taps gently on life's door, and it swings open. Or sin raps rudely and repeatedly till the lock breaks and the hinges bend. Isn't that how it goes so often?

Shifting the blame for temptation is nothing new. The comic phrase "the devil made me do it" is such an evasion. Of course, Satan has much to do with sin. But he's not the only or the closest one to blame when temptation comes. Others try shifting the blame to God. Like Pilate, reaching with dripping hands for a clean towel, they point to others. Adam tried it also in the Garden of Eden when he blamed Eve for his sin. All these say, "Don't blame me. Blame God who made the world and me the way we are. Blame him for the people and the things around me."

Yet James tells me, "God cannot be tempted by evil, nor does he tempt anyone." Because God is absolute holiness, he cannot have contact or contract with evil. Instead, he keeps temptation away from me or gives me the power to repel it. Not God but my sinful heart is the problem. The devil and world are always ready to put the match to temptation's charcoal within my heart.

What to do when temptation succeeds as it often does in my life? Above all, I need to remember that though I can't shift my sins to others, God can and did. He laid my iniquity on his Son and healed me with his Son's wounds. Because of Jesus, I'm welcomed back to my Father's house.

Lord, thank you for power when I try to walk
in your ways and for forgiveness when I fall. Amen.

> HE CHOSE TO GIVE US BIRTH THROUGH THE
> WORD OF TRUTH, THAT WE MIGHT BE A KIND
> OF FIRSTFRUITS OF ALL HE CREATED. *James 1:18*

Look What He Has Done For Me

Back in the endless day of eternity, God willed to save us. In his marvelous grace, without any worthiness in us whatsoever, he chose us of his free will out of the mass of all mankind to be his children and heirs of his heaven.

Then came the day when angels sang and shepherds saw in a manger the miracle of God's love. There lay the best God could give, his Son born of woman, burdened with our sins, that we might become God's children, unburdened of all our sin. Soon after that came another day, a black one with its crimson cross. On that cross, the Savior took the pains of hell we had deserved and drained the cup of sin we had filled. On Sunday came the victory. Since Easter, the risen Christ is at work in the world. In his Word of Truth he has deposited all we need to know of life and salvation. Through that Word of Truth his Spirit works in our hearts, giving the new birth of faith.

For me there's been another day, the one when God worked faith within me. At the baptismal font or through the spoken Word, he made me his firstfruit. Like some first sheaves of grain reserved for God's use in the Old Testament, I was set aside for his very own. Others may be his creatures. I am his child. The world may be his goods. I am his treasure. Now I wait for one more day—that eternal day. When it comes, he'll take me from the faint view of his face here to full sight of it in heaven—from stumbling in a vale of tears to standing at his side, his firstfruits forevermore.

Thanks, Lord, thanks so much
for all you have done for me. Amen.

> MY BROTHERS, AS BELIEVERS IN OUR GLORIOUS LORD
> JESUS CHRIST, DON'T SHOW FAVORITISM. *James 2:1*

No Difference In Jesus' Eyes

People are partial. Some like chocolate ice cream; others, vanilla. Some prefer classical; others, country music. Some play in the sun; others, in the snow. It's a good thing such partiality exists. How dull the world would be without it! With the souls of people, however, there dare be no partiality. All souls are equal in God's eyes and need to be in our eyes too.

Notice how quickly James focuses his topic. He cannot talk about living the Christian life without pointing to the Lord Jesus Christ. This Christ, who fills my heart and floods my life, is "glorious." His is the glory as of the only-begotten of the Father, yet he put aside that glory. A borrowed manger became his cradle. A borrowed boat his pulpit. A borrowed tomb his resting place. All this so that all people might share his glory with him. For all he came, since "all have sinned and fall short of the glory of God" (Romans 3:23). For all he died, paying the same price for each soul. For all he reaches, for Samaritan and Jew, for blind Bartimaeus and rich Nicodemus, for a penitent malefactor and ruling Pilate. In his eyes, all are the same, regardless of position or possession, culture or race.

"God is bringing the mission field right to our own backyard," someone put it. Around me in increasing number are people different from me in culture but not in need. Like me, they need the Savior from sin. Just as he reached for me, the Savior wants to reach them with his gospel of salvation. And he wants to do this through me.

Lord, open my eyes to see around me
the souls in need of your saving message. Amen.

> FAITH BY ITSELF, IF IT IS NOT
> ACCOMPANIED BY ACTION, IS DEAD. *James 2:17*

Does It Work?

Every year people contact the US Patent Office to seek patents for their inventions. Among the questions asked before such a patent is granted are "Does it work? Is your invention usable?"

James poses the same question. "Does it work?" he asks of my faith. Before I answer, I need to think of grace. For it is God's grace that saves me. God's grace planned my salvation in eternity, prepared it on Calvary, and proffers it to me through Word and sacrament. Even the faith through which I obtain the benefits of this salvation is a gift of God's grace. Such faith, James reminds me, involves more than taking Sunday trips to church. It involves my daily life. Faith that binds my heart to Christ also binds my life to his service.

With this emphasis James doesn't contradict Paul who wrote, "A man is justified by faith apart from observing the law" (Romans 3:28). Paul described the way of justification. James described the life of the justified. Paul warned against "law works" that the self-righteous sinner would use to earn his salvation. James encouraged "gospel works" that flow from a believer's thankful heart. Paul and James are complementary, not contradictory. Like colors at opposite ends of the spectrum, both are needed to show the full rainbow of Christianity.

James' point is clear. Works are never a cause of salvation but ever a result. No more than a rose can refuse to release its fragrance or a fire to radiate its heat can faith fail to produce works.

God of all grace, cause my
faith to show in my daily life. Amen.

> WHEN WE PUT BITS INTO THE MOUTHS OF HORSES TO MAKE
> THEM OBEY US, WE CAN TURN THE WHOLE ANIMAL. OR TAKE
> SHIPS AS AN EXAMPLE. ALTHOUGH THEY ARE SO LARGE . . .
> THEY ARE STEERED BY A VERY SMALL RUDDER. . . .
> LIKEWISE THE TONGUE IS A SMALL PART OF THE BODY. *James 3:3-5*

The Tiny Tongue

Two examples show what great effect the tiny tongue has. A spirited, strong-willed stallion is turned this way or that by the tiny bit in its mouth. A giant ship plows its furrow in the deep, going where the pressure on the tiny rudder indicates. So it is with the tongue, one of the smaller parts of the body. What power it has!

My tongue can compel the feeble and comfort the fainthearted. Or it can crumple reputations and compound recriminations. It can make songs that lift up hearts and deliver speeches that fire up heroes. It can wipe out human hope and leave whip marks on the heart. A few enticing words in Eden's garden plunged the whole human race into sin. But a few triumphant words in Easter's garden promise life to all believers. Who can measure the great power of the tiny tongue?

My tiny tongue, with the hand of the Spirit on it, has tremendous power for good. For my God, there can only be glory when I use my tongue to sing his praise. For myself, there can only be gain when I use my tongue to recite his Word. For my neighbor, there can only be good when I use my tongue to spread his story. But it all depends on whose hand "holds the reins" or "handles the rudder." Only when my heart is reached by Christ's salvation is my tongue restored to Christ's service.

*Lord, cleanse my heart and control
my tongue, that I may speak for you. Amen.*

ALL KINDS OF ANIMALS, BIRDS, REPTILES AND CREATURES OF THE
SEA ARE BEING TAMED . . . BY MAN, BUT NO MAN CAN TAME THE
TONGUE. IT IS A RESTLESS EVIL, FULL OF DEADLY POISON. *James 3:7,8*

Tongues Tamed By Christ

People can tame many things. In creation, God gave them dominion
over beasts and birds, serpents and sea creatures. Though sin blighted
their mastery, yet they exert it somewhat with force and cunning. They
can tame creatures of all kinds to serve as beasts of burden or to
entertain as pets of pleasure. People can master the animals around
them but not the tongue within them! For sinful people, the tongue is
a wild beast they cannot break or bring under control.

A brief glance into the shadows of sin in Eden shows this fact. After
the fall, Adam used his tongue to make excuse to his Maker and
accusation against his wife. A brief glance into sin's shadows in my own
life verifies what I've seen in Eden. The loving, glorifying tongue God
wants for me has become a buck-passing, blaming tongue. Like some
restless snake, it slithers around, darting and striking without warning,
puncturing and paralyzing with its venom.

And that's the point. When it comes to tongue taming, I'm not just
weak. I'm helpless. Tongue taming is a job for my Savior. It requires
digging deeper and doing heart transplanting. Only Jesus can create a
clean heart and renew a right spirit within me. Only when he does this
through Word and sacrament can the words of my mouth and the
meditation of my heart even begin to be acceptable in his sight. Only
then can I use my tongue for him.

Lord, open my lips and let my
mouth show forth your praise. Amen.

> OUT OF THE SAME MOUTH COME
> PRAISE AND CURSING. MY BROTHERS,
> THIS SHOULD NOT BE. *James 3:10*

Tongues Trained For Christ

"Show me your tongue," says the doctor. By looking at my tongue, he can tell something about my physical health. "Show me your tongue," Scripture also says. By listening to my tongue, people can tell something about my spiritual health.

So what does the use of my tongue indicate? To use my tongue in loving praise toward God is the lofty goal for which he has made it. Yet at times that same tongue is used to curse my fellowman. James is right, "My brothers, this should not be." Such "Dr. Jekyll and Mr. Hyde" use of my tongue is not what God had in mind when he gave me the marvelous gift of speech.

On Sunday my tongue can raise holy hymns and on Monday repeat smutty stories. In the evening it can speak pious prayers and in the morning spread ripe rumors. Such split use of my tongue can lead to spiritual bankruptcy. If I have been guilty, I need to plead in penitence, "God, be merciful to me, a sinner." God will hear and answer. His own living Word of love he placed into a stable and on a cross to cleanse me also from the sins of my tongue. Through the means of grace he will train my tongue, turning it from running after to running away from sin. He will turn it from cursing people to communicating to them the love of my God. Let the way I use my tongue show to whom I belong. Let it show plainly that I am alive and well in Jesus.

> *"Lord, take my lips and let them be*
> *Filled with messages from thee." Amen.* (CW 469:3)

So will it be with the resurrection of the dead. The body that is sown is perishable, it is raised imperishable. *1 Corinthians 15:42*

Better Than Popcorn

Last night I put the popcorn kettle on the stove. Before long I could hear the familiar popping. How does popcorn work, I wondered? Checking it out, I learned that inside the kernel is a bit of starch and a bit of water. When heated, the water in the kernel turns to steam. The steam builds up pressure until it pops the outer shell. The white popcorn that I enjoy is the starch that was inside. From that tiny kernel came something in entirely different form.

Something far greater is going to happen to my body in the resurrection. Just like that popcorn kernel, it'll be my same body, but marvelously different. Here on earth it's a perishable body. A needy child grows into a strong adult and then back again into weakness. The passing of time ravages my body's strength. Disease and accident leave their scars. Age plucks the hair and dims the sight. And soon it's back to the dust from which my body came.

How different with the body I'll have in the resurrection. In our verse Paul says it will be an imperishable body. In Philippians 3:21 he also said that Christ with his power "will transform our lowly bodies so that they will be like his glorious body." What this all means I can't fully comprehend. I live in a perishing world with a perishable body. How can I understand a body that no longer is subject to the results of sin? But this much I do know—Jesus is the One who will do it. He'll change my perishable body into one that is magnificently imperishable.

Lord Jesus, keep me in faith in you as my
Savior so that I can stand in heaven at your side. Amen.

> "ONE THING I DO KNOW.
> I WAS BLIND BUT NOW I SEE!" *John 9:25*

More Than Bifocals

Some days I get tired of my bifocals. I have to put them on to see the clock next to our bed. I can't read without them. I have to clean them or else put up with the smudges that smear them. How I wish that I could see as I did when I was younger. But then, I stop to think of what life would be like if I were blind.

Jesus had just healed a man born blind. That was already a noteworthy miracle. Far greater was Jesus' miracle of healing that man's spiritual blindness. When the healed man said, "I was blind but now I see!" he didn't just mean that he could see what Jesus looked like. He referred also to faith's seeing in Jesus the only Savior from sin. To see with the eyes is wonderful. To see with the heart is greater by far.

Thank God, I can say those same words: "I was blind but now I see!" Born with a heart totally blinded by sin, I had no ability to see in Jesus my Savior. I didn't even want to look at him and could only reject him. That's how blind unbelief made me. But then Jesus gave me the eyes of faith through the miracle of Baptism. My heart could now look upon my Savior's face and see how lovely it is. True, on this earth faith's eyesight has problems. Some days it suffers from astigmatism that blurs the sight of my beautiful Savior. Other days it's nearsighted and blocks out the view of the eternal home he has waiting for me. Then it's time for a visit to the "eye doctor"—time to turn to his Word where Jesus works on faith's eyes so that I see him more clearly.

Lord, thank you for faith's vision. Keep my eyes of faith focused on your salvation. Amen.

> "I DO BELIEVE; HELP ME OVERCOME
> MY UNBELIEF!" *Mark 9:24*

Flying Safely

We were in Billings, Montana, helping out at a congregation without a pastor. Across the street from the parsonage was a large park where every summer a hot air balloon festival was held. What a sight those balloons slowly taking off were. How I wished that I could go up in one of them. Did you know that at first people were afraid to ride in those balloons? So the first riders in the first balloon were a sheep, a duck, and a rooster. When these animals returned safely, people were the next to go up in the baskets of those balloons.

Sometimes I'm reluctant to trust in Jesus. Yes, I know he's almighty God, who can do anything. He's promised to watch over me and help me with my problems. I also know that he can handle all my sins. He's promised that his death and resurrection have covered every single one of them. But I hesitate at times to fly high with him. My particular problem seems so heavy that I don't think he can really take care of it. My sins seem so numerous that I don't know if his blood can really cover all of them. Yes, I know that I can fly safely with the Savior. But I hesitate to climb into the basket of his hot air balloon!

Time to pray those words again, "Lord, I believe; help me overcome my unbelief!" Time to turn to his powerful Word through which he worked faith in me originally and now works to strengthen my faith. My faith doesn't hold on to Jesus. He holds on to me. The more I live in his Word the more his promises strengthen faith so that I can fly safely with my Savior.

Lord, you know how weak my faith can be.
Strengthen it through your powerful Word. Amen.

[THE ORDINANCES OF THE LORD]
ARE MORE PRECIOUS THAN GOLD,
THAN MUCH PURE GOLD. *Psalm 19:10*

Digging For Real Gold

In 1896 gold was discovered in the Klondike region of the Yukon Territory, just across the border from Alaska. Thousands of people went by ship to Alaska to make the journey overland to the Klondike. Many of them died. Few of them struck it rich. Today, excursions take tourists to this area. One of the trip's highlights is panning for gold, just as those early prospectors did.

I can pan for gold anytime. In fact, I need to pan for the gold of which the psalmist wrote. When he said, "They are more precious than much pure gold," he was referring to God's Word. In that Word I have salvation's gold. God's forgiveness is far more valuable than gold specks panned out of a stream or gold seams dug out of a mine. A bag full of this world's gold may buy me many things. But God's salvation brings me heaven.

Prospectors worked hard to unearth a few nuggets of gold. In God's Word the nuggets of salvation lie open everywhere. Wherever I turn in that heavenly book, I find Jesus. He's the heart and center of the Bible. God gave me his book so that I could grow rich in his salvation.

But he does want me to go prospecting. He wants me to take shovel and pick in hand and dig into his book. When I do, I'll find gold like those prospectors in the Yukon never dreamed of. When I dig regularly and deeply into Scripture, God makes me rich beyond my wildest dreams.

Tourists pan once for gold in the Yukon. I want to pan in God's Word again and again.

Lord, what heavenly riches are
mine when I dig into your Word! Amen.

> WHEN [PETER] SAW THE WIND, HE WAS AFRAID AND, BEGINNING
> TO SINK, CRIED OUT, "LORD, SAVE ME!" IMMEDIATELY JESUS
> REACHED OUT HIS HAND AND CAUGHT HIM. *Matthew 14:30,31*

My Inflatable Vest

Every time I fly it happens. The flight attendant demonstrates the life vest I'm to use if the plane goes down over water. I watch the demonstration and then hope that I never have to wear that vest. It looks so flimsy and besides I can't swim. Will it really hold me above the waves?

Peter thought he didn't need a life vest that night out on the Lake of Galilee. When he saw Jesus walking on the water toward their boat in the midst of the storm, bold Peter asked to join him. When Jesus invited him, "Come," Peter stepped out of the boat onto the waves. As long as he looked to Jesus, he was safe. The wind might toss his hair, the spray might drench his robe, but all was well. When Peter looked at the boat out of reach and the furious waves beneath his feet, he began to sink. When he forgot about Jesus, who was so near, the solid water became fluid again under his feet. As the waters drew him under, he cried, "Lord, save me!"

How come I so easily forget what Jesus did for Peter that day out on the lake? In the storms of life, I make the mistake of looking at the waves instead of at Jesus. I feel the spray of the storm and fear that Jesus is so far away. I look at the life vest and wonder if it'll hold me. How I need to feel the touch of his hand as Peter did that day. When the Savior calls out to me through his Word, "Take courage! It is I. Don't be afraid," I know I'll be safe. His life vest always works.

Lord, when the storms of life beat down
on me, let me feel your powerful hand. Amen.

> THOSE WHO HAD BEEN SCATTERED PREACHED
> THE WORD WHEREVER THEY WENT. *Acts 8:4*

Spreading The Seed Of The Word

Where did oranges originate? While peeling several for our lunch yesterday, I got to thinking about this question. Seems that this delicious fruit, rich in vitamin C, came originally from China. The Spanish and Portuguese explorers carried orange seeds with them to our continent. Early Spanish settlers planted them in Florida and California. And the rest, as they say, is history.

The early Christians, forced by persecution to scatter from Jerusalem, spread something too—not orange seeds but the Word of God. Wherever those believers went, they preached the message of God's saving love in Christ Jesus. The vitamin C in oranges is good for my body, helping it stay healthy and also to fight off sickness. The vitamins of salvation in God's Word do even more for my soul. A gracious God has packed into his Word the news of my Savior. It's chock full with the forgiveness that Jesus has earned for my sins. It makes my heart, dead in sin, alive in faith through the work of the Spirit. It clears up my eyes so that they see beyond this ball of mud to the glory of heaven.

I could peel those oranges yesterday because years ago people brought seeds to the North American continent. Similarly, my soul has God's health-giving Word because others brought it over the years to my side. Now what about me? How many seeds am I scattering? Just as with those early believers from Jerusalem, God wants me to spread his Word wherever he puts me. I have it. People need it. God wants me to preach it.

Thank you, for those who brought your
Word to me. Use me to bring it to others. Amen.

> JESUS CHRIST IS THE SAME YESTERDAY
> AND TODAY AND FOREVER. *Hebrews 13:8*

No Changing For God

On a visit to the zoo with our grandchildren, we stopped in front of the glass case housing chameleons. This strange looking member of the lizard family comes from Africa. Its body is flat as if mashed out of shape. Its sticky tongue, about as long as its body, shoots out suddenly to catch its prey. Its skin can change color rapidly enabling the chameleon to hide in its surroundings. One moment it's green or yellow or brown. The next moment it might be a completely different color.

What if God were like that chameleon? What if he changed from one moment to the next? What if tonight when I prayed on my pillow, "Forgive us our trespasses," he would answer, "Not today. Try me again tomorrow"? What if in the day of trouble when I raised my anxious face toward him, he'd reply, "You've used up your quota of help for this year. Handle your problem as best you can"? What if when the devil comes tempting me, God would respond, "This time fight him on your own. I'm tired of always helping you out"? Or what if when death draws near, he'd turn his back on me and tell me to walk through the valley of the shadow alone?

I know none of the above will ever happen. How do I know? Because God has said so. He's told me that he never changes. He's told me that Jesus my Savior is the same yesterday and today and forever. Chameleons change color, and that's what makes them interesting. My God of love never changes, and that's what makes him so valuable.

Lord, in this ever-changing world,
fix my eyes on your unchangeable love. Amen.

WE KNOW THAT IN ALL THINGS GOD WORKS FOR THE GOOD OF THOSE WHO LOVE HIM, WHO HAVE BEEN CALLED ACCORDING TO HIS PURPOSE. *Romans 8:28*

Dried In The Sunshine Of God's Love

The elderly Christian had suffered a stroke after her hip surgery. Instead of walking with a new hip, she was immobile on one side. Visiting her in the hospital, I told her how raisins came to be. In the 1870s a severe drought hit the California grape crop. Instead of writing off the crop, the growers dried the stunted grapes in the sun and shipped them out as raisins. Today California produces yearly almost 500 million pounds of this fruit loaded with ten valuable food minerals.

God in his loving wisdom sometimes deals with us as if we were raisins. Trouble beats down like the hot California sun, seemingly sapping the moisture of my very being. But a gracious God tells me not to worry. He can and does turn bad into good. Notice, he doesn't make the promise of all things for good to everyone. Only to those "who love him." Only those whom he has called to faith in the Savior know his ultimate love. They know how his love has brought them out of sin's evil to salvation's good. So they know they can also trust his love in the lesser needs of life.

Perhaps this "raisin" talk about bad turning into good because of God's love doesn't grab me all that much right now. But just wait! God has not promised that his followers will be exempt from the burning heat of earth's problems. He does, however, promise that his love will turn that heat into good for those who love him. That's what I need to know, if not today, then in some tomorrow.

Lord, let the cross of my Savior be a plus sign, assuring me of your love for all my life. Amen.

> ALWAYS GIVING THANKS TO GOD THE FATHER
> FOR EVERYTHING, IN THE NAME OF OUR
> LORD JESUS CHRIST. *Ephesians 5:20*

A Thanksgiving Account That's Full

Someone has said, "A Christian is one who doesn't have to consult his bank account to see how rich he is." How true! Every beat of my heart and every breath I take, the water I drink and the food I eat, the home I live in and the loved ones I hold dear, the freedoms I take for granted and the country I often complain about—all this comes from God.

God gives me even more and even better. The Bible I read and the prayers I offer, the church I attend and the pure word I hear, the never ending supply of forgiveness for my sins and the always powerful help against temptation, the days he grants me to learn more about Jesus and the graves he will open because of Jesus—all this and more comes from God.

Would you believe there's still more? Sickness that hits me and pains that don't go away, the bad weather that damages and the crops that aren't quite right, a paycheck that doesn't quite stretch and the friends that don't last, the person I couldn't date and the spouse I had hoped for but didn't find—all this and more has come from God. "Always giving thanks," Paul wrote, including even those "disagreeable" events that come from a loving God. They serve my good or God wouldn't allow them.

This Thanksgiving, as I check my account, am I ready to say, "I'm rich! Thank God!"

Lord, thank you for all you have
showered upon me, both body and soul. Amen.

> ALWAYS GIVING THANKS TO GOD THE FATHER
> FOR EVERYTHING, IN THE NAME OF OUR
> LORD JESUS CHRIST." *Ephesians 5:20*

A Thanksgiving Check That Doesn't Bounce

A proper thanksgiving doesn't begin and end with one day's worth of inventorying the blessings God has showered on me. If it does, my thanksgiving is like a check that comes back marked "insufficient funds." If I don't put money behind my written check or deeds behind my thanksgiving, what's it worth?

This week people across our land will celebrate Thanksgiving in different ways. Some will make it a "flashbulb" thanksgiving. They'll be content with a small flash of gratitude for how good they have it, but then it's back to life as usual on Friday. For others it'll be a wrench-it-out-of-me observance. Thanksgiving comes slowly for those who don't have all they want and who worry about how long they can hang on to what they have. For still others it'll be a self-congratulatory day to consider what they have done and how hard they have worked. Such givers of thanks want to send a card of praise—to their own address.

Such thanksgivings are worthless checks made out to the wrong individual and not backed up by sufficient funds. Not mine! God wants my thanksgiving to begin with thanking him for all I have. Then he wants me to go down life's street and put my thanksgiving into practice. In my home with my loved ones, on my street with my neighbors, in my church with my offerings, out in my world with the missionaries I help send, he wants my daily life to be a thank-you "check" to him.

Lord, help me thank you daily
with my heart and hands and voice. Amen.

> BE IMITATORS OF GOD, THEREFORE, AS DEARLY LOVED
> CHILDREN AND LIVE A LIFE OF LOVE, JUST AS CHRIST
> LOVED US AND GAVE HIMSELF UP FOR US." *Ephesians 5:1,2*

Follow The Leader

Follow the leader. That's what children do. One of my favorite photos of our firstborn shows her as a three-year-old with my shoes on her feet, my tie loosely tied around her neck, and my hat on her head. Children watch and imitate. They follow their leaders.

What a leader I have in Christ! Paul might have pointed me to God's wisdom as shown in his planning, God's mercy as shown in his actions, and God's holiness as shown in his conduct. But instead, the apostle referred to just one area—to that which is the very essence of God's being. "Be imitators of God," he urged, "and live a life of love." Lest I misunderstand, he hurried on, "Live a life of love, just as Christ loved us and gave himself up for us."

Paul's not telling me that I'm to go to a cross or give myself up for sin. That only Christ could do. But he is saying that Christ's unselfish, sacrificing love is to be the pattern for my daily life. Knowing Christ's unselfish love, being totally dependent on his love and eternally grateful for it, I want to love in return. I begin by showing such love to my Savior. I show him that his Word and salvation are my treasures and that his work is my pleasure. Then I'll also show such love to those around me. Seldom, if ever, will I have opportunity to do the "great" things that make the newspaper headlines. More often, my love will express itself in the kind words, thoughtful deeds, common courtesies that make up daily life. But, as Jesus' grateful child, I will love.

*Lord, fill my heart with your saving
love so that I might love others more. Amen.*

CAST ALL YOUR ANXIETY ON HIM
BECAUSE HE CARES FOR YOU. *1 Peter 5:7*

All That Care

Yesterday, while grocery shopping with my wife, I paused before the display of fresh pineapples. On one trip to Puerto Rico, we had visited a pineapple field and learned what it takes to produce ripe, juicy pineapples. The shoots are planted in well-drained, acid soil. The soil is treated to control pests, and the plants are sprayed to remove harmful insects. The right amount of water is also important. Finally, after two years of such tender, loving care, the pineapple is ready to eat.

Like that pineapple, I need special care. And my loving God provides it richly. He sent the sunshine of his love into my heart at my baptism. He waters my faith through his refreshing, invigorating Word. He gives me his strength for pest control against the devil, the world, and my sinful flesh. He lets problems and pains beat down upon me, not to uproot the plant of faith or break off its leaves but to strengthen it. I don't always stop to think about it, but it's true. God's love cares for me every day in every way. He wants me to ripen into a "pineapple" that will be on display some day in his heaven.

How can I be so sure that he cares for me? Admittedly doubts arise when the storms in life are severe. Sometimes I may even wonder when only raindrops are beating down on my head. Then I need to look to Calvary. God cared so much for me that he sent his Son to save me. He will surely also care enough to keep me safe till I stand in his heaven. Two years to produce pineapple—that's nothing. God cares for me forever!

Lord, help me trust your care in all the
affairs of life, till you take me to your heaven. Amen.

WE DO NOT HAVE A HIGH PRIEST WHO IS UNABLE TO SYMPATHIZE WITH OUR WEAKNESS, BUT WE HAVE ONE WHO HAS BEEN TEMPTED IN EVERY WAY, JUST AS WE ARE—YET WAS WITHOUT SIN. *Hebrews 4:15*

Go To Jesus— He Knows How We Feel

When hard times strike, I need someone who can encourage me. One who hasn't walked in my shoes can scarcely say, "I know how you feel." One who after listening sympathetically responds, "I wish I could help you, but . . ." won't do me much good either. I need someone who listens, knows, and then helps. I need Jesus.

Do I wrestle with pain? Go to Jesus. He whose back was lashed, hands were pierced, and head was bloodied knows all about my pains. Do friends forsake me and dear ones fail me? Go to Jesus. He whose one disciple betrayed him and the rest fled from him knows about loneliness. Am I troubled by temptation? He who faced Satan's attacks for 40 days in the wilderness knows how clever the old evil foe can be. Do I hesitate to bear the cross, to do and dare for God? Go to Jesus. He knows all about such temptations. He even sweat drops of blood because of it in Gethsemane. Am I tested to the very limit by the pains of life and by the problem of dying? Go to Jesus. He's been there himself. The old spiritual is right, "Nobody knows the troubles I've seen. Nobody knows, but Jesus."

I can go confidently to Jesus because he knows how I feel. He faced what I face but with one important difference. He remained "without sin." Temptation and trouble never overcame him. He followed his Father's will perfectly. Thank God that he did. For now he can offer me what I need.

What a friend I have in Jesus to whom I
can go and who will shield me in his arms. Amen.

> LET US THEN APPROACH THE THRONE OF GRACE WITH
> CONFIDENCE, SO THAT WE MAY RECEIVE MERCY AND FIND
> GRACE TO HELP US IN OUR TIME OF NEED. *Hebrews 4:16*

Go To Jesus—
He Offers What We Need

People who have walked in my moccasins in life can sympathize with me. They know how I feel. But they can't always help me. Jesus can! That's what this verse tells me so beautifully.

At Jesus' throne I "receive mercy and find grace to help" in time of need. "Mercy" and "grace" say it all. "Mercy" refers to me and highlights my wretched spiritual condition. "Grace" refers to God and highlights what he does for me as something totally undeserved by me. Don't I see Calvary in those two words? There he poured out his Son's precious blood in payment for my sins. There he paved the way to his home above with Jesus' crimson blood. That's how completely his mercy and grace have taken care of my greatest needs.

Now I can also approach his throne of grace confidently with my other needs. Never can my cross be so heavy that Jesus' shoulders can't help me carry it. Never can temptation be so serious that Jesus' words can't help defeat it. Never can my tears be so bitter that Jesus' concern can't help dry them. Never can death's road be so dark that Jesus can't reach through it to carry me safely home.

Where to go when I need encouragement? Let the first answer always be "To Jesus and his Word." He knows how I feel and he offers what I need.

Lord, draw me confidently to your throne
of grace for all my needs of body and soul. Amen.

> GREAT IS YOUR LOVE, HIGHER THAN THE HEAVENS;
> YOUR FAITHFULNESS REACHES TO THE SKIES. *Psalm 108:4*

Higher Than The Heavens

While in California on church business, I had a half day to see the famous redwood trees. Many redwoods stand taller than 300 feet. Their trunks can measure more than 10 feet in diameter. Their bark can be 12 inches thick. A single redwood may give as much as 480,000 board feet of durable lumber. What an impressive sight those tall redwoods are!

The psalmist speaks about something even more impressive. God's love is so tall that I can't begin to measure it. "Higher than the heavens" is how the psalmist put it. People have soared miles high into the heavens but have never reached their end. So God's love, coupled with his faithfulness, has no end. It goes on forever. I can wrap a tape measure around a redwood's trunk and read the numbers. I can't, however, wrap the arms of my understanding around God's infinite love. I can determine the board feet each redwood may produce. I can't comprehend what God's love can all do and in whom.

Redwoods pale in comparison when placed next to God's amazing love. In love, he reached down for me in the form of his most precious gift, his own Son. In love, he reached out for me while I was still his enemy. In love, he reaches up with me all the way to his glorious heaven. Such love is higher than the heavens. I can't measure it or wrap my comprehension around it. But, in amazement, I can thank him for it.

*Lord, never let me stop marveling at
your amazing love for me in Christ Jesus. Amen.*

NOW TO HIM WHO IS ABLE TO DO IMMEASURABLY MORE THAN ALL
WE ASK OR IMAGINE . . . TO HIM BE GLORY IN THE CHURCH AND
IN CHRIST JESUS THROUGHOUT ALL GENERATIONS. *Ephesians 3:20*

A Well, Not A Reservoir

Near my wife's childhood home is an artesian well. It's been flowing for
as long as she can remember. People come from miles around to take
home some of its pure water. No one knows its capacity. Unlike a
reservoir whose contents can be calculated, this well is immeasurable.

So is the well of God's power. It just keeps on flowing. With God
nothing is impossible. I can never ask too much of him. Hasn't he
shown me this comforting truth on the pages of his Word? He can
create the world and then cover it with a flood. He can free his people
from slavery and drown their masters in the Red Sea. He can watch over
me each day and keep trouble from me. He can turn trouble into good
when he does allow it to come. Nor is his power finished yet in my life.
What his power can all do for me in the future, I can't even imagine.

So also with the well of God's grace. He can put his Son into the womb
of a virgin and onto a cross of pain. He can prepare forgiveness for each
of my many sins. He can turn my dead heart into life and make it his
very own in faith. He can robe me in his Son's righteousness and ready
me for his banquet room in heaven. Nor is his grace finished with me
yet. How his grace can keep covering me is far beyond my imagination.

At the artesian well of God's power and grace I find more than I can
ever need.

Lord, bring me to your Word to fill up
with your inexhaustible power and grace. Amen.

> THE HOUR HAS COME FOR YOU TO WAKE UP FROM
> YOUR SLUMBER, BECAUSE OUR SALVATION IS NEARER
> NOW THAN WHEN WE FIRST BELIEVED. *Romans 13:11*

Advent's Call To Be Awake

When it's my weekend to preach, I have to set the alarm clock. Otherwise I won't wake up in time to get to the early service. One of the perks of semi-retirement is that I can usually sleep later. But not on the Sundays I have to preach.

Advent is alarm clock time for Christians. It's the wake-up call urging me to wipe the sleep out of my eyes and get ready for the Lord's coming. Why should I listen to the Advent call? "Because our salvation is nearer now than when we first believed," Paul reminds me. The Lord in his grace brought me to faith some time ago. Each passing day brings me closer to faith's goal—my eternal salvation. Day by day, the Last Day, either of my life or the life of this world, is drawing nearer. Day by day I'm getting closer to the moment when I shall see my Savior's lovely face. I don't want to be caught napping when that blessed day comes.

Recently I read a news report about a young man who was killed by a train because he was walking on the tracks. Listening to his Walkman stereo through earphones, he never heard the train as it thundered down on him. I don't want to be a "Walkman" Christian, so absorbed in the affairs of daily life that I don't see my Savior coming. I want to be awake and ready for his return. And I know how. He has told me, "Faith comes from hearing the message, and the message is heard through the word of Christ" (Romans 10:17).

Lord, open my sleepy eyes to read and
my heart to hear your saving Word. Amen.

> THE NIGHT IS NEARLY OVER; THE DAY
> IS ALMOST HERE. SO LET US PUT ASIDE
> THE DEEDS OF DARKNESS. *Romans 13:12*

Advent's Call To Be Aggressive

Do you like aggressive people? You know the kind I mean—the ones who push hard to get their point across or to get what they are after. I may not always appreciate such pushers, but I have to admire them at times. Paul in our verse tells me that I should be aggressive too—aggressive in the fight against sin.

"Deeds of darkness," Paul labels sin. How true! Sin comes from the devil, the prince of darkness. Sin goes on constantly in our world where the darkness of unbelief rules. Sin has no connection whatsoever with the light and day of faith. Paul was even specific about some of the deeds of darkness he meant. In the verses after ours he warned against "carousing and drunkenness, sexual immorality and debauchery, dissension and jealousy." Sounds like he's been watching our TV, reading our magazines, viewing our thoughts, if not our actions. Seems like he knows how often I'm tempted, how hard I can fall, and how indifferent I can become to sin.

In the supermarket aisle, a mother scolded her little boy, "I don't like the way you're acting." Sheepishly the little boy asked her, "How should I act?" That crowded aisle was hardly the place for a lengthy lecture on right behavior, so the mother simply replied, "I want you to act like a child who belongs to me." Perhaps that little boy couldn't grasp the full meaning of his mother's words. But I know what Paul means this Advent when he sounds the alarm, "Act like a child who belongs to a Lord who has redeemed you with his own blood."

Lord, fill me with your power to walk as
your child and forgive me when I fail. Amen.

> PUT ON THE ARMOR OF LIGHT. . . .
> CLOTHE YOURSELVES WITH THE
> LORD JESUS CHRIST. *Romans 13:12,14*

Advent's Call To Be Armed

I was watching a movie on TV in which a SWAT team was called upon to storm a building. The team members hustled out of their van. But before taking up position and taking on the criminals, they very carefully put on their armor. They wanted to be as safe as possible against the enemy.

"Put on the armor of light," Paul urges me in my battle against sin. My walk as a believer in this world of darkness is no leisurely stroll. If I'm sincere about living for the Lord, I'll need some armor—not just any armor but the armor of light. In Ephesians chapter 6, Paul described this armor in detail. He wrote of the Christian putting the helmet of salvation on his head, the breastplate of righteousness on his chest, the shield of faith on his arm, and the sword of God's Word in his hand. Then he can go forth to battle the enemy who fights in darkness. Note well, though, all this gospel armor protects only the front of the Christian. As long as he stands and faces Satan and sin with this armor of light, he's safe. Let him turn his back, and he's vulnerable.

Do I want to win in the battle against the devil, the world, and my flesh? Paul clearly points out the only way. "Clothe yourselves with the Lord Jesus Christ," he says. I need Christ's pardon wrapped around me, covering all my sins and clothing me for heaven. I need Christ's power coursing in my life and compelling me more and more to live for him. I need to take the time to put my armor on by turning to his powerful Word as Advent reminds me.

Lord, this Advent season lead me deeper
into your Word for the pardon and power I need. Amen.

> "DO NOT BE AFRAID, LITTLE FLOCK,
> FOR YOUR FATHER HAS BEEN PLEASED
> TO GIVE YOU THE KINGDOM." *Luke 12:32*

How To Live Without Fear

How to Eat Heart Healthy, How to Succeed with Stocks and Bonds, How to Cope with Depression—seems like there's no end to the how-to books on the store shelves these days. How about the Bible? Isn't it the real how-to book? Its main message could be entitled "How to Receive Eternal Life." Parts of this book from God could be labeled "How to Cope with Trouble," "How to Pray," "How to Manage Your Possessions."

Jesus tells me "How to Live without Fear." Is that really possible? Perhaps only babies in their mother's arms can do so. How quickly worry, with accompanying fear, can creep into my life. I worry about my health, particularly if it's not what it should be. I worry about my money—how to make it, how to spend it, how to save it. I worry about my family—how to care for them, how to keep them safe. If asked whether I ever worry, I guess my hand would have to go up.

Would my hand also go up if asked whether I know how to get rid of my worries? I hope so. Hasn't Jesus told me, "Your Father has been pleased to give you the kingdom"? Can't I feel my worries evaporating as Jesus holds me close to his chest? As he reminds me, "Your Father has paid for all your sins with my holy blood. He has made your heart his own by putting faith there. He has prepared relief from your greatest worry, that of sin. Now don't think that he'll fail to care for your lesser worries. He cares well for the insignificant sparrow and the inconsequential lily. Even more so, he will care for you, his dear child and heir of his kingdom."

*Lord, pick me up and hold me close so I can
live without fear in this world of so much fear. Amen.*

> "PROVIDE PURSES FOR YOURSELVES THAT WILL
> NOT WEAR OUT, A TREASURE IN HEAVEN
> THAT WILL NOT BE EXHAUSTED." *Luke 12:33*

How To Live For Eternity

How many have wallets that stay brand new? Property that never needs fixing? I've officiated at many funerals, but never one where wealth was packed into a coffin. I've been at deathbeds, but never found one person whose goods brought him peace in that valley of the shadows. Christians know how fading earthly treasures are. That's why they look for advice about living for eternity.

Among my clippings is an article entitled "What Disturbs You Most?" It asked, "What disturbs you most, a soul lost in hell or a scratch on your new car? A sermon ten minutes too long or lunch a half-hour late? Your Bible unread or your daily newspaper not read? Your country in debt or your church in debt? To miss a Bible class or to miss a favorite television program? Your missing the Sunday service or missing a day's work?" Good questions, aren't they? How do I answer? For what am I living?

Certainly I have to live and work in this world. I have to use money and investments. Those are means God has given me to use for my livelihood. I have to use them but not let them use me. In the long run, such misuse of earthly goods can only rob me of heavenly treasures. More valuable by far is the salvation God has prepared for me in Christ. More durable by far is the heaven he has waiting for me. More worthy by far is the effort to be rich in Christ and his Word. That's the only way to live for eternity.

Lord, help me use my earthly treasures,
but even more help me use your Word. Amen.

"BE DRESSED READY FOR SERVICE AND KEEP YOUR LAMPS BURNING,
LIKE MEN WAITING FOR THEIR MASTER TO RETURN FROM A
WEDDING BANQUET, SO THAT WHEN HE COMES AND KNOCKS,
THEY CAN IMMEDIATELY OPEN THE DOOR FOR HIM." *Luke 12:35,36*

How To Live In Expectation Of Christ

Someone described the believer as the person with the suitcase. That's a good description because a Christian lives each day with his suitcase packed for heaven. Each day he wears his traveling clothes. Each day he has his lamp filled and burning. Like the servants in our verse, the believer goes about his daily life, but always with one ear turned to the door. Always he waits for the first sound of the Lord's return so that he may throw the door open without delay to joyously welcome his master.

What's in the suitcase? Need I even ask? Only one item is necessary. "Believe in the Lord Jesus and you will be saved" is how Paul once answered (Acts 16:31). Jesus' perfect life has woven the robe I need to wear to sit down at heaven's banquet. Jesus' precious blood has washed me clean so I can stand spotless before my Maker. Jesus, Jesus, only Jesus is all I need when my Lord returns.

The Lord is going to come. Is my suitcase packed? I may need it sooner than I think. Who of us knows how many more packing days are left? I need to live today, tomorrow if God gives me one, and whatever tomorrows may follow in expectation of Christ's return. That's what Advent with its message of Christ's coming reminds me.

Lord, preserve me in faith through your
Word so that I may be ready for your coming. Amen.

"THERE WILL BE SIGNS IN THE SUN, MOON AND STARS. ON
THE EARTH, NATIONS WILL BE IN ANGUISH AND PERPLEXITY
AT THE ROARING AND TOSSING OF THE SEA." *Luke 21:25*

The Signs Are There

Across the street there's a "For Sale" sign on a house. In our subdivision such signs sprout regularly. Young couples move in and then out as their companies transfer them. That "For Sale" sign is interesting. It tells me the family has to move. It tells me what realtor is assisting the owner in selling the house. It may contain a telephone number and even details about the house.

God uses signs too. Though in his loving wisdom, he doesn't tell me when Jesus is coming, he does give me signs to read. God doesn't tell me the exact day because he wants me to use every day as if it were the last. But let me not mistake the certainty of Christ's coming. When the world ends or my time on this world comes to an end, I need to be ready. Whichever comes first doesn't matter. What matters is that I'm ready when Jesus comes.

Rudyard Kipling wrote, "No one thinks of winter when the grass is green." We think summer will never end. When the frost hits and the flakes fall, we first start thinking about winter's certainty. So when tsunamis wipe out thousands, we suddenly are forced to think of Christ's return. When hurricanes hammer communities and mudslides demolish houses, we of necessity think of things eternal.

Thank God, he puts his signs out in the world. They remind me of what I should know but don't always remember. Moving day is coming, perhaps sooner than I think.

Lord, keep me in your Word and
living each day as if it were my last. Amen.

> "THERE WILL BE A TIME OF DISTRESS SUCH AS HAS NOT
> HAPPENED FROM THE BEGINNING OF NATIONS UNTIL THEN.
> BUT AT THAT TIME YOUR PEOPLE—EVERYONE WHOSE NAME IS
> FOUND WRITTEN IN THE BOOK—WILL BE DELIVERED." *Daniel 12:1*

Triumph Over Trouble

"Come on down and get some breakfast while it's still hot," the poacher called out from the porch of his backwoods cabin. Stunned, the game warden walked toward the house, asking, "How did you know I was out there?" "I didn't," the poacher replied. "I say the same thing every morning just in case you are." Could I learn something from him about being ready for the Last Day?

Daniel paints a bleak picture of the last days. In desperate fury the devil will lash out at God's people. I think we know what Daniel means. Has there ever been a time when evil has more dominated the world's thoughts, speech, and actions? Ever a time when love for others has been replaced more with love for self? A time when churches serve up a "soft slipper" sort of religion more than the "work boot" kind God's Word details? How will God's children survive?

Daniel tells me not to worry. God's people will triumph in the end. God has promised deliverance to "everyone whose name is found written in the book." That expression refers to his family register in which he has recorded the names of all who are his children through faith in Christ Jesus. Deliverance will come from their Savior, who rules over all and always in the interest of God's children. Of course, I need to think about those last days coming. Far better, though, for me to think about my Savior, who always triumphs over trouble.

Lord, in these anxious times, lift my eyes
to the Savior, who will come to claim me. Amen.

> "MULTITUDES WHO SLEEP IN THE DUST OF THE EARTH
> WILL AWAKE: SOME TO EVERLASTING LIFE, OTHERS
> TO SHAME AND EVERLASTING CONTEMPT." *Daniel 12:2*

Deliverance From Death

Daniel writes about death—not to terrorize me but to offer the hope of deliverance. He's not writing about the soul, which Scripture points out goes to heaven or to hell upon death. Instead, he takes me to the grave to show the final deliverance from death. He writes about the "multitudes" or as Jesus himself put it in John 5, "All who are in their graves" (28). He speaks about the "dust of the earth," whether it's some well-kept grave in a cemetery or people blown into dust by atomic bombs. Christ will raise and reunite all bodies with their souls for their eternal destiny.

Am I prepared for that day? I'd better be, because of what will happen to those who aren't. Those who wasted their lives evading God or not wanting him will be forever separated from him. "Shame and everlasting contempt" is how Daniel describes their future. The same Lord who at Noah's time drowned a whole world of people and who scorched Sodom and Gomorrah with fire still reigns in heaven. He still wants all people to share the joy of his heaven, but in his justice he'll send those who reject his salvation into hell's shame and everlasting contempt.

There's no second chance, no neutral place, only everlasting life in heaven or everlasting contempt in hell. I want to be ready for that great day's coming. I want to share in that glorious final deliverance from death. God, make and keep me ready through Jesus whose resurrection has conquered life's greatest enemy for me.

Lord, make me ready, both body and
soul, through Jesus, for the life to come. Amen.

"THOSE WHO ARE WISE WILL SHINE LIKE THE BRIGHTNESS OF THE HEAVENS, AND THOSE WHO LEAD MANY TO RIGHTEOUSNESS, LIKE THE STARS FOR EVER AND EVER." *Daniel 12:3*

Reward For Wisdom

On the wide porch of a certain restaurant are hand-crafted rocking chairs from the Blue Ridge Mountains area. Every time I walk past them, I think of Daniel's words. He reminds me that I'm not to be rocking in some nice chair with my eyes glued on heaven for Jesus' return. I'm to get busy. Even as I wait prepared for Jesus' coming, I'm to work so that others might be prepared also.

First, Daniel speaks to me when he talks about "those who are wise." He reminds me that true wisdom is found only in God's book and only in clinging to the Savior, who is at its center. Jesus is the only Way to the Father's house above. Nothing or nobody should distract or derail me from him. Jesus put this truth another way when he said, "He who stands firm to the end will be saved" (Matthew 24:13). God keep me numbered among the wise in this world filled with fools!

Second, Daniel talks about me when he points out how the wise "lead many to righteousness." Those wise unto salvation through faith in Christ know life's main goal is not just to marry and have a family but to share heaven's wisdom with their families. They know the main occupation in life is not just to make money but to view the workplace as another forum for sharing the Savior. They know that the preaching and teaching ministry is not just another profession but an excellent way to use life for the spreading of the Word of wisdom. Through the Word that I share, others can be prepared to shine like the stars in God's eternal heaven.

Lord, make me wise unto salvation and
use me to spread the wisdom of salvation. Amen.

> "I AM THE VOICE OF ONE CALLING IN THE DESERT,
> 'MAKE STRAIGHT THE WAY FOR THE LORD.'" *John 1:23*

Needed This Christmas–John's Finger Pointing At My Sin

"What does Mom need for Christmas?" is a question our kids ask me. I know I should be more observant over the year. I know I should be compiling a list. But somehow I have a hard time coming up with suggestions for what my wife needs for Christmas.

As a believer, I know what I need for Christmas. Before I climb out on a firefighter's ladder, I must be convinced the building is burning. Similarly, before I want a Savior, I must be convinced of my need for him. I need John's finger pointing at my sin! And that's not easy. I live in a world that is so sin-saturated and yet so little sin-conscious that it accepts sin as the normal way of life. "Everybody's doing it," people reason. "Why shouldn't I?" They try boldly to deny sin. Nudity today is daring dress. Adultery is indiscretion. Cheating is getting by. Drunkenness is feeling high. Homosexuality is alternate lifestyle. Nor does the world like that word *sin*. Counselors prefer to speak about life's circumstances, and guilt becomes rather some kind of mild failure.

In such a sin-denying world, I need John's finger pointing at my sins and pressing hard on my heart. I need to hear him thunder, "Make straight the way for the Lord." I need to get out the bulldozer of repentance and level the mountains of sin in my heart. Then I'll hold my soul's aching head in my hands as I moan, "My sins, oh, my sins." Then I'll thrill as John also shouts, "Look, the Lamb of God, who takes away the sin of the world!" (John 1:29).

Lord, let your law condemn me soundly
for my sins and your gospel cheer me sweetly. Amen.

"LOOK, THE LAMB OF GOD, WHO TAKES
AWAY THE SIN OF THE WORLD!" *John 1:29*

Needed This Christmas—John's Finger Pointing At My Savior

"Are you still mad at me?" asked Mark. In a fit of anger he had punched his fist through the window in the storm door on the porch. In no uncertain terms, I let him know that was not acceptable behavior. Now hours later, he needed to know that all was well again.

So do I. Separated from a holy God by my sins, I need to know that a loving God has taken care of them. I have to know that he has laid them all on his spotless Lamb whose blood has removed them forever. What peace God offers my troubled conscience when in his gospel he says, "Your sins are forgiven." What peace he offers my storm-tossed life when through his Word he touches my feverish brow and says, "I am with you always." What peace for my final day when his nail-pierced hand clasps my failing hand and he says, "I am at your side, even in the valley of the shadow."

That's what I need for Christmas. So does my world, though it doesn't know it. Like some stubborn child, the world closes its eyes, plowing persistently ahead in its own foolish furrow. To better mankind it's tried improving education, passing laws, providing better social benefits, espousing civil rights, and rehabilitating criminals. Still, people cheat and kill, pillage and pilfer, hurt and wound in increasing intensity. For the majority, life still remains a cruel joke and an existence without laughter. May God spread John's message of the Savior far and wide this Christmas season. And may he use me in some small way to point others to their only Lamb.

Lord, draw me close to the Savior this holy season.
Use me to point others to him too. Amen.

> "YOU . . . MUST BE READY, BECAUSE THE
> SON OF MAN WILL COME AT AN HOUR WHEN
> YOU DO NOT EXPECT HIM." *Matthew 24:44*

Ready And Waiting

We were on an all-day whale-sighting excursion out of Seward, Alaska. We had seen some magnificent sights but no whales. Finally my wife decided to go back inside the warm interior of the ship. Sure enough, that's when the whales appeared. She missed it because she stopped watching.

Just imagine if Jesus had told me he would return on August 29, 2008. How would I react? Would I conclude, "Well, there's no sense in my watching for his return till August 29 or August 28 at the earliest. Then I'll get busy getting ready for him." Would I forget to factor in that I might not make it to August 29, 2008? What if on the night of August 28 a heart attack would snuff out my life without my having taken the time to get ready for his coming?

"You . . . must be ready," Jesus says. He hasn't told me the time of his return because he wants me to be ready all the time. That day on the whale-watching excursion, I used the caffeine in a cola drink to help me stay awake. My eyes were wide open, and I saw the whales splashing their tails as they slipped beneath the waves. If I want faith's eyes wide awake and watching, I need more than cola with caffeine. I need God's Word with its message of Jesus' sure return to claim his own for heaven. I need eyes fixed on Jesus my Savior and returning Lord. Those whales that day were a magnificent sight but nothing like the sight of my Savior when he returns in his glory.

Lord Jesus, keep me in your Word and
wide awake for your unexpected return. Amen.

"SURELY THE DAY IS COMING; IT WILL BURN LIKE A FURNACE. ALL THE ARROGANT AND EVERY EVILDOER WILL BE STUBBLE, AND THAT DAY THAT IS COMING WILL SET THEM ON FIRE," SAYS THE LORD ALMIGHTY. *Malachi 4:1*

Advent's Look Into The Burning Furnace

Doesn't it seem like much of life is spent getting ready for something? In the fall it's time to trim the shrubs and tune up the snow blower. As the fall of life approaches it's time to reexamine retirement plans to see if financial cushions are thick enough. How about getting ready for judgment day? "Surely the day is coming," the prophet reminds me.

Malachi compares judgment day to the hot oven used by the Jews to bake their bread. Unbelievers are like the stubble used in wood-scarce Palestine as fuel in those ovens. When the righteous judge returns, unbelievers will be shoved like worthless straw into the bake oven of hell. What an oven that will be! One where the fire never goes out and the searing heat never cools down. What horror for them to hear from the lips of the Savior, through whom they could have avoided hell's heat, those drastic words: "Depart from me, you who are cursed, into the eternal fire prepared for the devil and his angels" (Matthew 25:41).

Talk about the fires of hell, regardless how vivid, doesn't scare people into heaven. It doesn't work that way. But such honest talk is necessary. It helps me realize my sins are serious and that I had better be serious about my sin. I need the Advent look into hell's hot bake oven so that I will realize all the more how much I need to look at the Savior, who came to rescue me from it.

Lord, this Advent season show me sin's
seriousness and then your pardon for my sins. Amen.

> "BUT FOR YOU WHO REVERE MY NAME,
> THE SUN OF RIGHTEOUSNESS WILL RISE
> WITH HEALING IN ITS WINGS." *Malachi 4:2*

Advent's Look Up At The Sun Of Righteousness

Yesterday I woke up early. My mind started whirring with thoughts of what I had to do. So I got up and went out into the family room. As I looked toward the east, I saw a welcome sight. The darkness of winter's night was being pushed back by the cheering, warming rays of the morning sun. What a picture of Christ, the glorious Son of heaven, bringing cheer and warmth to the sinner's darkened soul!

Have I felt the healing force of the Sun of Righteousness? As one whose conscience is scarred and scared by sin, do I know what cheer the Savior offers me when he says, "Friend, your sins are forgiven"(Luke 5:20)? As a sinner for whom judgment day is ever nearer, do I know what confidence the Savior offers me when he says, "There is now no condemnation for those who are in Christ Jesus" (Romans 8:1)? As a mortal being for whom each step on planet Earth might be my last, do I know what comfort the Savior offers me when he says, "I am the way and the truth and the life. No one comes to the Father except through me" (John 14:6)?

If this Advent season I'm standing in the warmth and cheer of the Savior, it's time to thank God again. It's his blessed work alone that enables my eyes to see the Sun of Righteousness whom he has sent for me. It's his grace, his undeserved gift, that I have found healing and heaven in the salvation that this Son brings. His love has made me ready for that last, great day.

Lord, thank you for bringing me into
the sunshine of your love through Jesus. Amen.

> THE TIME HAS COME FOR MY DEPARTURE. I HAVE
> FOUGHT THE GOOD FIGHT, I HAVE FINISHED THE
> RACE, I HAVE KEPT THE FAITH. *2 Timothy 4:6,7*

Faithfulness At The Crib And Cross Of Jesus

Not too many folks like to talk about life and death. Others, when they do, speak only cynically. The English satirist Samuel Butler, for example, described life as one long process of getting tired. A college student opined that life is a rapid transition from diapers to dignity to decomposition.

Better by far that I listen to Paul the apostle. Imprisoned at Rome for preaching the gospel, death was at his heels. Did he despair? Did he write off his life as a failure? No. Instead, with quiet composure, he looked back over his life and spoke of faithfulness. "I have fought the good fight," he said, noting that the Christian life of faith is a lifelong battle against horrendous enemies. "I have finished the race," he continued, again pointing out that the road to heaven takes all the stamina one can muster. "I have kept the faith," he concluded, holding high the most important part of his life. "I," Paul said. But really he was saying, "God did this for me and through me. He equipped me with faith and empowered me for faith's battle. I remained faithful only because of my gracious Lord."

Do I want to make Paul's words my own? Then I need to kneel before the crib and cross of the Savior. That's where Paul found his strength for a life of faith. So can I! Look what Christ does for me. When I stumble, he picks me up. When my faith flickers, he strengthens it. When I face death, he stands beside me. Only because of him can I speak of faithfulness to him.

Lord, keep me faithful and humble
by drawing me to your crib and cross. Amen.

NOW THERE IS IN STORE FOR ME THE CROWN OF RIGHTEOUSNESS,
WHICH THE LORD, THE RIGHTEOUS JUDGE, WILL AWARD ME ON
THAT DAY—AND NOT ONLY TO ME, BUT ALSO TO ALL WHO
HAVE LONGED FOR HIS APPEARING. *2 Timothy 4:8*

Confidence At The Crib And Cross Of Jesus

A life that doesn't end with heaven's crown is a failure. The world doesn't think so. Often it treats people who live with this crown in view as persons somewhat deficient in intelligence and unreal in values. But eternity will show the value of heaven's crown of righteousness.

When King Charlemagne died some 1,200 years ago, they propped him up on a throne in his sepulcher. On his head they placed his jewel-encrusted crown; in his hand, his royal golden scepter. On his finger glistened his signet ring, while on his lap lay a scroll. Centuries later, his tomb was opened. Only his skeleton was left. The crown had slipped off his skull. His ring lay on the floor in the dust. All that remained of his robe was small puffs of fuzz. The scroll on his lap had unrolled and the skeletal hand that had held the scepter now pointed to the words written in the scroll. What words, you ask? The words of Jesus' warning: "What good will it be for a man if he gains the whole world, yet forfeits his soul?" (Matthew 16:26).

The time is coming when all the world's crowns will be just so much faded cardboard and all the world's jewels just so much worthless glass. All who struggled and sweat for those perishable crowns will cry out to the hills, "Cover us," when they see the righteous judge approaching. But for those who have knelt at that judge's crib and cross, his return will be a joyous event. It'll be a day I love, because it'll mean my Savior has come to take me home.

*Even so come, Lord Jesus, and
crown me with your righteousness. Amen.*

> "SEE, THE LION OF THE TRIBE OF JUDAH,
> THE ROOT OF DAVID, HAS TRIUMPHED." *Revelation 5:5*

My King, The Lion Of Judah, Has Won

The Lion of Judah—what a picture of my Savior! It takes me back to Genesis chapter 49 where the aged patriarch Jacob in blessing his son Judah said, "You are a lion's cub, O Judah; you return from the prey, my son. Like a lion he crouches and lies down, like a lioness—who dares to rouse him?" (9). Then comes the passage we've all learned and recited in Christmas Eve services: "The scepter will not depart from Judah, nor the ruler's staff from between his feet, until [Shiloh] comes" (10).

Not only was Judah an ancestor of the promised Savior. He was also a picture of what that Savior would be. Jesus would be like some young lion crouching down with his captured prey in the bold security of his den. Even more, Jesus would be like the fierce lioness who has cubs to guard. Once this strong lion of Judah has settled down in triumph, who would dare to rouse him? How can I miss the picture? Jesus, the heavenly King, has triumphed over the foe and is seated at God's right hand in victory in heaven.

This Advent season John urges me to raise faith's eyes to that Lion of Judah. My King has won the one battle that counts. Through him the victory over sin, death, and the devil is mine. Now let the words of Proverbs 28:1 fit me: "The righteous are bold as a lion." God make me bold to claim my share in Christ's victory. God make me bold to close my eyes in peace each night and in the final night. The Lion of Judah has won sin's battle for me also.

Lord, let me thrill at the victory over
sin that your Lion has brought me. Amen.

> "DO NOT WEEP! SEE, THE LION OF THE TRIBE OF JUDAH,
> THE ROOT OF DAVID, HAS TRIUMPHED. HE IS ABLE TO
> OPEN THE SCROLL AND ITS SEVEN SEALS." *Revelation 5:5*

My King, The Lion Of Judah, Always Wins

If only I could open that scroll and see the future in this sin-drenched world. Because I can't, I might shrug my shoulders in tired resignation, saying, "It's always been that way. Evil flourishes and evil people move forward." I might give up, sighing, "You can only dog paddle against the prevailing stream so long before your strength gives out." I might selfishly thank God that I have gray hair and won't have to see what my grandchildren will live through.

Or should I look at my King, the Lion of Judah? "He has triumphed," the verse reminds me. "The One who is enthroned in heaven laughs," David said in Psalm 2:4, reminding me that the world's feverish attempts against God's church are so puny that the Lion of Judah doesn't even rise up from his throne of glory. My Lion of Judah always wins, even if I don't always see it because doubt's cataracts cloud faith's eyes.

Luther once wrote, "Who could have imagined that God laughed when Christ was suffering and the Jews were rejoicing?" The Reformer was right. What looked like utter defeat for the Lord's anointed turned out to be salvation's victory. With his great persecution, Diocletian of Rome was determined to put an end to the gospel. He boasted, "The name of Jesus is being extinguished." Diocletian's Rome has long since crumbled, but Christ's church still stands. When the dust settles in the future, as in the past, it's his victory I'll see.

Lord, still my anxious heart by showing
me the conquering power of your gospel. Amen.

I SAW A LAMB, LOOKING AS IF IT HAD BEEN SLAIN, STANDING IN THE CENTER OF THE THRONE. *Revelation 5:6*

Advent Praise To The Lamb Slain For Me

I have a jacket made of soft lambskin. But I've never held a lamb in my arms. My daughter had a stuffed lamb on her bed. But the only real lambs she's ever seen were in a petting zoo.

Though I'm not much acquainted with lambs, I need to know this one. John describes him as a Lamb "looking as if it had been slain." This picture reminded John of the day when his teacher had pointed at Jesus and said for all to hear, "Look, the Lamb of God who takes away the sin of the world!" (John 1:29). Jesus was the real Lamb of God. All the other lambs, sacrificed during all those Passover celebrations, had only pointed to this Lamb. All their blood had only pointed to the blood of God's real Lamb. Only the blood of the God-man could cancel all sin. Only those covered by his precious blood would be spared when God's eternal judgment passed over them.

John also described him as "standing in the center of the throne." A slain lamb can only sprawl lifeless in the dust. God's Lamb stands triumphant in the middle of his throne in heaven. He shares with his Father in all divine majesty and power. See what John is trying to tell us? Jesus is not just a lamb whose blood stained Calvary's cross but the Lamb who satisfied the penalty for all sin. He's not just a lamb who went silently to the slaughter but the Lamb who stepped out of the grave in loud victory over sin, death, and the devil. The question is, Is Jesus *my* Lamb? Praise God this Advent season that I know he was slain for me.

Thank you, Lord, for the faith to see Jesus,
your Lamb who has taken away my sin. Amen.

> "YOU HAVE MADE THEM TO BE A KINGDOM
> AND PRIESTS TO SERVE OUR GOD." *Revelation 5:10*

Advent Praise To The Lamb Served By Me

The other day while surfing on TV for some Christmas music, I happened on a show with more than 250 singers massed together in songs of praise to Christ. The music was beautiful and so were some of the thoughts expressed. But it was still a weak imitation of the praise I'll raise to the Lamb in heaven. Did you notice, though, that John in our verse encourages me not to wait till heaven to praise my wonderful Lamb? We are to do it now, as "a kingdom and priests to serve our God," he urges.

Don't his words give me the feeling that God wants me to be up and at 'em? I'm not just to be savoring what I have in the Lamb. I'm to be busy serving that Lamb. I'm to be a kingdom and a priest because of him. I'm not only to sing "Oh, that we were there," in that heaven above, where I shall reign with him in eternal joy. I'm also to roll up my sleeves and get to work spreading the gospel of his salvation here so that others may join me.

It's easy to talk about serving the Lamb in the safety of my church with its stained-glass windows and smell of candle wax. What about out in life, where the rubber hits the road and where life is lived in the raw? That's the real test of how real my praise for the Lamb is. By word and deed, at all times and under all circumstances, I'm to raise advent praise to the Lamb. Others may call such service work and sacrifice. For me it's life's purpose and love's privilege.

Songs of praise the angels sang. Lord, help
me join them in praising you with our lives. Amen.

> WE PROCLAIM TO YOU THE ETERNAL
> LIFE, WHICH WAS WITH THE FATHER
> AND HAS APPEARED TO US. *1 John 1:2*

Who's That Baby In The Manger?

"Who's that baby?" someone asked. I was handing out little plastic manger scenes to the children as the missionary preached. Strange as it may seem, here was a child who had never heard the story of the Savior's birth.

John answers that important question in no uncertain terms. He describes the babe of Bethlehem as one "which was with the Father and has appeared to us." In the original, John wrote that Jesus was "face-to-face with the Father." Before the world began, Jesus was there. After the world ends, he will still be there. From eternity to eternity, he who came into the flesh through the virgin Mary has existed as true God with the Father and the Holy Spirit.

The "life," John also calls him. Beautifully, John saw that Jesus is life itself and brings life to others. He is the Christ, who came into the flesh to die that man might live. Therefore he could promise positively, "I am the resurrection and the life. He who believes in me will live, even though he dies; and whoever lives and believes in me will never die" (John 11:25,26).

Who's that baby? Thank God, I can answer, "He is the true God and eternal life" (1 John 5:20). Without these important words, the babe of Bethlehem wouldn't be any different from any other baby. With them he is God's eternal Son come in love to be my Savior.

Lord, show me in your Word that Jesus is
your Son come to bring me eternal life. Amen.

"PREPARE THE WAY FOR THE LORD,
MAKE STRAIGHT PATHS FOR HIM." *Matthew 3:3*

Decorating The Right Way

My wife has grand ideas for decorating the outside of our house for Christmas. I then have to carry out her ideas. Balancing on the second to last step on my short ladder, I almost went over backward as I tried to attach some lights to our porch roof. Later, picking up the newspaper, I read a warning from the Centers for Disease Control and Prevention. They warned that decorating the halls for Christmas can be dangerous. The article noted that some 5,800 people each holiday season land in emergency rooms because of decorating mishaps.

The warning shouldn't stop me from decorating our house. It should remind me to do such decorating the right way. That's what John the Baptist says in our verse too. When he urged, "Prepare the way for the Lord," he wasn't talking about colored lights or plastic evergreens. He was pointing to my heart. A heart clogged with sin has little room for the Christ Child. A heart calloused by sin's denial feels little need for the Light of the world. A heart cluttered with the world's tinny treasures has scant shelf space left for the Savior.

"Make straight paths for him," John cries out to me. "Do the right kind of decorating," he's reminding me. Now's the time for me to recognize sin, repent of sin, and reach for sin's forgiveness. Now's the time to clean house, sweep the heart clean, and make ample room for the Savior. Such decorating for his coming is never dangerous. It's necessary preparation for a necessary gift—the Savior God sent in his love for me.

O dearest Jesus, make my heart
an undefiled, clean chamber for you. Amen.

SUDDENLY A GREAT COMPANY OF THE HEAVENLY HOST
APPEARED WITH THE ANGEL, PRAISING GOD AND SAYING,
"GLORY TO GOD IN THE HIGHEST, AND ON EARTH PEACE
TO MEN ON WHOM HIS FAVOR RESTS." *Luke 2:13,14*

A Special Time For Singing

I thought it was just my imagination till I read the news magazine article. Some radio stations are playing more Christmas music and earlier than before. Of course, the main reason for the switch is that "Jingle Bells" rings the cash register. Christmas songs are supposed to remind the listener that the season is all about giving—or, should we say, shopping.

For us as believers, Christmas is a special time for singing. I've often lamented that we have only a handful of weeks in which to sing favorite Advent and Christmas hymns. For us, though, the reason for singing is much different. Christ, not cash, causes our songs. Praising the Savior, not pushing sales, is why we sing our verses this all-too-short season. That's why the angels sang that first Christmas. They praised God for love's pure Light in the Bethlehem manger. They praised God on the day he opened heaven again and gave us his own Son. "Peace on earth and mercy mild, God and sinners reconciled" was the joyful content of their song.

As grandparents we eagerly attend the Christmas Eve services of our grandchildren. We love to see their joyous faces as they sing about their newborn Savior. Sitting there, we think back to the children's services in which we participated so many years ago. Even more, we think about why Christmas is such a good time for singing. "Christ our Savior is born."

*Lord, I have even more reason to sing than the angels.
Help me praise my newborn King. Amen.*

THANKS BE TO GOD FOR HIS
INDESCRIBABLE GIFT! *2 Corinthians 9:15*

A Gift That Never Stops Giving

Gift certificate cards seem like perfect gifts. They require little thought on the part of the giver and are fun to receive. Last Christmas, people spent more than $40 million on these easy-to-buy presents. Gift cards may also pose problems that can make one feel more gypped than jolly. Some expire after 12 months. Others may charge a monthly inactivity fee that subtracts from the card's value. And what if you should lose the card?

Paul calls God's Christmas present "indescribable." It, indeed, is just that. When I see in that baby asleep on the hay the eternal God come into my world, I have to shake my head in awe. When I realize why he came, my wonder increases still more. The Creator came to do what the creatures couldn't. He surrounded himself with my skin to rescue me from my sins. When I learn there's no time limit for this Christmas gift, praise and adoration are my response. He came into that manger over two thousand years ago, not just for the people of his time but also for me. God's gift of the Savior is as current today and will still be so tomorrow.

Best of all, there's no price tag on God's gift of the Savior—no price tag for me, that is. The cost was borne by my loving God. It cost him to send his Son. It cost his Son to go from the Bethlehem crib to the Calvary cross. Because God paid the price, I hold in my heart this Christmas Day a wonderful gift card. Every day I can present it at heaven's window and receive forgiveness. On my final day, I can turn it in to my loving Father whose gift to me it was.

Lord, thank you—thank you for your
gift that never stops giving, my Savior Jesus. Amen.

YOU KNOW THE GRACE OF OUR LORD JESUS CHRIST, THAT THOUGH
HE WAS RICH, YET FOR YOUR SAKES HE BECAME POOR, SO THAT
YOU THROUGH HIS POVERTY MIGHT BECOME RICH. *2 Corinthians 8:9*

Unwrapping Our Christmas Gift

My wife spends time wrapping Christmas gifts. She cuts the decorated paper, folds over the corners, and arranges the colorful bows. She doesn't like to put a present under the tree or into someone's hands without first wrapping it carefully.

God wrapped his Christmas present to me very carefully too. Every Christmas, I recall how a poor carpenter from Nazareth took his pregnant wife to the town of their ancestry. How, in that crowded town, no shelter could be found except some kind of stable. How, in such a lowly setting, surrounded by the smell of animals, her child was born. How she carefully wrapped her newly born Son in the strips of cloth used by poor people for their babies and gently laid him in a manger as a makeshift crib.

Bargain baby clothes, a manger crib, a lowly stable, a poor couple from Nazareth were the gift wrappings God used. And we remember them. Every Christmas, we look at them. But that's not just what God wants, no more than my family or friends do when they present me with their gifts. "Unwrap it," they urge me. So does my gracious God. He wants me to look at the gift itself. He wants me to see in the manger his own Son, the Christ Child, my Savior and King. He wants me to know how rich I am because his Son left his heavenly riches for that lowly Bethlehem manger.

Lord, help me look beyond the wrappings
to the gift of the Savior this Christmas. Amen.

> SO [THE SHEPHERDS] HURRIED OFF AND
> FOUND MARY AND JOSEPH, AND THE BABY,
> WHO WAS LYING IN THE MANGER. *Luke 2:16*

Marveling At Our Christmas Gift

Sometimes it's hard to marvel at a Christmas gift. What do you say when the gift tie doesn't quite match your suit? When it's a present that you secretly wanted, but didn't think you'd ever receive, it's much easier for eyes to light up.

Not too many eyes lit up that night at Bethlehem. Mary's eyes did. She knew who her child was because the angel had told her nine months earlier. Joseph's eyes lit up too. An angel had told him months earlier that the baby's name was to be Jesus, for he would save his people from their sins. Can we imagine how Mary cradled her Savior tightly to her breast and how Joseph hovered protectively over Jesus that night in the stable?

What about the shepherds? The humdrum darkness of their night watch had been gloriously interrupted. Never again would darkness rule over their hearts. Unto them had been born a Savior, who was Christ the Lord. Can we imagine their legs carrying them a bit faster than usual to that lowly stable? Or their hearts beating faster than usual as they knelt before their Savior?

I can't explain how the eternal God could be a little baby in a manger. Neither can I explain the divine love behind this miracle. But my eyes light up when I hold in hands of faith the present I so desperately needed but never thought I would get—my Savior, Christ the Lord.

Lord, never let me stop marveling
at your Christmas gift of my Savior. Amen.

> THE SHEPHERDS RETURNED, GLORIFYING AND PRAISING
> GOD FOR ALL THE THINGS THEY HAD HEARD AND SEEN,
> WHICH WERE JUST AS THEY HAD BEEN TOLD. *Luke 2:20*

Giving Thanks For Our Christmas Gift

What do I do with a Christmas gift that I really appreciate? Do I store it on some closet shelf out of sight? Do I hide it in some dresser drawer along with other odds and ends? Or do I use it? And when I use it, do I think of the giver? Do I perhaps even tell others about it?

Several days after Christmas, a mother and her little girl, shopping for bargains, stood outside the window of a large department store. As they watched, workers inside were dismantling the Christmas display. "Mother," the little girl asked, "what are they doing with the baby Jesus?" "Oh," replied the mother, "they're putting him away to keep him safe for next Christmas." That's what many in our world do with Jesus once Christmas is past. Perhaps even some members of my congregation. They take their annual look at the Savior and then store him away someplace as they go back to the business of living.

That's not what the shepherds did as they left the Savior's manger bed. I don't know how long they celebrated Christmas. I would guess their joyous response was ongoing. For me too! What better way to say thanks to God than by teaching my family to lay their sins on Jesus, the spotless Lamb of God. Or to tell my neighbors about the friend we have in Jesus, all our sins and griefs to bear. Or to help reach the heathen with Christ, the true and only Light. God's precious Christmas gift of the Savior is something I need every day. So do others in my world.

Thank you, Lord, for your most
practical and precious gift of the Savior. Amen.

"THE RISING SUN WILL COME TO US FROM
HEAVEN TO SHINE ON THOSE LIVING IN DARKNESS
AND IN THE SHADOW OF DEATH." *Luke 1:78,79*

A Time Of Light

Last New Year's Eve, on my walk around the block, I counted six Christmas trees out at the curb. Stripped of their decorations, they were waiting for the city truck to haul them away. The sight saddened me somewhat.

What can be lovelier than evergreen trees all lit up? They shine so beautifully through house windows and on spacious lawns. It just wouldn't be Christmas without them. When my mother in her last years hesitated to put up a tree, I told her she had to. So many memories are connected with the Christmas tree. It sparkles with thoughts of home and family, fun and surprises.

For us as Christians, the Christmas tree has deeper significance. Its lights twinkling in the darkness remind me of Christ, the Light of the world. He came so that I could have light in this dark world of sin. Its evergreen color represents the never-ending life I have in the Savior. Never will I be placed out at the curb to await the trash collector from hell. Its shape has meaning too. Toward heaven it points, reminding me from where my Savior came and to where he will take me.

Oh, one more thing—that lighted tree encourages me to shine too. Jesus isn't just my Light of love in sin and death's darkness. He's the Light of the world. Now he wants me to shine like a little Christmas tree with his light of salvation in a world of darkness and death.

Lord, keep shining on me, in me, and
through me with your light and love. Amen.

> "TODAY IN THE TOWN OF DAVID
> A SAVIOR HAS BEEN BORN TO YOU;
> HE IS CHRIST THE LORD." *Luke 2:11*

A Worldwide Birthday Party

When I reached a magical number, my wife surprised me with a birthday party. Not just one, but three—one with my colleagues, one with my family, and one with the members of my Bible class. That was a lot of cake to eat. But I enjoyed every minute of it.

Christmas is God's birthday. Sounds strange doesn't it? The eternal God has no birthday. I do, but he doesn't. For me, my birthday means the time of my life beginning on this earth. With God, there is no beginning or ending. Perhaps I should rather call Christmas the birthday of God's love on earth. At Christmas his love came down in human form for sinners like me.

My Savior's birthday is time for a party. He wants me to celebrate. And he wants the center of the celebration to be him. When I say "merry Christmas" at this time of the year, it's really a "happy birthday" to the world's Savior. It's really a "thank you" for the best gift ever given.

As my wife invited others for my party, so the Savior invites others to his. My *Guinness Book of World Records* is ten years old so I don't know if the fact still holds. It states that the biggest Christmas party ever was held by the Boeing Company with 103,152 guests invited. I know of an even bigger birthday party. It's the one held every December when more than a million Christians celebrate the birthday of God's love in human form.

*Lord, help me celebrate your birthday every
day till you take me to the eternal Christmas. Amen.*

> "MAY THE LORD OUR GOD BE WITH US AS
> HE WAS WITH OUR FATHERS; MAY HE NEVER
> LEAVE US NOR FORSAKE US." *1 Kings 8:57*

No Fortune Cookies For Me

We were in San Francisco seeing the sights. A friend had told us about a fortune cookie factory in the midst of Chinatown. We found it tucked off on a side street. At the end of the tour the proprietor gave us each a sample cookie. "Tomorrow will bring a bright beginning" was the fortune I found in mine. "You will meet an exciting stranger" was my wife's.

We had fun reading the fortunes. Of course, we didn't believe them. Only one person knows what tomorrow will bring. And I need only one person to be ready for tomorrow. That's the Lord, my faithful God. He was there for my fathers and he'll be there also for me. He didn't forsake me this past year when I so often slipped into sin. He was always there through Word and sacrament to pull me out of the ditch, with his Son's forgiveness to wipe me clean of sin's filth, and to put me back on heaven's highway. Thank God, my faithful God, that he doesn't leave or forsake his own.

Thank God that he'll be with me tomorrow as I enter another year. I don't have to worry about what will happen. I don't need a preview of what is coming. God knows and he'll take care of me. When he and I walk together, I have all I need. Better for me than knowing what the future holds is knowing who holds my future—the same faithful God who did not leave or forsake me this past year.

*Lord, help me trust your faithfulness as I end
one year and begin another. In Jesus' name. Amen.*